DR. TOM MALONE

PREACHES ON

CERTAINTIES

DR. TOM MALONE

P R E A C H E S   O N

CERTAINTIES

SWORD of the LORD
PUBLISHERS
P.O.BOX 1099, MURFREESBORO, TN 37133

Introduction

These sermons were preached in the early 1970's at Emmanuel Baptist Church in Pontiac, Michigan. They were not preached to convince the skeptic or infidel but to confirm and strengthen the faith of the saints. Reasoning and logic do not strengthen our faith. Only the living Word of God can strengthen the faith of a child of God.

Abraham's faith was strengthened because of his "being fully persuaded that, what he had promised, he was able also to perform" (Rom. 4:21). The unconverted mind "receiveth not the things of the Spirit of God: for they are foolishness unto him: neither can he know them, because they are spiritually discerned" (I Cor. 2:14).

So my purpose in preaching these sermons was not to try to appeal to the scholarly or intellectual mind but to help the saint of God to "know the *certainty* of those things, wherein thou hast been instructed" (Luke 1:4).

Some of the messages were of such length that it took both the Sunday morning and evening services to preach one of them. It was a period of great revival and evangelism in Emmanuel Baptist Church. Thirty or more people were baptized and united with the church every Sunday. Young men were called to preach, and many came from cold and formal churches to join the Emmanuel Baptist Church during these weeks.

There is nothing new here, but there is a strong emphasis upon the certainties of the Faith. Preachers should not feel that they must make some new theological discovery and appeal to the intellectual fancies of people. The saints need to be made certain and secure about what they already know and believe. When I was a young convert my heart would leap for joy when I heard some preacher preach on why he knew something was true.

"Have not I written to thee excellent things in counsels and knowledge, That I might make thee know the certainty *of the words of truth. . . ?"*—Prov. 22:20,21.

Table of Contents

I. How I Know God Wants Everyone to Be Saved .. 9

II. How to Know You Are Saved 19

III. How I Know Jesus Christ Is the Son of God....45

IV. Why I Know the Bible Is True 71

V. Why I Know God Answers Prayer 97

VI. Why I Know the Holy Spirit Is a Person 129

VII. Why I Know There Is a God 153

VIII. How I Know God Is Alive 175

IX. Why I Know Trouble Can Never Destroy
a Christian 201

X. Why I Know There Is a Place Called
Heaven 227

XI. Why I Know a True Believer Can Never
Be Lost 255

XII. Why I Know a Believer Shall be Delivered
From the Wrath of God 279

_____ Chapter I _____

How I Know God Wants
Everyone to Be Saved

I Timothy 2:1-8

"Who will have all men to be saved, and to come unto the knowledge of the truth."—I Tim. 2:4.

I have met a few people in my Christian experience who felt that they were excluded from the atonement and from the grace of our Lord Jesus Christ.

I never shall forget a sad experience I had with a man who came to this church many years ago. One night while riding with him in the car, I was talking to him about how he could know he was saved—how he could have assurance in his heart. He had said that at times he thought he was saved, but then again he did not know whether he was saved or not. In the darkness of the car, he said to me, "I am afraid, Brother Tom, that I am predestinated to be lost and that God did not intend for me to be saved in the first place."

I am absolutely positive that is not true, and I can take the Bible and prove that the will of God is that every man or woman be saved.

"Who will have _all men_ to be saved, and to come unto the knowledge of the truth" does not mean that everyone will be saved. The doctrine of universalism, which is a false teaching, teaches to the effect that sometimes God is going to change His mind and He is not going to let anyone be lost; He is not going to let anyone suffer; He is not going to let anyone go to Hell; and finally He is going to save everyone.

Not one verse in all the Holy Bible intimates such teaching. The Scripture says, "Who will have all men to be saved, and to come unto the knowledge of the truth."

There are two different verbs in the New Testament for *will.* One expresses *determination;* the other, *desire.* If the verb in this verse were the verb for *determination*—if God were determined that there would be no one in Hell—there would be no one in Hell. But this is not what the verb means. It is the word for *desire.* This verse teaches that God desires that everyone be saved, that no one be lost, that all come to the knowledge of the truth.

I find in the Scriptures five reasons why I know God wants and desires and longs for everyone to be saved.

I. WE ARE TO PRAY FOR EVERYONE

In I Timothy 2:1 we read, "I exhort therefore, that, first of all, supplications, prayers, intercessions, and giving of thanks, be made for all men."

God said we should pray for everyone. If there were no hope for a person to be saved, would God exhort us to pray for that person? No. Since there is a possibility for everyone to be saved, the Bible says that we are to pray for all men. I don't care how deep in sin they are, how hardhearted they are, how indifferent they are.

I heard just today of someone who is lost and needs the Lord, but who told one of our workers today, "Shut up! Go on your way! I don't want to hear about it!" That does not mean that we should not pray for him. The Bible teaches that we are to pray for all men everywhere. That fact leads me to believe that it is possible for any and all to be saved because God has told us to pray for them.

Many people have been saved because someone prayed. Many people are in Hell today because no one cared enough to pray for their salvation.

I never shall forget reading the accurate account of the mother of Tom Carter. Tom was a prisoner who was sent to prison for many years. While in prison, his mother, who had prayed for him all of his life, got a very special burden to pray that God would save him. She set aside other things and began praying for her lost boy in prison. She prayed that God would not let him die until he was genuinely saved.

In the midst of these four or five days of praying, fasting, waiting on God and travailing for the soul of her son, she received a telegram from the state prison. It read like this:

> Dear Mrs. Carter:
>
> We regret to inform you that your son Tom Carter died.

She took the telegram, went back to her knees again, laid it on the floor and bathed it with her tears. She told God, "God, I don't believe it! I don't believe it! I have prayed in faith believing. I have held my boy up to You, begging You to save him. I have had the confidence in my soul that my prayers were being answered. I don't believe this telegram!"

It is said that Mrs. Carter wadded up that telegram, threw it in the wastebasket and told God, "I still claim Your promises. I believe my boy will be saved."

In only a matter of hours a second telegram came from the state prison. it said:

> Dear Mrs. Carter:
>
> We are happy to inform you that we have made an error. There are two men in this prison by the name of Tom Carter. It was

not your son who died; it was another man with the same name.

That telegram was followed in a few hours by a letter from her son Tom saying:

> Mother, while here in this prison in recent days, I have felt the need of Christ in my life and I have been saved.

Friends, there is no way of knowing how many of us sitting in the house of God, singing songs of Zion and rejoicing in our hope in Christ, were saved because someone prayed. God in His Word says, "I exhort therefore, that, first of all, supplications, prayers, intercessions, and giving of thanks, be made for all men."

I know that God wants everyone saved because He wants everyone prayed for.

"Who will have all men to be saved, and to come unto the knowledge of the truth."

II. CHRIST GAVE HIMSELF A RANSOM FOR ALL

We read in I Timothy 2:6: "Who gave himself a ransom for *all*, to be testified in due time."

The Bible plainly teaches that Jesus died for all, died for every one of us—for the lost heathen, for the uncivilized, for those in the past, for those who live now, and for all those who will be born until the end of time. He "gave himself a ransom for all." When Christ died on the cross of Calvary, He died with you and me in mind.

A wonderful verse in connection with this thought is verse 5: "For there is one God, and one mediator between God and men, the man Christ Jesus." There is one God who manifests Himself in three different ways: Father, Son and Holy Ghost. Multitudes do not believe this verse and in a moment, you will know whom I am talking about. "For there is one God, and one mediator between God and men, the man Christ Jesus." Just one Mediator, not two, not three, not several—one God, one Mediator. Who is that Mediator? It is not the Virgin Mary; it is not a Protestant preacher; it is not a Catholic priest. "...one God...one mediator...." can mean only one glorious Person, Jesus Christ.

Mrs. Malone and I have visited the four largest and most historic churches in the Roman Catholic world: Saint Peter's Cathedral in the Vatican in Rome; St. John's Lateran Church, the most historic Catholic church on the face of the earth; Saint Mary's Basilica; and Saint Paul's Outside the Wall. While in Saint Mary's Basilica, I saw some things that I shall never forget. One was a large sculpture in beautiful stone. There is no telling how many thousands of dollars that piece of sculpture is worth. It was of a woman sitting, representing the Virgin Mary. Underneath her feet was an entanglement of men. One was an old haggard-looking man with long hair down to his back. That was John Huss. One with bulging eyes looked like an imbecile. Around both of these men snakes were wrapped. The woman's feet were upon Martin Luther, the Father of the Protestant Reformation.

While looking at that sculpture, I noticed some little booths, like telephone booths. I saw a Catholic nun, a young woman, in one of those booths. There was a perforated piece of board and then the enclosed booth on the other side. Through that perforation you could speak. In that booth was a Catholic priest, hidden from view of all who stood in that great church.

I saw that young Catholic woman come, kneel and cross herself. She had no sooner knelt, garbed in all her black attire, than she began to whisper and confess her sins to a man in that booth. I saw the big tears roll down her cheeks. Then I watched her arise, and with tears still on her cheeks and with the same sad look on her face, and with not one ray of hope or one glitter of peace or one bit of joy in her soul, I saw her walk out, stooped and weeping.

I said to myself that day, and I have said it thousands of times since, *Thank God for One to whom we can go who never sins!*

Not a man, but a God-man, the spotless perfect Lamb of God who bore my sins, the one and only Mediator.

Any man or woman who says there is more than one Mediator goes contrary to the Book of God. There is one God and one Mediator—no other. That Mediator is Christ Jesus.

You might say, "Oh, but I have heard all my life that you could confess your sins to So-and-So." "My little children, these things write I unto you, that ye sin not. And if any man sin, we have an advocate with the Father, Jesus Christ the righteous" (I John 2:1).

Don't think I am just "taking off" on the Catholic church. I have the truth at heart. I have as much right to preach what I believe, as they do to advocate what they believe. We see thousands of cars on the road that have a little Catholic image in them. People carry those images because they believe they have some efficacy, some atonement, for protection. Saint So-and-So is to protect you; Saint So-and-So is to help you when you are in sorrow; Saint So-and-So is to help you when you run out of money; Saint So-and-So is to help you when all of your friends have turned their backs on you; Saint So-and-So is to help you when you get sick; Saint So-and-So is to help you when you get old.

Gathered into one glorious, living Redeemer, we have all of those in "one God and one mediator between God and man, the man Christ Jesus." One Mediator. He gave Himself a ransom for everyone. No one can take this Bible and find anything that would indicate Jesus did not die for your sins. He wants everyone to be saved because He died for everyone.

III. THE TEACHING OF THE SCRIPTURE

In II Peter 3:9 we read, "The Lord is not slack concerning his promise, as some men count slackness; but is longsuffering to usward, not willing that any should perish, but that all should come to repentance."

Titus 2:11,12 says, "For the grace of God that bringeth salvation hath appeared to all men, Teaching us that, denying ungodliness and worldly lusts, we should live soberly, righteously, and godly, in this present world...."

So the Bible teaches that God is not willing that any should perish. There is a sense in which God has put everything He can between a lost soul and Hell—the Bible, a bloody cross, the church of Jesus Christ, gospel preaching, the prayers and tears of honest Christians. God is not willing that anyone be lost. He has put every barrier, every stop sign, every blockade, between you and Hell that He could possibly put. That He wants everyone to be saved is the teaching of the Scripture.

The Bible plainly teaches that the grace of God that bringeth salvation hath appeared to all men. He is not willing that any should perish. His glorious salvation is not confined to any one class of people. He loves the rich, the poor, the learned, the unlearned, the up-and-out, the down-and-out. God loves all sinners, every sinner, everywhere.

"But God commendeth his love toward us, in that, while we were yet sinners, Christ died for us" (Rom. 5:8). Jesus ministered to all classes of people while here on earth. His love and saving grace reached to the very lowest rung of the ladder of human society.

IV. HE HAS NEVER REFUSED ANYONE

I have never met anyone who came to Jesus and was refused. Have you? There are verses that teach that God has never refused anyone. I have often said that I can hardly preach without referring to John 6:37, "All that the Father giveth me shall come to me; and him that cometh to me I will in no wise cast out." The Lord never refuses anyone.

John Wesley was one of the greatest preachers who has ever

lived. He was a man and a human being, but he was a miracle himself. John Wesley crossed the Atlantic Ocean thirteen times when it was a miracle if anyone got across without disaster. He rode across this country on horseback and muleback, establishing Methodist churches and sowing the seed of the Gospel. John Wesley had an unusual voice. He never used a microphone. He would preach to as many as forty thousand people in an open field without a P.A. system. It is said that his voice would carry a mile. He would lift up his voice and it would fairly ring across the heads of thousands of people. He stood at his mother's grave and preached to many thousands.

One day when he had preached to a large open-air crowd, Lady Huntington and other royalty went up to him and said, "Mr. Wesley, we would like to entertain you for tea." So he went to tea. But just before he went into the home of this royalty of England, someone handed Wesley a little dirty piece of paper, which he stuck into his long Prince Albert coat.

While being entertained at tea, one of the royalty said, "Mr. Wesley, we think you went a little too far today in your preaching."

"Why do you say that?" this great Methodist preacher asked.

"Because you made the statement that God would never refuse anyone. You went so far as to say that Jesus would take people whom the Devil was even tired of. You said the Lord would take the Devil's castaways."

"Yes, I believe that," he answered. As she was talking, John Wesley reached into his pocket, got the note and read it.

> We are just two old, sinful women, two soiled doves of the London underworld who heard you preach today. We have lived in sin all of our lives. We heard you say that Jesus would take even the Devil's castaways. Hearing that and believing it, we have trusted Him and have been saved.

Mr. Wesley folded the note and looked through the glass of the large and beautiful doors. Out there he saw two old women with their rags gathered about them, standing shuddering in the cold. After reading the note to Lady Huntington and the other royalty, he said, "There are two people out there who have been away from God all of their lives, who have lived in the very gutters of this city. The Lord saved them today."

"All that the Father giveth to me shall come unto me; and he that cometh to me I will in no wise cast out."

My friends, there is no record of Jesus Christ ever refusing anyone. Thieves came to Him, and He took them in. When people flung a woman at His feet and said that she deserved to be stoned, He took her in. When a cursing, swearing fisherman crossed His path, He took him in. This Bible teaches that Jesus has never refused anyone.

"Who will have all men to be saved, and to come unto the knowledge of the truth."

V. BECAUSE OF THE GIFT OF HIS SON

Romans 8:32 says, "He that spared not his own Son, but delivered him up for us all, how shall he not with him also freely give us all things?" God gave His Son for you. That is why I know He wants you to be saved. "He. . .spared not his own Son." Can you possibly believe that God would give His only begotten Son to suffer and die on the cross of Calvary, then not want you to be saved?

"For God so loved the world, that he gave his only begotten Son, that whosoever believeth in him should not perish, but have everlasting life."—John 3:16.

Someone has told this beautiful and wonderful story:
Long ago, before the days of railways, people could travel only on horseback or by rumbling stagecoach. The arrival of the coach in town or village was a great event.

As Harry, a bright but careless boy, came out of school, he waited to see the visitors get out of the stagecoach. Among them was a queer-looking man who swayed from side to side as he walked. Harry laughed aloud and imitated the funny walk of the stranger to the rest of his chums. When he reached home, his father said, "Come into this room and see a dear old friend of mine."

Harry was glad to go, but oh, how ashamed he felt! There sat the stranger who had arrived on the stagecoach and at whom he had laughed. But the gentleman smiled and was very kind.

Then Harry's father told his son that when he (Harry) was quite little, he (the father) had fallen into the canal. A stranger plunged in to save him, but it left him crippled for life.

Harry flushed when he thought of his own bad behavior toward a man who had saved his father's life.

The Lord Jesus has more than risked His life to save you from sin. He gave Himself. Oh, such a cruel death He died upon the cross! He "gave himself a ransom for all."

You may not love Him now because you know Him not, but to know the Lord Jesus is to love Him.

'God is not willing that any should perish, but that all should come to repentance.'

Chapter II

How to Know You Are Saved

(Preached in the Emmanuel Baptist Church on Sunday, September 13, 1970)

READ: I John 5

"These things have I written unto you that believe on the name of the Son of God; that ye may know that ye have eternal life, and that ye may believe on the name of the Son of God."—I John 5:13.

I would like for you to seriously think about I John 5:10. Although it doesn't greatly relate to my message, if you are an unsaved man or woman, boy or girl, you should think about what this verse says: "He that believeth on the Son of God hath the witness in himself: he that believeth not God hath made him a liar; because he believeth not the record that God gave of his Son."

If you have never believed the Gospel as it is found in the Word of God and believed on the person of our Lord Jesus Christ, God's Son and your Saviour, then you are guilty of calling God a liar. The Bible says that, if you don't believe it, you make God a liar. Your belief is the same as saying, "I don't believe that Bible to be true. And I don't believe that Jesus Christ is the Son of God and was meant to be my Saviour." That is what I John 5:10 says.

Now notice a portion of verse 13: "These things have I written unto you that believe on the name of the Son of God; that ye may know that ye have eternal life...."

I remind you that this verse is addressed to those who are already saved: "These things have I written unto you that believe on the name of the Son of God...."

The writer, John, wrote the last book in the Bible, the book of Revelation, when he was in exile for his testimony on the barren Isle of Patmos out in the Mediterranean Sea (actually the Aegean Sea). Then he also wrote that great Gospel that magnifies Jesus as the Son of God, called the Gospel of John. Counting the three epistles of John and Revelation, he wrote five New Testament books.

These three epistles are letters dealing with the family of God. Many times in these epistles, John referred to the Christians as "my little children." That literally means in the original, "My little born ones" or, "I am writing to you that have been born the second time, and I am writing these things unto the family of God, unto people who are saved."

In the Gospel of John, he told people how to be saved. In this epistle of I John, he tells how to know that you are saved.

In the Gospel of John, we read a wonderful verse, John 20:31: "But these are written, that ye might believe that Jesus is the Christ, the Son of God; and that believing ye might have life through his name."

In the Gospel of John, he tells you how to be saved. In the epistle of John, he tells you how to know you are saved. In fact, the word *know* is found thirty-seven times in the first epistle of John. Thirty-seven times in one book God says, "You can know that certain things are true. You can know: you are saved, you have eternal life, you are not going to Hell, your sins are forgiven, and that you are on your way to Heaven."

That is what the Bible plainly declares.

Three great short statements in the New Testament go together, statements God put there in order to give you confidence and assurance so you could know you are saved.

For instance, the statement, "It is finished" (John 19:30)—just three words in the English translation of the Bible, but only one in the Greek New Testament. Actually He cried, "Finished! Completed! Accomplished! Performed!"

Thank God, the work of salvation has been completed! On the cross Jesus cried, "Finished!"

Another expression, "...it is I..." (Matt. 14:27). The Lord said, "Be of good cheer; it is I." You can have the person of the Lord in your life and know it.

Then Jesus said, "It is written..." (Matt. 4:4).

"It is finished"—salvation.

"It is I"—satisfaction.

"It is written"—security.

These three things assure us of salvation, satisfaction and security. The Bible plainly teaches that you can know you are saved. The Apostle Paul knew beyond any shadow of doubt he was saved.

There was a period in his life when he didn't know, a period when he was religious and thought he had what God had described in His Word, but Paul didn't have this.

Paul was most religious before he was saved, as religious as anyone might be. When he got saved, he knew he was saved. He constantly spoke of the fact that he knew beyond any doubt he had been born the second time, his sins were forgiven, his name was written in the Lamb's Book of Life, his body was indwelt with the Holy Spirit of God, and that he was a member of the family of God.

For instance, II Timothy 1:12 says, "For the which cause I also suffer these things: nevertheless I am not ashamed: for I know whom I have believed, and am persuaded that he is able to keep that which I have committed unto him against that day." Paul had given his soul to the Lord for safe keeping, and he said, "I know in whom I believe and am absolutely convinced that He will keep that which I have committed or deposited with Him until the time when He comes again.'' Paul knew he was saved. And he knew why he was saved.

Some things people say are not really scriptural, and some things people think are from the Scriptures, are not Bible at all. I will show you also how many traditional thoughts do not come from God.

For instance, I have heard many people say, ''You don't have to know where you were saved, just so you know you are saved.''

You don't get that out of the Bible. I am not going to say that salvation is such a minor experience that you can be saved and not know when it happened, or where. I think that I can prove that from the Bible.

Paul said in I Timothy 1:16, ''Howbeit for this cause I obtained mercy, that in me first Jesus Christ might shew forth all longsuffering, for a pattern to them which should hereafter believe on him to life everlasting.'' Paul said, ''In the providence and grace and sovereignty of God, He had saved me as a pattern for every believer.''

If he is a pattern for every believer, then we know what that means. If a lady is given a piece of material and a pattern and is told to make a dress according to the pattern, it means she is to make it just like that pattern. Paul, inspired of God, said, ''Christ has made me a pattern to them which should hereafter believe.''

If his conversion is a pattern conversion, a model conversion; if his life and his salvation are a pattern for us and our life is to be like his, then let's see what his is like.

Paul, as I have already said, knew he was saved. Romans 8 is one of the greatest chapters in the Bible. You could live in it forever. If all the Word of God were taken from a Christian except chapter 8 of Romans, you could spend the rest of your life meditating upon this fathomless well of truth and never reach the depth.

"There is therefore now no condemnation to them which are in Christ Jesus..." is the opening statement of chapter 8. Near the end of the chapter Paul cries, "Who shall separate us from the love of Christ?" (vs. 35).

It begins with no condemnation and ends with no separation. My honest opinion is that this chapter teaches that it is absolutely impossible for one to ever be shut off from Jesus Christ.

You are saved forever—but that is a different subject. I am not talking about how I know a believer can never be lost, but about how I know a child of God can have the assurance day and night, never changing, absolutely unalterable and implacable, that he is saved forever.

Just as settled as the fact of God and just as true as the Bible itself, you have everlasting life. How can you know that? Paul knew he was saved and was a pattern believer, and God wants every Christian to know he is saved.

Paul knew when he was saved, knew just exactly when and where it took place. Paul told it in a testimony, found five times in the New Testament, three times in the book of Acts, once in the Philippian letter and once in the epistles to Timothy. You find it given to the Jew, the Gentile, the church, to a preacher, etc. Five times he gives a personal testimony about what the Lord had done for him. He made it personal and real as to his salvation. Paul knew he was saved. "I can tell you exactly when it happened. It happened about noonday. I don't know whether it was 11:55 or 12:03, but I know when it happened." When Paul gave his testimony in Acts 22:6 he said, "It was about noon." He knew exactly when it happened, and where; for in Acts 9:3 he said it happened "near Damascus."

In the beautiful fields and plains about eight miles out of the

city of Damascus, a guide of the Bible lands pointed to a place
and said, "It is believed that here the arrogant young Saul of Tarsus, riding his charging horse toward Damascus and breathing out
threatenings against the church, was knocked from his horse and
where a resurrected Jesus Christ shined His undimmed light from
Heaven and heard Paul cry out, 'Who art thou, O Lord, and what
would You have me to do?' " He knew exactly where it happened.

He not only knew where he was saved and when, but he knew
how it happened.

From that day when he was saved until that day when he laid
his head on a chopping block outside the walls of the imperial city
of Rome and went out to meet God, and until that day when they
said, "Paul, what must I do to be saved?" Paul always knew the
answer, and he said, "Believe on the Lord Jesus Christ, and thou
shalt be saved" (Acts 16:31).

So Paul not only knew he was saved, he knew *when* he was
saved, *where* he was saved and *how* he was saved.

Bless God, he went even further than that; he knew *why* he was
saved.

There are literally thousands of believers scattered up and down
this land and around the encircled globe who do not have the
vaguest idea as to why they were saved. The Apostle Paul did,
for God made it clear to him in Acts 22:15, "For thou shalt be
his witness unto all men of what thou hast seen and heard."

God saved you so you could be His witness of what you have
seen and what you have heard. Anyone can tell that. Were you
put on a witness stand, the attorney would say to you, "Now tell
it like it is. Tell what you saw and what you heard."

God never told you to be a theologian. God never said you had
to be a Bible scholar. God never said you had to be an extrovert.
God never said you had to be knowledgeable. God never said you
had to have a great personality. But God did say, "I have saved

you to tell what you have seen and what you have heard.''

If Paul is a pattern believer, God wants every one of us to know these five things, as Paul knew them: know that we are saved, when we were saved, where we were saved, how we were saved, and why we were saved.

Then Paul knew how long he was saved. He kept talking about it.

Paul wrote to the church at Philippi, ''Being confident of this very thing, that he which hath begun a good work in you will perform it until the day of Jesus Christ'' (Phil. 1:6).

If God begins the work, He will finish it. But if some kind of ''religious experience'' has started in you, God didn't start it, so don't expect Him to give you the assurance of it.

In Philippians 1:6 we have: the commencing of salvation—''hath begun''; the continuing of salvation—''will perform it''; the consummation of salvation—''until the day of redemption.''

Paul not only knew how long he was saved; he knew what he was saved from.

Says I Timothy 1:15, ''This is a faithful saying, and worthy of all acceptation, that Christ Jesus came into the world to save sinners; of whom I am chief.''

One reason why the Apostle Paul got so gloriously saved was that he became convicted that he was so totally lost. And you can't be saved until you get lost. If you do not know that you are lost, forget about being saved. If you do not know that you are a sinner, don't expect to be a saint, because Christ's transforming, redemptive work is making saints out of sinners.

Someone has said, ''You can't get people saved until you get them lost.'' That is why we have to do so much preaching on the total depravity of man.

''For all have sinned, and come short of the glory of God.''— Rom. 3:23.

''As it is written, There is none righteous, no, not one: There

is none that seeketh after God.''—Rom. 3:10,11.

"...for there is no difference.''—Rom. 3:22.

If the drunkard on the curb in the gutter and the upright moral man have not been saved, God says in this matter there is no difference. You must realize that you are a sinner in order to be saved.

Those things Paul knew.

Now there are three great truths that all of this whole subject can be hung upon, three great truths or systems of truth which have much to do with your assurance.

1. *His completed work at the cross.*

John 19:30: "When Jesus therefore had received the vinegar, he said, It is finished: and he bowed his head, and gave up the ghost.''

Isaiah 53:6: "All we like sheep have gone astray; we have turned every one to his own way; and the Lord hath laid on him the iniquity of us all.''

First Peter 3:18: "For Christ also hath once suffered for sins, the just for the unjust, that he might bring us to God, being put to death in the flesh, but quickened by the Spirit.''

2. *His constant work at the throne.*

Romans 5:10: "For if, when we were enemies, we were reconciled to God by the death of his Son, much more, being reconciled, we shall be saved by his life.''

Hebrews 7:25: "Wherefore he is able also to save them to the uttermost that come unto God by him, seeing he ever liveth to make intercession for them.''

First John 2:1: "My little children, these things write I unto you, that ye sin not. And if any man sin, we have an advocate with the Father, Jesus Christ the righteous.''

3. *His coming work at the rapture.*

Philippians 3:20,21: "For our conversation is in heaven; from whence also we look for the Saviour, the Lord Jesus Christ: Who shall change our vile body, that it may be fashioned like unto his glorious body, according to the working whereby he is able even to subdue all things unto himself.''

First Corinthians 15:51,52: ''Behold, I shew you a mystery; We shall not all sleep, but we shall all be changed, In a moment, in the twinkling of an eye, at the last trump: for the trumpet shall sound, and the dead shall be raised incorruptible, and we shall be changed.''

How you can know you are saved can be hung, first of all, upon His finished work at Calvary. It hangs, second, upon His constant work at the throne. And in the third place, it hangs upon His future work at His coming. We can look back to a finished work; we can look within to the work of the Spirit in our lives; we can look upward to His advocacy at the throne; but we must also look forward to His future work at His coming.

You ask, ''What does that have to do with it?''

When you get saved, your body doesn't get saved. Your body is to be in subjection to your soul or to your spirit, and the spirit is to live in triumph over the body. When you got saved, your body did not get born again.

Some people like to argue about that and want to act pious, when all they do is show their lack of understanding. They say, ''Well, when I got saved, I got saved all over.'' I have had them say, ''When I got saved, it broke out on me like a case of measles.''

When I got saved, I knew God had given me a new nature. I knew Christ lived in my heart. I knew my sins were forgiven. I knew my name was written in the Lamb's Book of Life. I knew I was not going to Hell. But I knew I still lived in a body that was not yet saved.

You say, ''Not me.'' Well then, take off your specks.

''Not me!'' How come you have lost all your hair?

''Not me!'' How come you have lost your teeth?

"Not me!" What doeth all those wrinkles, bulges, bunions, bridges and bi-focals, if your body got saved? How come you have dandruff and have to use deodorant if your body got saved?

How come sometimes you don't talk like you ought to talk? How come sometimes you don't act like you ought to act? Why? You are a good man or a good woman in a bad body. Paul said, "O wretched man that I am! who shall deliver me from the body of this death?" (Rom. 7:24).

So there are three great systems of truths—His finished work at the cross, His constant work at the throne and His future work of His coming. All three contribute to the child of God having the assurance that he is saved.

You say, "Well, preacher, if all this be true, why is it that every Christian doesn't know positively that he is saved?"

First, some folks are not saved. Some folks have been in the baptistry who are not saved. There are others who have had some sort of religious experience who are not saved.

Proverbs 14:12 says, "There is a way which seemeth right unto a man, but the end thereof are the ways of death."

So the man or woman who says, "I am going to get saved by getting a little better every day," is losing ground. You had as well take me out to a big old oak tree, give me a little pair of manicure scissors and say, "Kill that tree by cutting one leaf off at a time." While you are dealing with one sin, God is looking at a thousand more. You will never get saved that way.

Many think they are saved because they have to their credit so-called "good works." They have been baptized, they have followed others in joining the church, they have learned a certain language; some even carry their Bibles, and some don't do the things that lost people do. But the Bible says, "There is a way which seemeth right unto a man, but the end thereof are the ways of death."

Every once in awhile someone says, "Preacher, you go your

way and I'll go mine, and we'll come out at the same place.''

No, we won't! In the first place, I don't have a way. I have no plan, no scheme, no road, no avenue, no way to be saved except God's way. There is only one way, and that is the way that Jesus spoke of in John 14:6: ''I am the way, the truth, and the life: no man cometh unto the Father, but by me.''

There are folks who are not saved who may be religious, who may be church members and who may be somewhat moral and honest. They pay their debts and live good enough to stay out of jail. But one can't live good enough to be saved, because he is a rotten, dirty sinner, cut off of the same bolt of cloth as this preacher and every other person ever born.

Then some folks are trying to know they are saved by the wrong basis of assurance. For instance, many say, ''Now, if you don't feel saved, then you will never have the basis for assurance.''

There is a sense in which I feel saved, but let me be honest with you. Just suppose someone gets on my nerves or I get on his and all of a sudden I lose my temper. Right in the middle of it all someone comes up and asks, ''Brother Malone, do you feel saved?'' Do you know what I would say? ''No. Get away from me until I get through with this argument.''

It is like a fellow one time who was having a fuss with another man and said, ''Let's have a word of prayer.'' He said, ''No. I don't want to have anything to do with God while I'm mad!''

This business of feeling saved is the wrong basis of assurance. I am happy in the Lord. I have the peace of God in my heart. While I am preaching this sermon, if this heart should give out, I know I would go out and meet God saved.

The basis of salvation is not feeling.

You say, ''Well, don't you believe in feeling?'' I sure do. I believe you ought to feel saved, ought to act like you are saved, and you ought to rejoice like you are saved; but this is not the basis of assurance. The basis of assurance is clearly set forth in the passage that I read.

"And this is the record, that God hath given to us eternal life, and this life is in his Son" (I John 5:11). This "record" is: "These things have I written unto you that believe on the name of the Son of God; that ye may know that ye have eternal life, and that ye may believe on the name of the Son of God" (vs. 13).

The basis of assurance is the blessed Word of God.

So if someone asks, "How do you know you are saved?" tell him you know it because the Bible tells you so.

Naturally, you are not going to know that you are saved by trusting in your works. Why doesn't everyone know he is saved? Some don't know what happens when a Christian sins. Many have been taught what is called the doctrine of sinless perfection. But there is no such thing taught in the Bible.

Take the greatest men and women of God and let them walk out of the pages of the Scriptures. Take Moses, whom God says was the meekest man that ever lived. One day mighty Moses smote the rock when he had been commanded to speak to it. God said, "You call these people rebels, yet you have rebelled against Me yourself. You are not going into the Promised Land. You will lead the nation Israel to the border, but Joshua will take them in."

Take David whom God said was a man after His own heart. But read that great penitential psalm that came pouring from the heart of this sinning saint.

Take the Apostle Paul. If you will examine the Scripture, you will hear him say, "When I would do good, evil is present with me." Paul says, "There is a law in my body that tells me to do bad." And Paul cried out for deliverance: "O wretched man that I am! who shall deliver me from the body of this death?" (Rom. 7:21,24).

Many people are not aware of what happens when a Christian

sins. He regrets his sin, repents, laments of it, goes to the secret place and makes it right with God; but he does not cease to be a Christian.

Someone says, "Preacher, have you gotten to where you can't sin?" "No, but I have gotten to the place where I don't want to sin."

We read in I John 1:9 and 10:

"If we confess our sins, he is faithful and just to forgive us our sins, and to cleanse us from all unrighteousness. If we say that we have not sinned, we make him a liar, and his word is not in us."

If any of you were to say, "Preacher, I'm a Christian, but I have never sinned," I will pull this Scripture on you.

God doesn't put a person out of His family when he sins against Him. The second chapter of the first epistle of John begins like this:

"My little children, these things write I unto you, that ye sin not. And if any man sin, we have an advocate with the Father, Jesus Christ the righteous: And he is the propitiation for our sins: and not for our's only, but also for the sins of the whole world."

Many people don't know what happens when a Christian sins. They think, *Well, God is through with me.* No, He isn't. God will deal with you, but you are still a member of His family.

Some people don't have assurance of their salvation because of the lack of understanding of the work of the Spirit of God in their lives. Jesus said:

"And I will pray the Father, and he shall give you another Comforter, that he may abide with you for ever; Even the Spirit of truth; whom the world cannot receive, because it seeth him not, neither knoweth him: but ye know him; for he dwelleth with you, and shall be in you."—John 14:16,17.

Once the Holy Spirit takes up His abode in the life of a believer, He never leaves.

Some people don't know they are saved because they are weak for lack of nourishment and teaching through the Word of God. That is why we read in I Peter 2:2, "As newborn babes, desire the sincere milk of the word, that ye may grow thereby."

I give you five reasons why I know I am a child of God. It goes without saying that these are five reasons why any born-again believer can know for sure that he is a child of God, and that forever.

I. THE WITNESS FROM WITHIN

First, there is a witness of the Spirit from within. Notice Romans 8:16: "The Spirit itself [himself] beareth witness with our spirit, that we are the children of God." This verse is talking about the witness of the Spirit from within.

I was asking some members of my family how they would explain this verse. They know as much how to explain it as any of you, but I had a reason for asking. I have never yet found anyone who could elaborate very much on this verse: "The Spirit itself [himself] beareth witness with our spirit, that we are the children of God."

There is not much you can say about it because it is such a conclusive verse. It is such an inevitable result of being saved that the Spirit bears witness with our spirit that we have been adopted into the family of God.

Many times young people come to me to be married. If they are both saved and have Bible grounds for marriage and are in love with one another, I don't feel there is a great deal that I can say to them. I am the poorest marriage counselor you ever listened to! I don't think you have to teach two people how to love each other, and I don't think there is a great deal that can be said about it.

When you come to this verse, you come to such an inevitable and conclusive truth of God that even God prohibits very much to be said about it. Within the body of a born-again Christian there is a testimony, a witness, a living, personal, dynamic witness, that he is a child of God.

You ought to know whether you have that witness from within or not. This is fact. You talk about feeling. You talk about inspiration. This is something that is felt in the heart of a truly born-again child of God.

One time in an ordination service they were asking each person, "How do you know you are called to preach?" No one can give a real theological answer to that question. But a young man in this particular ordination gave the best answer I have heard, with no exception. With feeling, emotion and fervor, he said, "I just know it, that's all!"

In this verse we find that the Spirit of God makes a Christian know that he is saved. If you suppress Him or if you crowd Him to an obscure place in your life or if you ignore Him or are ignorant of the Bible truth about Him, you won't have the assurance that you can have. If you know Him, exalt Him, surrender to Him, yield to Him and stay empty, He can fill you.

"The Spirit itself beareth witness with our spirit, that we are the children of God."

In the Old Testament days, when the great high priest went beyond the veil with a basin of blood in his hands, he was unseen by human eye. He went all alone once a year and never without blood. The Bible speaks of a bell and a pomegranate, a bell and pomegranate, a bell and pomegranate, all around the hem of his priestly garment.

The people in the outer court put their hand to their ear, listened and said, "If that priest were to die in there all alone, then we too would die and would never know the assurance of our sins forgiven. But as long as that bell rings, we know that the high priestly work goes on, and we know that atonement will be made."

This verse is talking about the bell ringing in the human heart: "The Spirit itself [himself] beareth witness with our spirit, that we are the children of God."

There is a wonderful illustration of how the Spirit of God indicates your assurance and gives you reason to know that you are God's child. In reference to the Lord Jesus Christ, God wanted people to know how they could recognize Jesus and know He was the Son of God and that, when the Son of God stepped on the stage of human history, He was the fulfillment of the Old Testament. God wanted the people to be able to recognize the Son of God.

How did they do it? We read in John 1:32, "And John bare record, saying, I saw the Spirit descending from heaven like a dove, and it abode upon him."

Now listen to the next verse: "And I knew him not: but he that sent me to baptize with water, the same said unto me, Upon whom thou shalt see the Spirit descending, and remaining on him, the same is he which baptizeth with the Holy Ghost."

Let's break that down. God said to John, "I will tell you how you will know when you see the Son of God. When you see the Holy Ghost descend on Someone and stay on Him, He is the One. You need not look any further."

When Jesus waded out in the muddy water of the River Jordan to this John the Baptist and when He submitted Himself for baptism, John the Baptist saw the Holy Spirit like a heavenly dove descend upon the Lord and stay on Him. By that, the writer, John the apostle, and John the Baptist both knew this was God's Son because the Holy Ghost of God said, "This is the Son of God."

That is an illustration of what God can do in the life of every believer. The Holy Spirit within says, "You are a child of God," and though there is not a great deal of explanation, you better know that you have the witness of the Spirit in your life. You better know that the Holy Spirit of God says, "Yes, you are saved and you are a child of God."

"These things have I written unto you that believe on the name of the Son of God; that ye may know that ye have eternal life, and that ye may believe on the name of the Son of God."

II. SCRIPTURAL SIGNS FROM WITHOUT

Then we have the scriptural signs from without. By that I mean, there are certain things, certain Bible signs, that a Christian ought to look for in himself. You ought to see if you have these outward signs. There are some outward signs mentioned in the Bible that a Christian ought to have. Seven of these are in the first epistle of John.

In II Corinthians 5:17 we read, "Therefore if any man be in Christ, he is a new creature: old things are passed away; behold, all things are become new."

This new creature is characterized by seven signs that you can see: 1. It says in I John 2:3,4: "And hereby we do know that we know him, if we keep his commandments. He that saith, I know him, and keepeth not his commandments, is a liar, and the truth is not in him."

One of the signs that you are saved is obedience to the commandments of Christ and to the Word of God. If you are a disobedient Christian, you have no right to ask God to give you the assurance of salvation. If you are not obeying the Lord and the Scripture that you know a Christian ought to obey, you have no right to ask God to make you know that you are saved. This matter of obedience is an indication that you are a child of God.

2. The first epistle of John, in chapter 2:29, mentions also, "If ye know that he is righteous, ye know that every one that doeth righteousness is born of him." Talking about the new nature, I John 3:9 says, "Whosoever is born of God doth not commit sin." The new nature which a believer receives cannot sin, does not sin, never does sin, cannot continue in sin. You can know that

you are born of God because you do righteousness.

3. We know we are born again because we love the brethren:
I John 3:14—"We know that we have passed from death unto life,
because we love the brethren. He that loveth not his brother abideth
in death."

This is one of the most misunderstood passages in the New Testament: "We know that we have passed from death unto life, because we love the brethren." I don't believe this is speaking about some individual. We ought to love every born-again individual because Christ is in him, though this is not easy. But it is not talking about an individual. "We know that we have passed from death unto life, because we love the brethren" means to love the family of God. That means going to church. That means where the children of God are, you ought to be and want to be if you are saved. If you are saved, you will want to act right when you get there. But if you don't love the family of God, the household of faith, the fellowship of the saints, you have no right to know if you are saved or not.

4. Then I John mentions the witness of the Spirit: I John 3:24—"And he that keepeth his commandments dwelleth in him, and he in him. And hereby we know that he abideth in us, by the Spirit which he hath given us."

Then I John 4:13: "Hereby know we that we dwell in him, and he in us, because he hath given us of his Spirit."

Then Romans 8:16: "The Spirit himself beareth witness with our spirit, that we are the children of God."

5. We know we have passed from death unto life because we believe in the deity and Lordship of Christ: I John 5:1—"Whosoever believeth that Jesus is the Christ is born of God...."

It says in Acts 9:5,6:

"And he said, Who art thou, Lord? And the Lord said, I am

Jesus whom thou persecutest: it is hard for thee to kick against the pricks. And he trembling and astonished said, Lord, what wilt thou have me to do? And the Lord said unto him, Arise, and go into the city, and it shall be told thee what thou must do."

Paul immediately believed in the Lord Jesus Christ, that He was the Son of God.

6. Then, we know we have passed from death unto life because we overcome the world: I John 5:4—"For whatsoever is born of God overcometh the world: and this is the victory that overcometh the world, even our faith."

Mark 8:36 says, "For what shall it profit a man, if he shall gain the whole world, and lose his own soul?"

And I John 2:15 tells us, "Love not the world, neither the things that are in the world. If any man love the world, the love of the Father is not in him."

7. Then, we know that we have passed from death unto life because we do not continue to practice sin: I John 3:9—"Whosoever is born of God doth not commit sin; for his seed remaineth in him: and he cannot sin, because he is born of God."

III. THE ATONING BLOOD FROM THE PAST

We can know that we are saved because of the atoning blood from the past. Notice a great verse in I John 5:8: "And there are three that bear witness in earth, the Spirit, and the water, and the blood: and these three agree in one."

Ecclesiastes 4:12 tells us, "A threefold cord is not quickly broken."

The first epistle of John is talking about how you can know that you are saved. "These things have I written unto you that believe on the name of the Son of God; that ye may know that ye have eternal life...."

Verse 8 of I John 5 says, "And there are three that bear witness in earth. . . .'' Witness to what? Witness to the fact that you are a Christian. First, the Spirit; second, the water—that is, the Bible; and, third, the blood. These three agree in one. Here is a threefold witness you can expect from God to know that you are saved.

The third one of these is the blood of Jesus Christ. The old-time saints used to make so much of the blood. So many of the old songs were about the blood. When so many of the saints of God testified, they testified about the blood. They were always looking backward to the finished work of Calvary. They reckoned on it; they trusted it; they believed in it; they leaned on it; they staked their souls on it; they fought the Devil with it, and if the Devil assailed them, they pleaded the blood.

That is what it means in Revelation when the Devil assails the elect, chosen people of God. Look at Revelation 12:11: ''And they overcame him by the blood of the Lamb, and by the word of their testimony; and they loved not their lives unto the death.''

Here is an illustration of this. The Lord said to the children of Israel, ''I am going to deliver you this night from over four hundred years of bondage and servitude in Egypt under these cruel taskmasters.'' God had sent plagues to soften the heart of an indignant unbeliever, the wicked Pharaoh, but none of those plagues had softened his heart; he only became harder in his rebellion against God. God said, ''This night I will deliver my people, and I will do it with the blood of a little lamb.''

God told them to take a basin of blood and a piece of hyssop—that little vine that grows in the crevices and cracks of a stone wall and in between the rocks—and for every family to shed the blood of a lamb and take that blood—all of it pointing to the Lamb of God who taketh away the sin of the world—and put that blood over the door of every home.

God had said, ''I will pass over this land tonight and slay the firstborn of every home where there is no blood.'' I can imagine a crippled son in a Jewish home, bedridden and an invalid, not able to walk. Maybe this crippled boy said to his father, "Father, are you sure that the blood is on the door?"

The Jewish head of that home had taken the hyssop, put it in the blood and then put the blood on the lentil, the crosspiece at the top of the door where God said put it. Down the door it ran, making a steady stream of scarlet.

God said, "Put it on either side." He dips it on this side and splashes it on that side and standing back he, looking at it and seeing a bloody cross on that door, looked forward to the cross upon which Jesus would die.

Perhaps this crippled son insisted, "Father, are you sure the blood is on the door? It is the life of the firstborn that is at stake tonight." Finally, the father sweeps the boy up into his arms, takes him to the door and says, "My boy, see for yourself." That son sees that bloody cross upon the door of his home and is satisfied.

His father takes him back into the home and puts him down in his bed of affliction. The boy looks at his father and says, "I have no fear of the judgment of God that will come tonight, for I have seen the blood and have all the confidence in the world that all is well."

Hallelujah to God! Ten thousand praises to the Lamb! I can look backward and see the bloody cross, and though all the demons of Hell and all the fires of darkness assail this poor ransomed soul, I cry to the highest Heaven and the deepest Hell, "The blood, the blood is my only plea!" "...without the shedding of blood is no remission" (Heb. 9:22).

You say to me, "Preacher, how do you know you are saved?" "...the blood of Jesus Christ his Son cleanseth us from all sin" (I John 1:7).

I know it because of not only the witness within and the sign from without, but for the redeeming blood of the past.

IV. THE INTERCESSOR FOR THE PRESENT

Then I know I am saved because of the Intercessor for the present moment. When the Lord arose from the grave and forty days later ascended back into the presence of the Father, He entered into the heavenlies to take up His mediatorial work. I don't know of any phase of this wonderful salvation that has been more neglected than the mediatorial work of our Lord.

Romans 5:10 contains a tremendous statement: "...we shall be saved by his life." It is not speaking of His death on the cross; it says, "...we shall be saved by his life."

The modernist picks that up and says, "What you need to do is imitate Jesus and take Him for an example. Walk like He walked. Live like He lived if you can. Talk like He talked. Think like He thought. Be like Christ and you will go to Heaven because the Bible says you are 'saved by His life.'"

But it is not talking about His life on the other side of that cross. It is talking about His life this side of the cross. His life the other side of the cross was for only one purpose, and that was to go to Calvary.

He said, "To this end was I born, and for this cause came I into the world" (John 18:37). When He said, "...we shall be saved by his life," it was this side of the cross, at the throne. He is our Advocate.

If someone ever asks if you have an attorney, you can say you have the best One in all the world. Every Christian has the same Attorney. That is what *advocate* means. It means *paraclete*, same word as *Comforter*; "one called alongside to help." He put One inside down here and put One at the throne at the Father's right hand to maintain my cause day and night, world without end. He is there, and His present work is to keep us and to make us know we are His forever.

That is what I John 2:1 and 2 is talking about:

"My little children, these things write I unto you, that ye sin not. And if any man sin, we have an advocate with the Father, Jesus Christ the righteous: And he is the propitiation for our sins: and not for our's only, but also for the sins of the whole world."

Jesus is what Job said he wished he had. In the midst of all his afflictions, when he knew that God was dealing with him, Job cried, "Neither is there any daysman betwixt us that might lay his hand upon us both" (9:33). A "daysman," as it is used in the book of Job, is a go-between, a mediator, an attorney, an advocate, a representative. That is what a Christian has—an Advocate with the Father, even Jesus Christ the righteous.

The Lord's Prayer, which many people think begins, "Our Father, which art in heaven . . . ," is not the Lord's Prayer but the disciples' prayer. The Lord's Prayer is found in chapter 17 of the book of John where He renders up His work to God just before His crucifixion and says in verse 12, "While I was with them in the world, I kept them in thy name: those that thou gavest me I have kept, and none of them is lost, but the son of perdition; that the scripture might be fulfilled." Judas Iscariot was the only one.

There is a beautiful picture in this chapter. You read where Jesus said, "I pray for them . . . ," talking about the other eleven disciples. I am on shouting ground when I read, 'I pray for them which Thou hast given Me; for they are My own.' "

But in verse 20 in John 17, He comes to something else. In that great high-priestly prayer Jesus said, "Neither pray I for these alone, but for them also which shall believe on me through their word." That reaches down across the unborn years and lays its truth on every Christian. Back in the shadow of the cross, Jesus said, "I am praying for Tom and for every Christian."

Another beautiful picture is when Jesus told the disciples to cross the Sea of Galilee while He goes yonder to the mountain to pray. They start rowing and a storm comes up. While they are in the storm, Jesus is on the mountain in prayer. He is now in the Mount of God praying for every believer.

Listen! Don't you know the Lord will get His prayers answered! What the Lord asked of God, God will do for His Son. In that great high-priestly prayer He said, "That they all may be one; as thou, Father, art in me, and I in thee, that they also may be one in us: that the world may believe that thou hast sent me" (John 17:21).

God is going to answer that prayer. I am just as sure to be with Jesus as two and two make four. I am just as sure to be with Jesus as the Bible is true. And so are you, if you are a Christian. "He ever liveth to make intercession for them" (Heb. 7:25).

I know that I am saved not only because of the witness within, the signs from without, the blood from the past, but by the Intercessor at this very moment.

V. THE SAVIOUR FOR THE FUTURE

In closing, I know that I am a child of God because of the guaranteed work of the Saviour for the future. The Lord is going to do something else for the believer. If you believe the Bible, you can reckon on it and depend on it. He is going to save our bodies. Every time I think of this carnal body and the depraved, fleshly tabernacle of every Christian, I remember God said that the body is going to be redeemed.

In Romans 8:23, where it speaks of waiting for the redemption of our body, it tells about this. Our *body* is going to be born again when the Lord comes, just like your soul was born again when you were saved. "And not only they, but ourselves also, which have the firstfruits of the Spirit, even we ourselves groan within ourselves, waiting for the adoption, to wit, the redemption of our body."

Philippians 3:20 and 21 says:

"For our conversation is in heaven; from whence also we look for the Saviour, the Lord Jesus Christ: Who shall change our vile body, that it may be fashioned like unto his glorious body, according to the working whereby he is able even to subdue all things unto himself."

Someday we will have a body just like Jesus'. When I am in the battle against this body, I think of the work of the future. Not only do I think of the witness from within, the signs from without, the blood from the past, the Intercessor at the present moment; but I also think of what I know He is going to do for us when He comes. This body will be redeemed.

I heard a wonderful story years ago of a mother and her teenage boy who were saved. After they were saved, they went home rejoicing together and saying, "Praise the Lord! We have been saved! Our sins forgiven! We are on our way to Heaven! The Lord is in our life! Praise the Lord!"

The next morning at the breakfast table, the mother said to the son, "Son, do you suppose we are really saved?"

He said, "Wait just a moment, Mother."

He left the table and went to his bedroom. The night before, a personal worker had given him a card with John 5:24 written on it: "Verily, verily, I say unto you, He that heareth my word, and believeth on him that sent me, hath everlasting life, and shall not come into condemnation; but is passed from death unto life." He brought the card with him back to the table and read it to her. Then he said, "Mother, it hasn't changed one bit from last night."

"Then," she said, "we must still be saved."

He said, "We sure are, because His promise hasn't changed one bit."

Thank God for His immutable Word that says that we are His children.

So I say again, what I have said hundreds of times: How do

I know I am saved? Because the Bible tells me I'm saved.

You can know that you are saved and that you are a child of God.

"These things have I written unto you that believe on the name of the Son of God; that ye may know that ye have eternal life ...."—I John 5:13.

_____ Chapter III _____

How I Know Jesus Christ Is the Son of God

Matthew 16:13-18; John 6:60-71

"And we believe and are sure that thou art that Christ, the Son of the living God."—John 6:69.

Matthew 16:13-18 and John 6:60-71 must be discussed together because there are some similarities about them. In both passages Jesus asks the disciples a question. In both passages Simon Peter comes forth with a thrilling answer.

In Matthew 16:13 Jesus asked, "Whom do men say that I the Son of man am?" Simon Peter answered, "Thou art the Christ, the Son of the living God" (vs. 16).

In this passage in John, chapter 6, Jesus asks, "Will ye also go away?" The multitudes had heard who He was and what He came to do, and they had turned and by the thousands had walked away. "Will ye also go away?"

Once again Simon Peter answered, "Lord, to whom shall we go? thou hast the words of eternal life." Then Peter said, "And we believe and are sure that thou art that Christ, the Son of the living God" (John 6:67-69).

Thus, from the lips of Simon Peter come probably the two greatest statements ever found in the Bible as to the testimony of who Jesus Christ is. Peter said, "And we believe and are sure that thou art that Christ, the Son of the living God."

I want to discuss "Who Jesus Christ Is," or, "How I Know Jesus Christ Is the Son of God."

How do we know that Jesus Christ is deity? *Divine* is a misused word. People in our day make some kind of concoction of candy and call it divinity fudge. Sometimes a person sees another and says, "Oh, isn't she divine!" or, "Isn't he just divine!" So I will dispose of that word and talk about the deity of Jesus Christ or why I know He is the Son of God and just as much God as if He had never been a man.

Three things need to be distinguished when we discuss the deity of Jesus Christ. I am not talking primarily about what is called the virgin birth of our Lord. The virgin birth was prophesied many times in the Old Testament, such as in Isaiah 7:14, "Behold, a virgin shall conceive, and bear a son, and shall call his name Immanuel." The Bible says that Jesus would be virgin-born, but I am not talking primarily about the virgin birth of Christ.

When that night of the annunciation or announcement came, the angel of God appeared to Mary, saying, "The Holy Ghost shall come upon thee, and the power of the Highest shall overshadow thee: therefore also that holy thing which shall be born of thee shall be called the Son of God" (Luke 1:35).

Neither am I talking to you about that which is often referred to as the incarnation, that is, Jesus is both God and man in one body. The Bible plainly teaches the incarnation: "And the Word was made flesh, and dwelt among us, (and we beheld his glory, the glory as of the only begotten of the Father,) full of grace and truth" (John 1:14).

Paul said in I Timothy 3:16, "And without controversy great is the mystery of godliness: God was manifest in the flesh...."
That is the incarnation—that is, both God and man dwelt in one

body and walked among men physically for thirty-three years. We must distinguish between the virgin birth and the incarnation and deity of Jesus Christ. I am talking to you about why I know Jesus is God.

One of the great problems that confronts people when you start talking about the deity of Jesus Christ is the same problem that causes many to doubt the Bible. You see, the Bible has both divine and human authors. Now the Bible is a divine Book, inspired of God and is the Word of God; but the Lord spoke to some thirty-eight or forty men over a period of some fifteen hundred years on three different continents and commanded them, ''Write what I tell you to write.'' Says II Peter 1:21, ''...holy men of God spake as they were moved by the Holy Ghost.'' *Moved* means ''borne along or carried along.'' God said to these men, ''Write what I say to you''; and here we have the Bible with both a human and divine authorship, although it is a divine Book.

Had God never used a man to write it, many people would not doubt that this Book comes from God. You take the Holy Bible— that is the written Word. You take Jesus Christ, the living Word— that is true also of Him. The mind of the natural man asks, ''How can a man with a human body, subject to all the limitations of a human body, be God Himself?'' You have the human, divine Jesus. That is what causes many to doubt the deity of Jesus Christ. I shall illustrate it this way.

Back in 1822 there was a most interesting man who, at that time, wasn't very prominent. In fact, he was a German monk similar to what Martin Luther was. His name was Gregor Mendel. Today we have what is called Mendel's Law or Mendelism. This studious man with a brilliant mind began a study in the field of biology and somewhat in the area of chemistry.

From that time, all the great students and scholars in the fields of biology have been exploiting and exploring, enlarging, building on and developing what is called Mendel's Law. Mendel's Law is simply this: "Every individual is the sum total of the characteristics, recessive or dominant, in its immediate progenitors."

To put that law in your language and mine, it means that every individual has all the characteristics, either dominant or recessive, in both his mother and father. The dominant one probably has come from the parents, and the recessive one might have come from the grandparents.

In fact, one great Bible scholar, now with the Lord, had a suggestion related to Mendel's Law for young couples. If the couples' children behave more like animals than children, the couples might say that the children are acting more like their grandparents than like their parents.

If you think about Mendel's Law for a minute or two, you can come to several conclusions. You can take man plus man equals man. That is all there is to it. Had Mary been just as the Bible says she was—the mother of our Lord Jesus Christ, a human being—Jesus would have gotten from her all the human characteristics. If Joseph had been Jesus' father and Jesus had been born of Joseph and Mary in wedlock—which is not the case—you have man plus man equals man. You end with nothing but a man. But such is not the case.

Take this Law and look at it in another instance. Had Mary been divine—as some people claim, and spotless, sinless and immaculate—and with the Holy Ghost being as the Bible teaches, then God plus God equals God. You would have a Christ whom no one could ever approach.

Then take this Law and look at it from the Bible standpoint. Mary was a human being. Jesus was born of the Holy Ghost. You have man plus God, which is a God-man. That is the Christ of the Bible. That is the Christ of my heart. That is the Christ of Calvary. That is the Christ who walked out of the grave, conquering death.

Jesus was the divine Son of God, just as much God as God the Father and God the Holy Spirit.

You ask, "Preacher, how do you know Jesus was deity?" First, let me say that I believe what the Bible says. I am not one who goes off in some other direction and digs up a piece of stone somewhere and says that archeology proves the Bible. This Bible doesn't need archeology to prove it. I don't go outside the Bible to find proof that I know Jesus Christ is the Son of God; I go to the Bible. Remember that Peter said, "And we believe and are sure. . . ." That is just the opposite from the average person wanting to approach this subject. He or she will say, "Well now, you make me certain that Jesus is the Son of God; then I will believe." Peter said, "And we believe and are sure. . . ." Whatever I preach and whatever I get, I get it right out of the Bible. I believe that Jesus Christ is the Son of God and that to any open mind we can make it plain and clear that Jesus Christ is deity.

"And we believe and are sure that thou art that Christ, the Son of the living God."

I. HIS DEITY IS PROVEN BY HIS POSSESSION AND MANIFESTATION OF ALL THE ATTRIBUTES OF DEITY

He possessed and manifested all the attributes of deity. Jesus Christ possessed and manifested every attribute that God has.

There is a wonderful verse in Colossians 2:9: "For in him [Jesus] dwelleth all the fulness of the Godhead bodily." Great Greek scholars say that the word *fulness* can be translated *attribute,* not *attributes,* because *fulness* is singular. The Greek word is *attribute.* So this verse can be read this way: "In him dwelleth all the attribute of God."

The Bible says that every attribute or characteristic that the Father has, Jesus has. The Bible claims that Christ has every attribute that God the Father has. The attributes of God are those distinguishing characteristics which are inseparable from the idea of deity and which constitute the basis for His manifestations to His creatures. Jesus had every one of them. That is why Jesus was able to say, "...he that hath seen me hath seen the Father..." (John 14:9).

Don't ever be persuaded into believing the things the liberalists say: "Yes, we will consent that Jesus was a great teacher and a great man. We will consent that he lived a great life." That is foolishness! If Jesus was not God, He was not good, for He claimed to be God. If Jesus was not God, the Bible is not true, for the Bible says that He has every distinguishing characteristic that is related to the idea of God Himself and to the deity. Jesus has all the attributes of God.

Now what are the attributes? I am no theologian or scholar, but I am a student of the Bible. For over thirty-five years, I have sought, with a hungry heart, to know what the Bible says.

If you were to ask people what God's greatest attribute is, many would say, "The greatest attribute of God is His omnipotence. He is all-powerful." On the morning of creation, He stood and flung from His omnipotent fingers countless worlds into space. He is the omnipotent God. Many Bible-believing and fundamental people would tell you they believe God's greatest attribute is His omnipotence. But that is not His greatest attribute.

If you were to ask the uninstructed people who do not know or believe the Bible, such as the liberalists and modernists, what God's greatest attribute is, they would answer, "Love." They paint a picture of God as a God of love who cannot punish sin and condemn anyone to the Hell described in the Bible. But neither of these is true.

1. The greatest attribute, according to the Bible, seems to be God's **holiness or purity.** The chief attribute of God, my friends,

is holiness, and Jesus Christ possessed this attribute. Christ Himself was the holy Son of God. Psalm 145:17 says, "The Lord is righteous in all his ways, and holy in all his works."

When we talk about holiness, we are talking about "the self-affirming purity of God." I could take a good man as an example. I could say that he is a holy man. He is robed in the righteousness of Jesus Christ. He is clad in the garments of salvation. He is washed in the blood of the Son of God. He is indwelt by the Holy Ghost of God. And He is in the process of being made like his Lord. I could say that he is holy, but he must get that holiness from another. It is not naturally his own; it is an imputed righteousness.

The holiness of God is a self-affirming purity that is inherent with and a part of God. The same was true of Jesus Christ. So the Bible says that "The Lord is righteous in all his ways, and holy in all his works" (Ps. 145:17). That statement could never be said about any other person born of woman, created by God.

It is like Isaiah, in Isaiah 6, when he got that glorious illuminating vision of God and saw the Lord lifted up. He saw Him as I wish all of us could see Him. Isaiah cried, "Holy, holy, holy, is the Lord of hosts: the whole earth is full of his glory" (vs. 3).

Holy in His person, holy in His ways and holy in His works—Jesus Christ has this attribute of God called holiness or purity.

Hebrews 7:26 declares, "For such an high priest [speaking of Jesus] became us, who is holy, harmless, undefiled, separate from sinners, and made higher than the heavens." The Bible says that Jesus had this first, this primary, this all-important attribute of God: He was absolutely holy. We see this holiness all through the Bible.

Sometimes in reading chapters in the Old Testament, I will take a chapter and in it underscore this one statement: "without blemish and without spot." Exodus 12:5 says, "Your lamb shall be without blemish...." When we get to the amplification of that statement in Peter's epistles, we read where Peter said:

"Forasmuch as ye know that ye were not redeemed with corruptible things, as silver and gold, from your vain conversation received by tradition from your fathers; But with the precious blood of Christ, as of a lamb without blemish and without spot."—I Pet. 1:18,19.

Every lamb of the Old Testament which typified Jesus Christ and pointed forward to the Lamb of God that would take away the sin of the world was without blemish. No blind eye, no crooked limb, no torn flank, no twisted ear, no distorted feature—no lamb with any blemish could ever be sacrificed upon the altar. Why? It pointed forward to One in whom there is no blemish. When Peter spoke of Him, he said, "...without blemish and without spot."

A blemish is a defect that is originally in something. If you buy a suit of clothes and find a flaw where the lining is twisted and torn as it came from the factory, that flaw is a blemish. If you buy a suit at a store and drop it in a mud puddle on the way home and get dirt on it, that is a spot.

Jesus had no blemish. He was pre-existent with God and had been as perfect as He was when He said, "Which of you convinceth me of sin?" (John 8:46).

While walking thirty-three years from the cradle in Bethlehem's lowly manger to that hour when He died robed in blood and crowned with thorns upon the hill called Calvary, He picked up not one spot—not one. Thank God, we have a Saviour who is without spot and without blemish! That is the reason that Jesus said what no other intelligent being would ever say when one day, in the face of His enemies, He stood and said, "Who convinceth Me of sin?" *Convinceth* is synonymous with *convicted.* What He said was, "Who convicteth Me of sin?"

Thank God, no one! When He died, a centurion said, "Truly, this was the Son of God" (Matt. 27:54). When He died, a thief said, ". . . this man hath done nothing amiss" (Luke 23:41).

I want to go on record that I believe I have a perfect Saviour, the divine Son of God, who possessed and manifested all the attributes of God.

2. Theologians say that the second great attribute of God is that of **justice.** The word *justice* is often not defined as it is defined in the Bible. In the Bible, *justice* is defined as "the certainty of the punishment of wrongdoing." Since God is holy, He must punish everything that is unholy. God the Father possesses the attribute of justice. Ezekiel 18:20 says, "The soul that sinneth, it shall die." Death speaks of separation. Physical death is the separation of your soul from your body. Spiritual death is the separation of your soul from God.

Have you ever sinned in word, thought or deed since you came into the world? If so, the Bible says, "The soul that sinneth, it shall die." That is why Romans 3:26 says, "To declare, I say, at this time his righteousness: that he might be just, and the justifier of him which believeth in Jesus."

I speak reverently when I say that God faces the greatest dilemma that anyone could ever face. Here is a holy, righteous God who absolutely cannot look upon sin. Here are people, without one single exception, from the original dye cast in Adam to the youngest babe this very hour—every one of them has been born in sin. ". . . for there is no difference: For all have sinned, and come short of the glory of God" (Rom. 3:22,23).

God faces a dilemma. A just God has said, "The soul that sinneth, it shall die." Then how is man going to get to God and ever be one in Him? That is the dilemma. The book of Romans teaches us that God in Christ has bridged that gulf fixed between the righteousness of God and the unrighteousness of man. That bridge is Jesus Christ. That is why Jesus said, "I am the way...." He didn't say, "I will point you to the way." He didn't say, "I will show you the way." He said, "I am the way...." He said, "I am the way to God." Jesus is the bridge that spans over that chasm. Man, by believing, comes out of the area of unrighteousness and comes to a God who is righteousness personified. So Jesus possessed the attribute of justice.

I want to say that the justice of God is inexorable, implacable and impartial. No person, no family, no nation, no generation has ever escaped the justice of God. Neither will you. "...be sure your sin will find you out" (Num. 32:23). Jesus had that wonderful attribute of justice.

3. The third great attribute of God, according to theologians, is the attribute of **mercy.** That attribute makes my heart tender. Thank God for His mercy! Mercy is what Jesus taught the man in the Temple who came at the same time as the publican. Both came to pray.

The Pharisee prayed, "God, I thank thee, that I am not as other men are... I tithe, I fast, I pray." The publican prayed, "God be merciful to me a sinner" (Luke 18:11,13). Thank God that He has the attribute of mercy!

Jesus Christ has this attribute also. Men tried to prove that Jesus would not be merciful. One example is the beautiful passage that tells of someone getting saved.

One early morning when Jesus was in the Temple, the woman who was taken in the act of adultery was brought to Him. The enemies were His, not hers. What did they care about one little woman? This sin of adultery was being committed in a multiplicity of ways and by thousands of people. These enemies were not righteous and holy. They hated Jesus Christ and wanted to place Him upon the horns of a dilemma upon which they thought He could never get off.

So they brought this woman, flung her at the feet of Jesus, and said, "The law of Moses demands that this woman be stoned: but what do you say?"

Think of it! They said, "The Bible says this: but what do you say?" How would you like to have that presented to you? I would have to say, "Do what the Bible says." But they are talking to the One who wrote it!

Jesus wrote something on the floor in the sand of that outer court of the Temple with His finger, as if to say, "Don't you remember the Old Testament says that the Decalog given to Moses was written with the finger of God?" Jesus said it was "written with the finger of God" (Exod. 31:18).

The woman stood there quivering and weeping, broken, lost and ashamed. The carping critics and enemies of the Lord Jesus said, "The law of Moses said that she be stoned to death: but what do you say?" Jesus said, "He that is without sin among you, let him first cast a stone at her." The Bible says that they began— from the eldest to the youngest—walking out.

There she lay, quivering and ashamed, at the feet of the Son of God. Jesus asked, "Woman, where are those thine accusers? hath no man condemned thee?" In other words, "Is there none left to condemn you?" She answered, "No man, Lord." And Jesus said, "Neither do I condemn thee: go, and sin no more" (John 8:5-11).

Before you ever say that answer is a compromise, read verse 11 again: "Neither do I condemn thee: go, and sin no more." Yes, He is just and merciful. None of the attributes of God conflict one with the other. Friends, He will be merciful to you as He was to me who, just short of twenty years of age, was lost, without God and without hope. I was ever conscious of my sin, as David was, who declared, "My sin is ever before me" (Ps. 51:3).

I knelt at the old-fashioned altar and asked God to save me. The mercy of God, that wonderful, beautiful attribute that is as deep as the deepest sea, high as the highest sky and broader than the east is from the west, saved me!

Jesus possessed and manifested all the attributes of God.

4. The next attribute is that of **love.** "... for God is love," says I John 4:8. So was Jesus Christ. "For God so loved the world, that he gave his only begotten Son, that whosoever believeth in him should not perish, but have everlasting life" (John 3:16).

The Christian scientist Dr. Harry Rimmer told a most wonderful story. He was speaking not long after World War II. (Let me say this: Just before Pearl Harbor was bombed, the Pacific Fleet of the United States Navy had been given small white New Testaments by the Gideon Association. On that black day on December 7, 1944, when the Japanese bombed at Pearl Harbor, many were killed, large ships were sunk, and the World War officially began.)

Dr. Rimmer had been given one of those white Testaments, which he carried with him in his pocket. The inside cover read: **"To the Pacific Fleet of the United States Navy."**

As he preached that day, the war was still fresh on people's minds. During his sermon he held up the Testament and said, "I have here in my hand a white Testament given by the Gideons to all our boys in the Pacific Fleet in the Navy."

The service closed. A man came forward with a sad expression on his face. He stood by waiting while others talked to Dr. Rimmer. Then he came up to Dr. Rimmer and pulled out a white Testament from his pocket just like the one Dr. Rimmer had held up, except for one difference: An unmistakable brown stain and dye were on that white Testament. No one could ever question that they were the stains of blood.

When everyone else had walked away, this man held the Testament and fondled it, as if it were his most prized possession; then he said, "Dr. Rimmer, my boy was at Pearl Harbor and had this in his pocket. My son stood at his post until death came. His body was riddled through with many bullets. When they gathered up all of his personal effects, they shipped his body back for burial and sent this Testament stained with his blood." Then he said, "Preacher, this book, stained with the blood of my son, is the most wonderful possession I have ever held in my hand."

Moved by the story and not knowing exactly what to say, Dr. Rimmer paused for a moment, then said as he held out his own Testament, "And that one was stained with the blood of God's Son."

Two men stood with their two Testaments. The one man said, "Stained with the blood of my son"; the other said, "Stained with the blood of God's Son."

My friends, I hold in my hand a Book that tells me Jesus died in love and mercy and pity for you and wants to save you. You are dealing with God, for Jesus is God—the deity of Jesus Christ.

5. The fifth attribute of God is that of **truth.** Jesus said in John 14:6: "I am the way, the truth, and the life: no man cometh unto the Father, but by me."

It is absolutely impossible to associate falsehood or deceit or error with the character of God. One of the attributes of God is truth, and Jesus had that attribute. In fact, He said, "I am the truth."

Someone could ask the question that Pilate asked, "What is truth?" The Bible has the answer, as it has all other answers essential to the salvation of your soul. Jesus had the attribute of truth.

I could say many things about this attribute. Everything that Jesus Christ ever said is true. Mark that down! Everything that He ever said is absolutely true, and His truth is absolute.

Jesus said that He saves people—and He does. Jesus said that He could keep people—and He does. Jesus said that we are to be raised with Him—and we will be. Jesus said He is the resurrection—and He is. Jesus said that someday we are to be like Him—and thank God, we are going to be!

These are the five moral attributes of God, all of which Jesus had.

Then there are three attributes of God which we might call physical attributes.

Jesus was **omniscient.** Coming to the closing verse of the second chapter of the Gospel of John, we read: "...for he knew what was in man" (vs. 25). He knows all things. Seven miles away from Nathanael, who was sitting under a fig tree, Jesus said, "...when thou wast under the fig tree, I saw thee." When Nathanael realized that seven miles away, on the other side of a hill and through all that granite and soil, Jesus looked and saw him, Nathanael said, "Rabbi, thou art the Son of God" (John 1:48,49).

The omniscience of Christ made Nathanael know that this was God to whom he was speaking.

Then there is the **omnipotence** of the Son of God. Matthew 28:18 says, "All power is given unto me in heaven and in earth." Jesus Christ is all-powerful.

Then Jesus is **omnipresent.** He can be everywhere at the same time: "For where two or three are gathered together in my name, there am I in the midst of them" (Matt. 18:20).

A teacher was trying to teach a lesson on the omnipresence of the Lord Jesus Christ. She was saying, "The Lord can be everywhere at the same time. He is with us here in our Sunday school class."

A little boy spoke up. "Well, is He with the Methodists over on the other side of town?"

"Yes, He is with the Methodists, too."

He was a little skeptical, as a lot of people are. "Is the Lord back home in my house where I live?"

"Yes, He is there, and He is here, too."

"Is the Lord in the barn? We have a big barn."

"Yes, He is in your barn. The Lord is omnipresent. He can be everywhere."

The skeptical little guy couldn't understand that. And as many modernists and liberalists do, he thought that he ought not believe it if he couldn't understand it. He continued his query, "Is the Lord in our cellar?"

"Yes, the Lord is in your cellar, too."

Now he said, "Uh huh, I thought so! We ain't got no cellar, so I know that that's not true."

Nevertheless, the Lord is omnipresent. He can be anywhere at the same time. The burden of the message on the deity of Christ was that He possessed all the attributes that God the Father and God the Spirit also possessed.

"And we believe and are sure that thou art that Christ, the Son of the living God."

II. HIS DEITY IS PROVEN BY HIS RESURRECTION

Notice also that His deity is proven by His resurrection from the grave. One of the great statements of the book of Romans is Romans 1:4: "And declared to be the Son of God with power, according to the spirit of holiness, by the resurrection from the dead." The thing I have mentioned is set forth there as it is set forth many places in the Bible.

In verse 3 we read these words: "Concerning his Son, Jesus Christ our Lord, which was made of the seed of David according to the flesh." This is talking about His human body. "...which was made of the seed of David according to the flesh."

The next verse speaks of His deity: "And declared to be the Son of God with power, according to the spirit of holiness, by the resurrection from the dead."

I mentioned earlier that some people cannot understand how the Bible can be the Word of God because it had human-divine authorship. Some people cannot understand the deity of Jesus because He was both God and man—just as much God as if He had never been man, and just as much man as if He had never been God.

"And declared to be the Son of God with power, according to the spirit of holiness, by the resurrection from the dead." This verse says that the resurrection of Christ out of the grave proves that Jesus Christ is deity and that He is God. Let us see a wonderful example of this.

Here is the Apostle Paul, a bigoted Jew. He did not believe Jesus Christ was the Son of God. He did not believe He was divine or was deity or that He was God. Paul went about to kill everyone who did believe it. Paul opposed those who believed that this Christ was the promised Messiah of the Old Testament.

One day after Jesus came and died and went back to Heaven and the Holy Spirit came on the day of Pentecost, that bigoted young rabbi was riding along the Damascus Road. About twelve o'clock, at the noon hour, a light from Heaven shone upon him and a voice from Heaven spoke to him.

Paul asked, "Who art thou, O Lord?"

The Lord answered, "I am Jesus whom thou persecutest."

Paul said, "Lord, what wilt thou have me to do?"

The Lord answered, "Arise, and go into the city, and it will be told thee what thou must do."

The Apostle Paul was saved by a living, resurrected Jesus. Acts 9 gives a record of his testimony. Notice that immediately he begins to preach. What do you think he begins preaching? The first thing he preached is found in verse 20: "And straightway he preached Christ in the synagogues, that he is the Son of God."

Paul had heard from Him in Heaven. Paul had seen the light of the divine glory that day on the Damascus Road. So the first thing Paul ever preached was that Jesus Christ is the Son of God.

It is a wonderful thing to read Matthew 28 about Christ's resurrection and Matthew 27 just before His entombment. After Jesus had died upon the cross, we read what was said to Pilate: "Sir, we remember that that deceiver said, while he was yet alive, After three days I will rise again" (Matt. 27:63).

The people became frightened. I don't blame them. If you had watched someone die as Jesus died, you would begin to doubt whether you were right in rejecting Him and in denying His deity. Frightened, they said, "Sir, we remember that that deceiver said, while he was yet alive, After three days I will rise again."

Pilate answered, "Ye have a watch: go your way, make it as sure as ye can" (vs. 65). Now verse 66: "So they went, and made the sepulchre sure, sealing the stone, and setting a watch." They put a Roman seal over that stone, set a Roman guard at that tomb and said, "See that this man never comes out of that grave."

Listen! The Devil would have given all he could to have kept Jesus from coming out of the tomb. Even the Devil knew that, when Christ came from the grave, He would conquer death and would prove for all time the deity of the Son of God.

Thank God that after three days the stone rolled away and Jesus walked out. Those who watched Him die—even His enemies— had to say, "Truly this was the Son of God" (Matt. 27:54).

The resurrection of Christ proves His deity. Not only did Jesus arise from the grave, but others arose. There is a part of the resurrection that we rarely hear mentioned or discussed. I don't recall ever hearing a sermon on it. Four miraculous things happened when Jesus died.

First, there was the miracle of darkness. From noonday until three o'clock in the afternoon the sun refused to shine. God reached yonder in the heavens and pushed that light back into oblivion. A cloud of darkness covered this world. It is said that, because of the darkness, Diogenes down in Egypt said, "Either the world is coming to an end, or God is dying." Little did he know the truth of his words.

Not only was there the miracle of darkness, but there was the miracle of an earthquake.

Then there was a third miracle. That veil—not just a curtain because it weighed tons—was rent from top to bottom, not from bottom to top because it was God who rent the veil.

Then the fourth miracle was the opening of the graves. "And the graves were opened; and many bodies of the saints which slept arose" (Matt. 27:52). It is He who said, "I am the resurrection, and the life: he that believeth in me, though he were dead, yet shall he live: And whosoever liveth and believeth in me shall never die" (John 11:25,26).

While He hangs upon the cross, robed in blood and crowned with thorns, the resurrection comes and men walk out of their graves. No wonder the centurion, head of a hundred soldiers and the one who helped put Jesus on that cross, said, "Truly, this was the Son of God." The resurrection proves the deity of Jesus Christ.

"And we believe and are sure that thou art that Christ, the Son of the living God."

III. HIS DEITY IS PROVEN BY HIS ASSERTIONS

Third, His resurrection is proved by His own assertions. Think of some of the things that Jesus asserted. One time I read where a man was preaching on the deity of Christ and catalogued all his information under three headings: "First, Christ claimed to be; second, He seemed to be; third, He proved to be."

I would like for you to see how He not only claimed to be, and not only seemed to be, but, bless God, how He proved to be the Son of God.

In John 10:30 Jesus said, "I and my Father are one." He claims equality with God. Immediately His enemies took up stones to stone Him because He claimed equality with God. They have never quit stoning Him for that assertion. Today men hurl their stones of liberalism, intellectualism and rationalism at the Son of God because He said, "I and my Father are one."

Then in John 14:9 Jesus said, ". . .he that hath seen me hath seen the Father." Jesus claimed to be God. He seemed to be God. He proved to be God. Let us notice some of His assertions.

1. He claimed He was worthy of worship. Every human being in the Bible—without exception—was unworthy of worship. No man can ever accept worship. Any man who does is as far from God as a man can be. When the people sought to worship the Apostle Peter, he absolutely forbade it. When we see in the Bible an attempt to worship angels, even they would never accept worship. But Jesus claimed that He was worthy of worship and accepted it on many occasions.

I read in Matthew 2:11 that the Wise Men "fell down, and worshipped him." Here is not the babe in a manger, because Matthew 2 is not about a babe in a manger but about a child in a house. The Wise Men came and "presented unto him gifts; gold, and frankincense, and myrrh."

These potentates from other nations fell down at the feet of a little Child, two years old or less, recognized Him as deity and worshiped the Son of God.

The next thing we read is that they (the Wise Men) went home another way because God had warned them. If they had been doing wrong by worshiping the Son of God even in His infancy, do you think God would have told them, "If you go back home the same way you came, you will be killed"? No, He would not have. But God in a revelation warned these good men because they were doing right by worshiping God.

So Jesus always accepted worship.

I read again in Matthew 8:2, "And, behold, there came a leper and worshipped him, saying, Lord, if thou wilt, thou canst make me clean."

I read in Matthew 9:18, "...there came a certain ruler, and worshipped him."

In Matthew 14:33, "Then they that were in the ship came and worshipped him, saying, Of a truth thou art the Son of God."

So, if Jesus is not deity, He is the greatest imposter the world has ever known. Don't ever let anyone say to you, "Well, I don't believe He was deity, but I believe He was a good man."

A man said to me at the Sea of Galilee, "I am going to agree with you that Jesus was a great teacher. He was a really sharp man and must have been a good man." (Those were his words.)

I answered, "No, that won't do. That can't be. In fact, that is an absurd statement. Jesus claimed to be God. He claimed equality with the Father. He accepted worship. And if He was not the Son of God, then He was no good. You must come down to this sober, solemn decision: either you accept Him as deity or brand Him as demon, one way or the other."

With all my heart, soul, body, mind and strength, I will worship Him as the Son of God. He proved His deity by His assertions.

2. He claimed to forgive sin many, many times in the Bible.

Four neighbors brought a paralytic man who could not come by himself and laid him at the feet of Jesus. When Jesus saw their faith, He said, "Son, be of good cheer; thy sins be forgiven thee" (Matt. 9:2).

I read again in Luke 7:48 where they criticized Him. A woman (maybe not one of great reputation, for a Pharisee said, "If you were the Son of God, you would have known that this woman was a sinner") came to Jesus. And what does Jesus say to her? "Thy sins are forgiven" (Luke 7:48).

He forgave mine also, thank God! Oh, yes, when I was nearly

twenty years of age I labored with sin. I labored with sin a long time for my age. I would think of it every night. I would get out of my bed at night, kneel and pray, "O God, let me see the light of another day." I prayed many times, "O God, don't take me now; I am not ready to go. I am lost." I had an awful burden of sin. My heart was as heavy as lead.

Thank God, the second week of August, 1935, I believed what Jesus said: "All that the Father giveth me shall come to me; and him that cometh to me I will in no wise cast out" (John 6:37). I gave myself to Christ and went home with my sins gone. Now for all these years I have had a deep conviction that they are gone, gone, gone! Hallelujah! They are gone forever, removed as far as the east is from the west, buried in the depths of the sea, put behind the back of God, buried in divine forgetfulness. God promised to remember them against me no more, forever.

He proved His deity by His assertion. He said, "I am worthy of worship. I can forgive sin."

3. He goes further than that. The divine audacity found here is beautiful. Jesus said that you get prayers answered through Him. He claimed He could answer the prayers of His God. Only God can do that!

John 14:13,14 says, "And whatsoever ye shall ask in my name, that will I do, that the Father may be glorified in the Son. If ye shall ask any thing in my name, I will do it."

The Bible says that there is one God and one Mediator between God and man—the man Christ Jesus. Have you ever tried asking Jesus to answer your prayers? I have asked Him to do things for me. I have heard the bells of Heaven ring as my High Priest yonder in the Holy of Holies ministered for me, advocated my cause. I can testify that Jesus answers prayer. Hallelujah! He proves His deity.

Yes, He defied the laws of nature by His own assertions, by

His own deeds and by His own miracles. He walked on the water; He calmed the storm. Jesus Christ proved His deity by His assertion.

"And we believe and are sure that thou art that Christ, the Son of the living God."

IV. HIS DEITY IS PROVEN BY HIS UNERRING PREDICTION OF THE FUTURE

Then, Jesus proved His deity by His unerring prediction of the future. He told the people of His day some things that were going to happen. In fact, He said some things were going to happen through the course of these two thousand years. And these have come to pass just as He said they would.

One day Jesus went to Capernaum. It used to be a commercial, thriving, bustling city at the north end of the Sea of Galilee. It was a crossroad of commerce and tourism even in Jesus' day.

One day Jesus said, "And thou, Capernaum, which art exalted unto heaven, shalt be brought down to hell: for if the mighty works, which have been done in thee, had been done in Sodom, it would have remained until this day" (Matt. 11:23).

In and around this great city, this strong city, this thickly populated city, this commercial center, Jesus wrought some seventeen miracles. And in sight of Capernaum Jesus had walked on water.

But Capernaum didn't repent, so Jesus said it would be brought down to Hell. Today, every stone in Capernaum is a mute remains of a city cursed by God. Just exactly what Jesus said would happen, did happen to Capernaum.

In Jerusalem was Solomon's beautiful Temple that had been the glory of the people of God.

As some spoke of the Temple, how beautiful it was, how it was adorned with goodly stones and gifts, Jesus said, "As for these things which ye behold, the days will come, in the which there shall not be left one stone upon another, that shall not be thrown down'' (Luke 21:6).

(These stones are for real. They are 45 feet long, 15 feet one way and 22 feet another and weigh literally hundreds of tons—a miracle that they could ever be placed there in those days.) Oh, they must have thought, *By what unknown power, by what unusual power, can such stones be removed from their place?*

People came and asked Him, ''Master, but when shall these things be? and what sign will there be when these things shall come to pass?'' (vs. 7).

In A.D. 70, thirty-five years later, Titus, the Roman militarist, came against Jerusalem and leveled it to the ground, leaving not one stone upon another. He sowed the fields with salt until neither tree nor grass could grow for many decades.

The words of Jesus came to pass just as He said they would.

Jesus said, ''But woe unto them that are with child, and to them that give suck, in those days...'' (Luke 21:23).

Women were ripped up. Jesus had said that people would die by the sword, and it is said that at that siege of Jerusalem under Titus in A.D. 70, trees were cut down to make crosses on which Jews were nailed. Not a tree was left.

The words of Jesus came to pass.

Listen to Jesus tell about His own death and who would kill Him: 'I must go to Jerusalem and suffer many things of the elders and chief priests and scribes, and be killed...' (Matt. 16:21).

Then He told of His own resurrection and ascension and betrayal.

The twelve men closest to Him one day were told that one of them wasn't saved, that one of them was a demon, that one of them wasn't clean, that one of them would betray Jesus.

Thomas said, ''Lord, is it I?''

James said, ''Lord, is it I?''

John said, "Lord, is it I?"

They didn't know, but Jesus knew. The night before His death on the cross of Calvary, while sitting at the Last Supper, the darkest hand of human history dipped in the dish with Jesus, who had already said, "He who dips with his hand in the dish, it is he that will betray Me." Judas knew who it was.

Listen! It is said that Jeanne Dixon claims that 70 percent of her predictions are accurate. That means that Jeanne Dixon is not of God, for God is 100 percent right all the time.

You know, a sweet and wonderful verse is Isaiah 34:16, "Seek ye out of the book of the Lord, and read: no one of these shall fail, none shall want her mate: for my mouth it hath commanded, and his spirit it hath gathered them." Not one! No one will ever show me or anyone else one error in the Bible. The Bible is as impeccable as Jesus Himself. It is without spot and blemish, just as Jesus is. It is without error, without contradiction, just as Jesus is. Everything that Jesus said came to pass just as He said it would. He proved His deity by His knowledge of the future.

"And we believe and are sure that thou art that Christ, the Son of the living God."

V. HIS DEITY IS PROVEN BY HIS IMMUTABILITY

Then His deity is proven by His immutability. That is a Bible word, found twice in chapter 6 of the book of Hebrews.

We read in Hebrews 13:8, "Jesus Christ the same yesterday, and to day, and for ever." Thank God for that! He is unchanging, just as God the Father is. He is absolutely immutable.

I read on about the immutability of Jesus Christ, in Hebrews 6:18: "That by two immutable things, in which it was impossible for God to lie, we might have a strong consolation, who have fled for refuge to lay hold upon the hope set before us."

Now, if you will read that passage, you will see that the Lord

wants to affirm His Word. It says, "For when God made promise to Abraham, because he could swear by no greater, he sware
by himself," that is, by His person, for His person is immutable.
He swore, as it were, that His Word was as unchanging as His
person.

He is always the same. Hallelujah for an unchanging Saviour!
There is a beautiful passage in Psalm 102:26,27:

"They [earth and the heavens] *shall perish, but thou shalt endure: yea, all of them shall wax old like a garment; as a vesture
shalt thou change them, and they shall be changed. But thou art
the same, and thy years shall have no end."*

Hallelujah for a Saviour who never changes! He is immutable.
Only God is unchanging. Says Malachi 3:6, "For I am the Lord,
I change not; therefore ye sons of Jacob are not consumed." There
are two great statements here. "I am the Lord, I change not,"
and, "therefore ye sons of Jacob are not consumed."

Israel is the burning bush that burned but was not consumed.
Here the Lord says, 'I am the Lord, I change not; therefore you
Jews shall never be destroyed,' and they never have been.

Hitler couldn't destroy them, though it is said he destroyed six
million Jews. Rather, he caused them to multiply. He caused them
to flee back home. He helped to fulfill Bible prophecy. But they
are not consumed, and never will be. And that verse tells you why.
The Jews are not consumed because of the immutability of God.
The Jews will live on forever. The Lord never changes.

I used to hear an expression, "As solid as the Rock of Gibraltar."
All my life I had wanted to see the Rock of Gibraltar. Jutting up
out of the waters, the Rock of Gibraltar was pointed out to me
one day. That huge rock, which has stood there all these centuries,
was created by God out in His vast, expansive ocean.

I began reading about that rock. I read where once the Rock
of Gibraltar started crumbling away. People got afraid that it might

begin to disappear beneath the water's surface. Large boatloads of concrete were hauled in the hold of great boats and people patched the Rock of Gibraltar like a dentist patches a tooth to keep it from decaying and crumbling away.

Thank God, I know one Rock that never changes!

> **Rock of ages, cleft for me,**
> **Let me hide myself in Thee;**
> **Let the water and the blood,**
> **From Thy wounded side which flowed,**
> **Be of sin the double cure,**
> **Save from wrath and make me pure.**

I thank God that I stand on a Rock that is immutable, unchanging. Jesus proved His deity by His immutability.

"The same yesterday, and to day, and for ever."—Heb. 13:8.

"Thou art the Christ, the Son of the living God."—Matt. 16:16.

"And we believe and are sure that thou art that Christ, the Son of the living God."—John 6:69.

Chapter IV

Why I Know the Bible Is True

(Preached in the Emmanuel Baptist Church, October 18, 1970)

READ: II Timothy 2:15; 3:15-17

TEXT: II Timothy 2:15; 3:16

". . . rightly dividing the word of truth."

"All scripture is given by inspiration of God. . . ."

I want to talk on "Why I Know the Bible Is True," or, "Why I Know the Bible Is the Word of God." There are two statements that I will use. One is the closing statement of II Timothy 2, ". . . rightly dividing the word of truth." Notice that God says it is the Word of truth. Then in verse 16 of chapter 3, this statement, "All scripture is given by inspiration of God. . . ."

The Bible claims to be true, claims to be inspired. There is no telling how many times all through the Bible we read, "Thus saith the Lord," or, "The word of the Lord came unto me saying. . . ." The Bible claims to be the Word of God, and the Bible claims to be inspired.

Here is a verse that says ALL Scripture is given by inspiration of God.

If the Bible be not true, just think of the importance of this subject.

If the Bible be not true, we know nothing of the one and only true God.

If this Bible is not true and this Bible is not the Word of God, we have no assurance, because everything stands or falls on whether the Bible is true or not.

If this Bible be not true, there is no revelation of God so that you can know God and the forgiveness of sin.

If the Bible be not true, we know nothing of life beyond the grave. At the very best, all we know about life is for this very moment, and we know nothing about life beyond the grave.

If the Bible be not true, we have absolutely no answer to the depravity of the human heart and the universality of sin.

If the Bible be not true, we have no true answer as to our origin. We know not where we came from and have no explanation of our purpose on earth and no assurance of our state in eternity, if the Bible be not true.

If the Bible be not true, we have no message of hope in the lonely hours of sorrow, no message of life in the deep valley of death.

If the Bible be not true, there be no such thing as a moral code, no guide to human relationships and no sense of right and wrong.

So it is all-important to know whether the Bible be true or not.

Many people do not believe the Bible is true. Please don't say, "Well, Preacher, nearly everyone believes the Bible." That is not true anymore. Many in our day—and I guess it has always been that way—do not believe the Bible is true, and many do not believe the Bible is the Word of God.

There is a wonderful study in II Timothy, this little epistle written by one great preacher to a younger preacher, of how people get away from the Bible.

For instance, verse 18 of chapter 2 says some have "erred" from the truth. They make an error in the study of the Bible. Paul mentioned some people who said that the resurrection is already past. They didn't divide it rightly, didn't get it straight. When they found that they were wrong, they became confused about much of the Bible.

Then we see in II Timothy 3:8 that some resist the truth—". . . so do these also resist the truth, men of corrupt minds, reprobate concerning the faith." Sometimes people make a mistake and resist the truth.

Then in chapter 4 of this epistle, Paul writes to the young preacher:

"For the time will come when they will not endure sound doctrine; but after their own lusts shall they heap to themselves teachers, having itching ears; And they shall turn away their ears from the truth, and shall be turned unto fables."—vss. 3,4.

Paul said that their time would come, and it has come. You and I are living in it right now. Men deny that the Bible is the Word of God. So I speak on "How I Know the Bible Is Inspired and True."

"All scripture is inspired of God," says the Bible. Someone says, "What is inspiration?" The word *inspire* or *inspiration* means "God breathes" or that God has breathed into this Book and inspired it in a unique and miraculous way.

Many people say, "But there are different versions of the Bible." This definition of inspiration has been accepted by great fundamental scholars throughout many generations:

> The Bible as we now have it, in its various translations and revisions, when freed from all errors and mistakes of translations, copyists and printers, is the very Word of God and consequently, wholly without error.

Inspiration has also been defined in this manner:

> Denotes that secret action of the Spirit on the faculties of a living messenger by which he is enabled to receive, utter or

record the divine message. Scripture is the result of that sacred influence embodied and recorded in written form.

I must say that I not only believe in the inspiration of the Bible but in the preservation of the Bible. God's Word is perfect as it claims. "The law of the Lord is perfect, converting the soul: the testimony of the Lord is sure, making wise the simple," declares Psalm 19:7.

We are often reminded that none of us have ever seen the original manuscript. While this is true, yet God saw them and authored them. He has preserved His Word in one Book—the Bible. "For ever, O Lord, thy word is settled in heaven," says Psalm 119:89. We don't have to consult various translations by men to assure ourselves that we are reading the pure Word of God. The authorized King James Version is the Word of God. God has preserved His Word, else inspiration would mean nothing to us. Given the fact that it is inspired, what would that mean to us if parts of that inspired Word were either lost or hidden away in some ancient manuscript in a language most of us could not read? We have now a perfect Bible. We believe that the Bible in its original manuscripts is absolutely the pure and true Word of Almighty God. We know that the Bible is true and that it is inspired, as it claims to be. "As he spake by the mouth of his holy prophets, which have been since the world began" (Luke 1:70).

You say to me, "Preacher, it is one thing to say that you know something but another thing to be able to give an intelligent answer as to why you know it."

If a person asked me a question about why I know something, I ought to be able to give him the answer.

If a person says to me, "How do you know you are saved?" I ought to have the answer to that question.

If someone says to me, "How do you know that there is a God?" I want to have the answer to that question.

If a man or woman, saved or unsaved, comes to me and says, "Preacher, how do you know the Bible is true?" I, as a Christian, ought to know why I believe the Bible is true and the very Word of God.

WHY I KNOW THE BIBLE IS TRUE

1. Its Endurance Through the Centuries

That is a miracle when you think of how the Bible has endured and how it stood and how it remains and how its enemies come and go and the battles against it rise and fall. But the Bible still stands all down through the years. That is the way God said it would be in His Word.

Psalm 119:89 says, "For ever, O Lord, thy word is settled in heaven." God said that in Heaven it is settled that His Word is to last forever. It is not a temporary Book. This is the Book of all ages, of all centuries, of all times. The Bible is this world's Best-seller.

Read again Psalm 119:160: "Thy word is true from the beginning: and every one of thy righteous judgments endureth for ever." Not some Christian, not some preacher, but God said this Book would endure forever, and it has. I don't know exactly how old the Bible is. I know that, if you go back to the very beginning of the Bible, you are probably going back about 6,000 years from where we stand today. For 6,000 years either parts or all of the Bible has stood all the assailing of enemies, all the vain philosophies of men, all the unbelief and infidelity of modernism and all the hatred, satanical hatred of lost people. It has stood like the mighty rock that it is, the mighty foundation of our faith. Nothing has ever been able to destroy the Bible. It has been burned in a huge bonfire; it has been sunk by the boatload in the sea; it has been cut by the penknife of modernism, unbelief and liberalism; but, just like the Bible says, the foundation of God stands sure today, and the Bible is still true.

I know it is true because it has endured down through the centuries. Jesus took up this theme when He said in Matthew 24:35, "Heaven and earth shall pass away, but my words shall not pass away." It has not only endured in past history, but it will endure in the ages to come.

Jesus said, "Heaven and earth shall pass away...," and they will. The stars will someday fall from Heaven. The moon shall turn to blood. The sun will refuse to shine. But Jesus said, "...my words shall not pass away." Thank God we have in our hearts and lives a Book that shall stand the test of all the storms!

Recently I was preaching in a city of 170,000 people. There they told me one of the most wonderful, yet tragic, stories I have ever heard.

They described the great tornadoes that had hit that city. On May 11, 1970, three tornadoes swept through the downtown section of that city of 170,000 people and moved out across the suburbs causing such damage as you have never seen. Thirty some people had lost their lives in the storm. Everyone in town marveled that hundreds were not killed.

Recently, I saw that city and where it had been cleaned away. A friend said to me, "A large hotel used to sit there, but it was completely destroyed."

One riding in the car with us said, "Dr. Malone, see that big skyscraper there in the downtown section? No one occupies it. That skyscraper is leaning because of the great storm. The strongest buildings were shaken and moved."

Then they told me this wonderful story. During the fierce storm and strong wind, one home was completely destroyed, blown to smithereens. But there was a table in that home and, strange as it may sound and unbelievable as it may seem, that table was still in the same spot where it had been before the storm, and on it was a Bible opened to Psalm 83. Verse 15 of that Psalm reads, "So persecute them with thy tempest, and make them afraid with thy storm." There it stood, while destruction and debris lay everywhere. That says that no storm shall ever be able to destroy the Word of God.

I believe the Bible because of its endurance through the years. It has stood the storm of satanical hatred. It has stood the storm of human unbelief. It has stood the storms of religious perversion. I know the Bible is true because no man has ever been able to destroy it.

The civilizations and empires of ancient history are gone, and their silent remains lie smoldering in the earth. Everything that has threatened to extinguish the Bible has only served as testimonies to its indestructibility and eternal nature.

> **One day I passed beside a smithy's door**
> **And heard the anvil sound the vesper chime;**
> **Then, looking in, I saw upon the floor**
> **Old hammers worn with beating years of time.**
> **"How many anvils have you here," said I,**
> **"To wear and batter all these hammers so?"**
> **"Just one," the blacksmith said, with twinkling eye;**
> **"The anvil wears the hammers out, you know."**
> **And so, said I, the anvil of God's Word,**
> **For ages skeptic blows have beat upon;**
> **Yet, though the sound of hammers thus was heard,**
> **The anvil yet remains; the hammers gone.**

"All scripture is given by inspiration of God."

2. Endorsement by the Son of God

I believe that the Bible is true not only because of its endurance through the centuries, but because of its endorsement by the Son of God.

Stop and think for a moment. When you question whether or not the Bible is true, you are questioning whether you can depend on Jesus telling the truth. His whole testimony, His character, His deity, His reliability is at stake, for Jesus endorsed the whole Bible.

You say, ''You mean Jesus put His endorsement upon every book in the Bible, from Genesis to Revelation?'' He certainly did! To the Old Testament Jew, the Old Testament was divided only into three ways: the Books of Moses, the Prophets and the Psalms. When the Jew referred to the Old Testament, he referred to it as the Law of Moses, the Books of the Prophets, both major and minor, and the Psalms.

Two thousand years ago, when Jesus was teaching the Word of God to people, He quoted Abraham as saying, ''If they hear not Moses and the prophets, neither will they be persuaded, though one rose from the dead'' (Luke 16:31). He said that to a man at a most crucial hour, a man who had died without God and without hope and was in Hell begging for someone to go to his five brothers and tell them how to be saved. Abraham said, 'It wouldn't do any good for one to go from the dead. For if they believed not Moses and the prophets, neither will they believe one who came to them from the dead.'

Jesus goes on in the same book of Luke, in Luke 24:27, ''And beginning at Moses and all the prophets, he expounded unto them in all the scriptures the things concerning himself.'' Jesus Christ, the Son of God, took His omnipotent hands of deity, laid them on the Old Testament and said, ''The Old Testament is the Word of God, and you can believe that the Old Testament is true, for I endorse it.''

Think of all that Jesus said about the Old Testament. For instance: the Lord knew that when we came to this day, many would not believe the book of Genesis, so He talked a lot about Genesis. He talked about Lot and Sodom, about Noah and his ark. He talked about Abraham, Isaac and Jacob. He talked about Joseph and other characters in the book of Genesis. He talked about the institution of marriage: 'Have you not read that God made them one, both male and female?' He put His hand on the book of Genesis and all the Old Testament.

Jesus knew that a lot of people would not believe the book of Jonah, where a fish swallowed a man and had him in his stomach for three days and at the command of God, deposited him out again.

A man by the name of Bullinger has written a book describing certain whales that are able to swallow an object twelve times the size of a man. But because it is in the Bible, some oppose it. Besides, God never said that it was a whale. God said He prepared a great fish, and He can make a fish as big as He wants to. Some of you go fishing and catch a wee little thing, and you make it as big as you want to when you tell the story! So God can make one as big as He wants. He can make one big enough to swallow the Emmanuel Baptist Church if He so wishes. God made a fish to swallow Jonah, and he lived inside it three days before the fish deposited him out.

Folks in this day and time laugh at that little book of Jonah and say, "Preacher, you mean you believe things in the Bible, like the book of Jonah?" I sure do! Why? Because Jesus believed it. Jesus, one day, when He was going to speak of His resurrection, said, "For as Jonas was three days and three nights in the whale's belly; so shall the Son of man be three days and three nights in the heart of the earth" (Matt. 12:40). (*Whale* here could accurately be translated "large sea monster.") Jesus reached back across the dusty years, laid His hand upon the book of Jonah and said, "The swallowing of Jonah by that fish was a type, ordained of God, of the bodily, literal, visible resurrection of the Son of God out of the belly of the earth." I believe the book of Jonah because Jesus Christ believed it.

Now wait just a moment! You say, "Preacher, when Jesus came, there was no New Testament, and for several decades after He was here there were no New Testament books written. So how could Jesus endorse a New Testament which was not yet written?" The Bible makes that plain and clear. He endorsed not only the Old Testament, but the New. There is no room for doubt or confusion as to whether or not Jesus put His endorsement upon the New Testament. For instance, we read in the book of John, "But the Comforter, which is the Holy Ghost, whom the Father will send in my name, he shall teach you all things, and bring all things to your remembrance, whatsoever I have said unto you" (14:26).

All the apostles who saw Him alive heard Him say that God the Spirit would come, bring all things to mind and show things yet to come. Thus, Jesus reaches out by His infallible statements, puts His hand upon the New Testament, yet unwritten, and endorses it.

The Bible, so to speak, is on trial. Imagine a trial going on and someone saying, "We will bring you a witness, the most widely known person in all the world. He has never been proven wrong, and he has always been fair. He has never been biased or prejudiced, and he has never used deceit or falsehood. We will bring into this courtroom the most widely known witness in all the world, put him on the witness stand and ask him, 'Is it thus and thus or not?'" Any judge, any jury, any court, any attorney, would say that that kind of a witness is acceptable.

I bring to this court Jesus, the Son of God, and I ask Him the supreme question of the ages, "Is this Bible true? Is it the Word of God or not?"

Jesus Christ, with one nail-scarred hand, lays it upon the Old Testament and with His two omnipotent hands, brings these two books together in one unified, miracle Book that is nothing short of the living Word of God.

So, when you come to ask, "Is the Bible true or not?" you come to ask, "Can you believe what Jesus said or not?"

"All scripture is given by inspiration of God...."

3. Its Enabling in the Lives of Men

The Bible does what no other book can do. Bring me the writings of the Mohammedans; bring me the writings of the Buddhists; bring me all the writings of the world's religions: they are all younger than the Bible, and none have gained the worldwide recognition that this Book has gained. The Bible is the only Book that can do in the lives of men what we see it do.

This Book enables people to be saved—Romans 10:17: "So then faith cometh by hearing, and hearing by the word of God."

This is the only Book that can lead men out of darkness into light, out of sin into grace; the only Book that can give men peace in their hearts. The enabling power of the Bible!

It not only saves, but it assures. This Book makes a person know that he is a child of God, that his sins are forgiven, and that that question is eternally settled in his life. Jesus said, "Verily, verily, I say unto you, He that heareth my word, and believeth on him that sent me, hath everlasting life, and shall not come into condemnation; but is passed from death unto life" (John 5:24).

So the Bible enables men to be saved, and the Bible assures them that they are saved.

This Bible cleanses. Jesus said, "Now ye are clean through the word which I have spoken unto you" (John 15:3).

Not only that: no book can direct a man through the dark days of his life like the Bible can. "If any of you lack wisdom, let him ask of God, that giveth to all men liberally, and upbraideth not; and it shall be given him" (James 1:5).

How many times I have not known the way to go, then found it in this Book! Like the man after the storm one night prayed,

"O God, show me the safe way home." He crossed a bridge and the next day saw he had crossed the narrow little span of bridge that had been left, the only safe way he could have gone. God directed his feet that night.

I could testify that in the many crises of life through the valleys and over the mountaintops down through the years, this Book has showed me the way to go. Oh, its enabling power in the lives of men!

It not only directs, but there is no comfort like the Bible. Thank God for the comfort it gives! Mark 5:36 exhorts, "Be not afraid, only believe."

Then it gives hope when I bury my Christian dead. It gives hope when my heart is broken beyond human repair. This Book gives comfort and this Book gives hope.

"But I would not have you to be ignorant, brethren, concerning them which are asleep, that ye sorrow not, even as others which have no hope. For if we believe that Jesus died and rose again, even so them also which sleep in Jesus will God bring with him. For this we say unto you by the word of the Lord, that we which are alive and remain unto the coming of the Lord shall not prevent them which are asleep. For the Lord himself shall descend from heaven with a shout, with the voice of the archangel, and with the trump of God: and the dead in Christ shall rise first: Then we which are alive and remain shall be caught up together with them in the clouds, to meet the Lord in the air: and so shall we ever be with the Lord. Wherefore comfort one another with these words."—I Thess. 4:13-18.

So this Book gives comfort and it gives hope. It gives warmth and it gives life. This Book gives light. The enabling power of the Book of God cannot be explained in any other way.

The dear old saint of God was reading her Bible when the skeptic asked, "Is that Book the Word of God?"

"Yes, it is."

"How do you know that?"

She said, "Is there a sun?"

"Yes, there is."

"How do you know that there is a sun?"

"I feel its warmth, and I see its light," he replied.

She said, "Oh, when I read this Book, it warms my heart and gives me light. That is why I know it is the Book of God."

Thank God, the Bible is true! I know it because of its endurance through the years, its endorsement by Jesus Christ, and its enabling in the lives of men.

I was in my office some years ago when there came a knock at the door. I opened it, and there stood a man I had never seen, a handsome man, well dressed.

"Are you the pastor of this church?" he asked.

"Yes, I am."

"I saw the sign out there that this was the Emmanuel Baptist Church, and I need help."

He didn't look like a man who, physically speaking, needed help, but he told me this story, as I remember it.

He was a traveling man who had never known the Lord. He lived for the dollar and lived for the moment; and, "I guess I could say that I have lived for myself," he said.

He went on to say that he knew what the world was like and had tasted of all its glitter, "but last night I sat in the loneliness of my motel room and got to looking at a Book," he said. Then he told me there was a Bible in that room, and he got to looking at that Bible. He asked himself, "Is that Bible true?" Then he said to himself, "If that Bible is true, there is a God. If that Bible is true, I am a sinner. If that Bible is true, there is an eternity. If that Bible is true, I will have to meet God."

He then said, "Preacher, I need help. Can you tell me the way out? My family doesn't know God. I have never known joy and peace though I have had everything the world has had to offer. If the Bible is true, is there anything for a man like me?''

Down on his knees in my office he went and in a moment I heard him pray, ''O God, I believe Your Word. I need to be saved, and I want You to save me.'' He trusted the Lord. Then I saw him turn and walk away. I knew our paths would never cross again in this life, but I knew he was saved. Thank God for the old Book and its enabling power in the lives of men!

4. Its Enclosure of Things to Come

The fourth reason I believe the Bible is true is its enclosure of things to come, or the prophetic part of the Bible and its accurate fulfillment down across the centuries.

Some years ago a man said to a believer, ''Give me one word that will make me know the Bible is true and the Word of God— just one word.''

The believer said, ''Jew.''

That leads me to this discussion of the prophetic part of the Bible. Here is an unanswerable argument as to its truth and accuracy. No human being could possibly explain how the Bible is history prewritten. The Bible tells what will come to pass hundreds of years before it comes to pass and always does it with minute accuracy.

Take, for instance, the prophecies related to the nation of Israel or to the Jew. You remember in Genesis 12 what God said to an oriental sheik, a great leader by the name of Abraham:

''. . .Abram, Get thee out of thy country, and from thy kindred, and from thy father's house, unto a land that I will shew thee: And I will make of thee a great nation, and I will bless thee, and make thy name great; and thou shalt be a blessing: And I will bless them that bless thee, and curse him that curseth thee: and in thee *shall all families of the earth be blessed.''*—vss. 1-3.

Now there is a sevenfold prophecy in what is called the Abrahamic Covenant. God said that seven things will come to pass. God said that He would make Abraham a great nation. God said to Abraham nineteen hundred years or more before Jesus was born that in him would all the families of the earth be blessed. This is the prophecy of the coming of the seed of Abraham, of the Lord Jesus Christ as a Messiah.

God said to Abraham, "I will make you a great nation," and God made Abraham a great nation. Wherever the sun runs a circuit and wherever the sun rises and sets, it rises and sets upon a people called the Jews. The Jew is as eternal as God and His Word, for God said, "I will make of the Jew a great nation."

God also said, "And I will bless them that bless thee. . . ."

I have often asked myself, "Here is America, a nation of drinkers and rioters, a nation of immorality and lawlessness. What is the explanation that it is still a free nation? The Bible can still be preached; it is still a nation of great churches and a nation of freedom of worship. What is the answer to that?" The kindness shown in this nation toward the Jew, God's elect, God's chosen race, accounts for the fact that God has so wonderfully blessed America. "And I will bless them that bless thee. . . ." God has blessed every nation that has been kind to the Jew, just like He said He would.

Then God said to Abraham, "And I will curse him that curseth thee." Down across the centuries and down across the course of history, every nation that has sought to destroy the Jew lies in crumbling ruins and in the dust of a forgotten past.

In modern times, there is the nation of Germany. In Germany is the great dividing wall. [Preached in 1970.] Thousands have lost their lives in Germany, and their freedom, for a great part, has been lost. Why? because Adolph Hitler said, "I will destroy the Jew.'' It is believed that as many as six million of God's chosen people were burned in the ovens of concentration camps in Germany. Now today it is a parted land, a divided land. The curse of God lies upon Germany today because of fulfillment of prophecy. God said, ''I will bless them that bless thee, and curse him that curseth thee.''

No one has the human ingenuity to explain the prophecy of the Bible and how it came to pass, except that Christian who admits this Bible is written by and inspired of God and is a miracle Book.

Take the prophecies related to Jesus Christ. Before Jesus came into the world and walked among men and incarnated His deity with men in the confines of a human body, the Bible described and gave all the names of His complete ancestry.

The Bible tells us where He will be born—in Bethlehem.

By reading the book of Daniel, one could have even known, hundreds of years before Christ ever came, the very year He would be born in Bethlehem's manger.

Not only the place, but the time and the manner. God said that a virgin would conceive and bear a Child and would call His name Jesus and that that Child would be born without union of a woman with a man, God's natural way to inhabit the earth—a thing unheard of. That is just how it took place.

Not only that; God said He would name His forerunner. Back in the book of Malachi it says that a man would come before Jesus saying, ''I am the voice of one crying in the wilderness, Make straight the way of the Lord, as said the prophet Esaias'' (John 1:23).

John the Baptist, the forerunner of Jesus, is prophesied in the Bible. A first cousin to Mary, the mother of Jesus, was with child in her old age and had a son born, and they called him John. He became that thundering preacher that went up and down the Jordan Valley saying,

"Repent ye: for the kingdom of heaven is at hand. For this is he that was spoken of by the prophet Esaias, saying, The voice of one crying in the wilderness, Prepare ye the way of the Lord, make his paths straight."—Matt. 3:2,3.

All this was prophesied in the Bible hundreds of years before it took place. If you do not believe the Bible is the Book of God, that the Bible is the miracle Book, that the Bible is inspired of God, explain to me how even His betrayal and the very amount of money for which He was to be sold (thirty pieces of silver)— all prophesied in the Bible—came to pass just like the Bible said it would, hundreds of years before it ever happened.

Explain to me how the book of Isaiah could tell that Jesus would die between two thieves and be buried in a rich man's tomb, this at least seven hundred years before it ever came to pass.

The Bible predicted His resurrection, prophesied of His ascension and gave a perfect picture of what Jesus would be like before He was ever born. This word picture, miracle of miracles, was not painted by one man, but by many men, most of whom never saw the other; some lived on a different continent; some spoke a different language; but all painted the same picture. When Jesus stepped out on the stage of human history, He was just like the Bible said He would be.

No man can gainsay the miracle of fulfilled prophecy in the Bible. One could take a whole evening and speak on the prophecies of the Word of God that no one ever thought would come to pass, but which came to pass just like God said they would.

There used to be a nation called the Edomites, the descendants of Esau, a wicked race of people who wanted to conquer and perpetuate themselves. But one day God made an announcement in Obadiah 1:18: ". . . and there shall not be any remaining of the house of Esau; for the Lord hath spoken it."

These descendants of Esau defied God and said, "We will prove that God is wrong."

They went to a place now called "Petra," which is one of the seven wonders of the world. Out of the mountainous rocks they hewed their homes and public buildings—one of the most beautiful sights ever beheld by human eye. Men said, "This nation of people will live forever; they will never be conquered."

But when I rode a horse down through that valley some years ago, there was nothing in those magnificent carved buildings but hoot owls, birds, jackals and animals. No descendant of Esau lives there now.

You see, this Bible, the inerrant, accurate Word of God, has always come to pass just like God said it would.

Someone has written this poem:

> **Almighty Lord, the sun shall fail,**
> **The moon forget her mighty tale,**
> **The deepest silence, hush on high,**
> **The radiant chorus of the sky,**
> **But fixed for everlasting years,**
> **Unmoved amid the wreck of spheres,**
> **Thy word shall shine in cloudless day,**
> **When a heav'n and earth have passed away.**
>
> **—Unknown**

No man can gainsay the miracle of prophecy which proves that the Bible is true. That is exactly what the Bible claims in Isaiah 34:16, where God said, "Seek ye out of the book of the Lord, and read: no one of these [prophecies] shall fail, none shall want her mate." Isn't that beautiful? Then God said, "...for my mouth it hath commanded, and his spirit it hath gathered them." Not one prophecy of all the Bible will ever want for its fulfillment, for His mouth spoke it and His Spirit will bring it to pass.

The Bible is a miracle Book because it writes history before it takes place. How many instances of this we find in the Word of God.

Take, for instance, what God said about the city of Jericho: "I want that city destroyed"; and through the miracle of God, He destroyed it. Not only that, but God said this city will never be rebuilt. He said the man who tries to rebuild it will lay the foundation in the death of his firstborn and build its walls in the death of his secondborn. Just as foretold: every man who tried to rebuild it—the Bible tells us of more than one—lost his children. His sons were destroyed just like God said they would be.

There is a wonderful accuracy here, one of the most minute and beautiful things about fulfilled prophecy. The Bible says that the wall of Jericho fell down "flat." Walls which are ten or fifteen feet wide do not usually fall down flat. They are more apt, through the decay of centuries, to crumble down. But the walls were to fall down "flat." When you see the walls of Jericho, you see that is exactly what happened.

God told the people of Israel that when they went into that land, they could take only the metal, nothing else. They were not to take the spoils of that city (Josh. 6:18,19). So when the excavators came and dug in the ruins and debris of Jericho, they found no metal whatsoever, only a wall standing and an apartment-like building on the top of it where Rahab lived and where the scarlet cord was let down—all of it just like the Book of God says that it is.

When you stop and realize that seventy-five percent of the Bible is prophetic and three-fourths of that has already been fulfilled, what a fool to say, "The rest of it will not come to pass just like God said it would"!

I believe the Bible because of its enclosure of things to come.

"All scripture is given by inspiration of God...."

5. Its Enraged Enemies

You say, "Preacher, what do enemies of the Bible prove? Why do they prove to you that the Bible is true and inspired and the Book of God?"

Go back to the beginning of the Bible, to Genesis 3, in the very Garden of Eden where man and woman were miraculously created by God, and read: "Now the serpent was more subtil than any beast of the field which the Lord God had made. And he said unto the woman, Yea, hath God said, Ye shall not eat of every tree of the garden?" (vs. 1).

There we find the first time anyone ever drew a big question mark at what God had said, and from that hour to this, men have been raising questions about the Bible. We even find it described in the Bible.

A man by the name of Jehoiakim, a wicked unbeliever, had a scribe, Jehudi, take the Book of God and sit and read to him. While Jehudi read, Jehoiakim took his penknife, cut out portions that he didn't like and threw them in the fire. "And it came to pass, that when Jehudi had read three or four leaves, he [Jehoiakim] cut it with the penknife, and cast it into the fire that was on the hearth, until all the roll was consumed in the fire that was on the hearth" (Jer. 36:23).

We read that God told Jeremiah to not only write what Jehoiakim had cut out, but to write more than he cut out: "Then took Jeremiah another roll, and gave it to Baruch the scribe... who wrote therein from the mouth of Jeremiah all the words of the book which Jehoiakim king of Judah had burned in the fire: and there were added besides unto them many like words" (vs. 32).

Every time man has fought against the Bible, he has only helped to prove that it is a miracle Book.

Men do not hate Shakespeare's writings nor the works of Milton, but they hate the works of God and seek to prove that it is a lie because this Bible brings man into the light of the holiness of God and assures him that, unless he repents, he must stand at a judgment bar and face God in the white light of His holiness. Thus man says, "I will question the Bible, and I am not going to believe it."

If all the bad people hated a person and all the good people loved that person, I would be prone to believe that that person was a good person. And when wicked people hate the Bible and good people love the Bible, it makes me know that it is a Book that comes from God.

Let man hate it if he will; he cannot destroy it, thanks be unto God forever! Let man take his little penknife and clip at its leaves, but he cannot destroy the Bible.

A man asked an Irishman to build a fence for him, "if you can guarantee me that it will be four feet high and will always be that high." The Irishman guaranteed it! He built the fence four feet high and five feet thick and said, "If they turn it over, it will be a foot higher than it was in the first place!"

That is the way it is in the Bible. Man has fought it, but the Bible has mounted and mounted and mounted like the great foundation Rock that it is, and it still stands today as sure as ever.

I know that it is the Word of God, and I know it is true because of its enraged enemies.

"All scripture is given by inspiration of God. . . ."

6. Its Excavated Silent Witnesses

I am not much on archeology, and I do not know a lot about it. A good many years I made my living digging in the rocks, trying to raise a few ears of corn and a few blackeyed peas, but I am not much of an excavator.

Millions of dollars have been spent excavating in Bible lands. Some years ago it was an actual fact that through all the excavations and all the historical works, no one had ever found a person named Pilate. So the critics and enemies of the Bible said, "The Bible said there was a man named Pontius Pilate before whom Jesus was sentenced to die. If that man didn't exist, then the Bible is not true."

Then a few years ago, in Caesarea, in digging up that great Roman colony in the great amphitheatre built there on the Mediterranean Sea, they discovered a box seat, a prominent seat, and inscribed on it in the stones buried beneath the sands for hundreds of years was the name **Pontius Pilate.** Man then had to go back and say, "We were wrong in saying Pilate never existed. History does not prove he existed, but archeology says he existed just like the Bible says he did."

Go down into the land of Egypt, and you will see a place called Tel-el-Kebir. It is the ruins of a city called the Treasure City of Pithom, built during the days of one of the Rameses. There is a strange thing about the excavation of this Treasure City. We read in the Bible where the wicked Pharaoh had the Jews make these buildings of mud bricks, consisting of mud, clay and also straw. They placed the straw in the mud and clay, then baked it, making the bricks as hard as stone.

One day the wicked Pharaoh said, "Now they will make just as many bricks as ever, but they will not gather any straw to put in them."

So when this city was excavated years ago, to the astonishment of excavators, they found some buildings made of blocks that had straw in them, and some blocks that had no straw—just exactly like the Bible said took place in the book of Exodus. They made some with straw and some without.

"And Pharaoh commanded the same day the taskmasters of the people, and their officers, saying, Ye shall no more give the people straw to make brick, as heretofore: let them go and gather straw for themselves.... So the people were scattered abroad throughout all the land of Egypt to gather stubble instead of straw."—Exod. 5:6,7,12.

There was a day in history when no one could actually prove that there was a man named Belshazzar, as is taught in the book of Daniel, a Belshazzar to whom God spoke and said, "Thy kingdom is divided. This night you are going to meet God. Thou art weighed in the balances, and art found wanting."

Sir Henry Rawlinson, digging in the ruins of Babylon in 1854, found the stones and inscription and writing that bore the name Belshazzar which placed him right in Babylon just where God in His holy Word said he was.

Not only is this true, but no man has ever turned the stone that proved an error in the Bible. Every stone that has ever been turned has said as a silent witness down across the years, "The Bible is the Word of God."

"All scripture is given by inspiration of God...."

7. Its Enormous Wealth of Truth

It is a fathomless Book which no man has ever mastered. Those who love it never tire of it. Those who read it find something new in it every time they read it. It has a wealth of truth.

A verse in I Corinthians says, "But as it is written, Eye hath not seen, nor ear heard, neither have entered into the heart of man, the things which God hath prepared for them that love him" (2:9). If you will read the context, you will see it is talking about the Bible, not about Heaven. 'Eye hath not seen it all; ear has not heard it all; the heart has not understood it all, because it is a bottomless well of fathomless truth, and it is deeper than the human mind.'

Oh, the wealth to be found in this sweet and wonderful Book! I believe that it is the Word of God because of its enormous wealth of truth.

I have not read the Bible as much as I should, but I have been reading it for thirty-five years. In the early days of my life I made a covenant with the Lord that I would read His Word if He would bless my life.

I can honestly say that somewhere between fifty and sixty times, I have gone through the Book of God. I have read it standing. I have read it seated. I have read it lying on my face. I have read it on bended knee. I have read it shouting. I have read it with tears. Yet I find it as fresh today as I did as a new convert thirty-five years ago, when I began to search its treasures both old and new. Oh, the fathomless wealth of this wonderful Book!

Men have done with the Bible just exactly like they did with Jesus. Stop and think. Jesus is the Living Word; this Bible is the written Word. Just as Jesus is the truth, this written Word is the truth. Man has treated this Bible, the written Word, just like they treated Jesus, the Living Word.

Men scrutinized the Living Word, hung upon His conversation, saying, "We will find something wrong with what He says," but they never did. Men have scrutinized the written Word, hung upon all of its precepts seeking to find some error, but they never found a one. Man hated the Living Word; man has hated the written Word. Men tried to destroy the Living Word, as they have tried to destroy the written Word; but they have failed in both. Just as men bruised Jesus, they have battered this Book. Just as men falsely accused Jesus, they have falsely accused the Bible, saying, "It is a book with dirty words and stories of immorality; it has ugly things in it."

That is not true. When you get saved and know that man has a depraved nature, then you realize that all God is doing is pulling the veneer off man and showing his awful, rotten depravity, all of his hideous sin, and his lost and carnal condition.

Oh, what an enormous wealth there is in this wonderful Book!

One great man years ago said, "Ninety percent of all good literature is nothing but the Bible diluted." In other words, he was saying, "Ninety percent of all good literature in the world is based upon the Bible."

You cannot explain how no man can master this Book, how no mind can sound its depths, how no one person can untangle all its mysteries and parables and riddles. No one can because it is a miracle Book. There is no bottom to it, no limit to it. Higher than the highest heavens, deeper than the deepest sea, broader than the circuits of the sun is this miracle Book.

The Bible is true because of its enormous wealth of truth.

I read a story years ago about a godly mother whose young son was going into acting. The mother said, "Son, I want you to take this Book and believe on the Jesus it tells about."

It is said that this actor, who became very famous, threw down in the bottom of his trunk, with his costumes and props, the Bible that his mother had given him. It lay on the bottom of his trunk and traveled thousands of miles.

But success turned to mediocrity and mediocrity to failure.

One night after a poor performance, he came and sat upon the trunk, put his head in his hands and thought, *Here I am, with health gone and no money. Success has faded away. The glitter has gone. Which way shall I look now?*

Then he thought of the old black Book lying in the bottom of his trunk which he had carted for thousands of miles. Penniless, broken in health, empty in life, hungering in heart and thirsting in soul, down into the trunk he dug for that little black Book which tells about life eternal, life more abundant. As he began to thumb the pages of the Bible his mother had given him, he found notes worth hundreds of dollars, sweet letters from her, and wonderful truth from Him.

That night by his trunk he turned to Jesus and to a Book that knows no end of wealth.

I know the Bible is true because of the enormous wealth of this wonderful Book. Thank God, I believe the Bible—from Genesis to Revelation. I am even like the old country preacher who said,

"I believe the two words on the front: HOLY BIBLE."
I believe the Bible is true.

"All scripture is given by inspiration of God...."—II Tim.
3:16.

Chapter V

Why I Know God Answers Prayer

James 5:7-20

"The effectual fervent prayer of a righteous man availeth much."—James 5:16.

There is a great deal in that verse, but I would like for you to think of it this way: "The...prayer of a righteous man availeth much."

This is one of many great passages in the Bible on prayer. Seven times in this great passage we learn something about prayer.

In verse 13: "...let him pray." Do you have a problem? Then pray about it. Is there something you need? Then pray about it.

Verse 14: "...and let them pray." Pray together.

One must have faith as he prays—verse 15: "And the prayer of faith shall save the sick."

Verse 16 says, "...and pray one for another."

Here is where there is a tremendous breakdown in the work of God and among the Lord's people. The Bible says that we are to pray one for another. I have the idea there may be a lot of *preying* upon one another instead of *praying* for one another. James said that we should pray for one another.

Prayer should be fervent—that is, with energy, travail and supplication before God. A man in the Old Testament, Elijah, prayed earnestly, and God heard his prayer. For three and one-half years the heavens gave no rain. I read that Elijah prayed again, and the drought ended and the floods came.

You ask me why I am preaching on "Why I Know God Answers Prayer." Because I know of nothing else in the world more important. Prayer is a great resource. Prayer is a great comfort. Nothing in this world can comfort the heart of a Christian more than getting on his/her knees and praying.

Prayer is a great source of supply. I do not know of any other way that God has promised to supply the needs of His people except through prayer. It is a great soul-conditioner. Sometimes you may pray and not receive the answer that you expected, but something will happen that you did not expect.

I have often prayed; and when God did not do exactly as I prayed, He did something else for me.

I like the story of a teacher teaching little boys. Once when she was not getting the attention of one little boy, she said, "Son, is there something on your mind?"

He answered, "Yes, I lost a marble. Would you mind if I just prayed to the Lord and asked Him to find my favorite marble?"

She said, "Go ahead."

He bowed his head and prayed, "Now, Lord, I have lost my marble. I don't know where to find it. I pray that You will lead me to it."

The teacher went on with the lesson. The next day she was almost afraid to ask, "Son, did you find your lost marble?" for fear he had not found it. But she boldly said, "Son, did God answer your prayer?"

"Yes, He did," he said, "but not in the way I thought He would. I didn't find my marble, but I am not concerned about it anymore; I really don't care whether I find it or not."

God always does something when people pray. Prayer is the

greatest soul-conditioner there is. Prayer honors God. Just think how God is honored when people come to the throne of grace. Prayer promotes His cause. It is so often said, "The church must go forward on its knees, or it will not go very far forward." Prayer promotes the cause of the Lord. It develops the soul. It is the greatest thing I know anything about.

You may ask, "Do you know God answers prayer?" I certainly do. I give you seven reasons out of the Bible and out of Christian experience why I know God will hear your prayer and do for you what needs to be done.

Let us notice some things about prayer.

First, the Bible plainly teaches that it is a sin not to pray. I remember one time when Israel was disobedient to God. They cried for a king when God had never wanted them to have a king. Samuel was told of the Lord to go ahead and anoint them a king, and Samuel anointed Saul. Saul was disobedient. There was heartache and confusion within the kingdom. Then, with a broken heart and with disappointment in these people, Samuel said, "Moreover as for me, God forbid that I should sin against the Lord in ceasing to pray for you: but I will teach you the good and the right way" (I Sam. 12:23).

The Bible teaches that it is a sin not to pray. It is a sin not to pray for your family, a sin not to pray for your church. It is a sin not to pray for the lost, a sin not to pray for the leaders of your country.

There is a reason why God does not answer everyone's prayer. The psalmist hit the nail right on the head when he said in Psalm 66:18, "If I regard iniquity in my heart, the Lord will not hear me." David is saying, "If I harbor iniquity, if I love it, condone it, accept it, the Lord will not hear my prayer."

God does not hear everyone's prayer. I have heard people discuss whether the Lord hears a sinner's prayer. I don't believe He does.

I know God will hear the sinner when he prays, "God, be merciful to me a sinner." Since prayer is in the name of Jesus, how can an unsaved person pray in the name of Jesus unless he knows Him as his personal Saviour? God does not always answer the prayers of people.

I have reason to believe that God does not hear all the prayers of Christians. David said, "If I regard iniquity in my heart, the Lord will not hear me." Isaiah said:

"Behold, the Lord's hand is not shortened, that it cannot save; neither his ear heavy, that it cannot hear: But your iniquities have separated between you and your God, and your sins have hid his face from you, that he will not hear."—Isa. 59:1,2.

The Lord's hand is no less powerful than it has always been; God hears today as well as He has ever heard; but He does not hear everyone's prayer because of iniquity and sin.

I shall give you an illustration. In Luke 18:10 Jesus said: "Two men went up into the temple to pray; the one a Pharisee, and the other a publican." Two are going to the Temple, and both are going to pray. God is going to hear one, but not the other. One is a publican—God hears him; the other is a religious man—God does not hear him. The religious Pharisee, who has a prominent place in the Temple, says, "...God, I thank thee, that I am not as other men are, extortioners, unjust, adulterers, or even as this publican" (vs. 11). Right there the Lord shut him off. When you come to the throne of grace, you must see your own needs first before God hears you pray. The Pharisee said, "I thank thee, that I am not as other men"—then he began to brag on himself: 'I tithe all I possess; I fast twice a week; and I pray three times a day.'

Then the publican standing in another corner cannot even lift up his head, so smitten is he with his own needs and under such condemnation. Rather, he smites upon his sinful breast and cries, "God, be merciful to me a sinner" (vs. 13). That man went down to his house justified. God heard the sinner but turned a deaf ear to the Pharisee.

If you are not getting your prayers answered, if God doesn't do something when you pray, then it is your fault, not God's. He doesn't hear everyone's prayer.

We are to pray for one another.

Some years ago when I was preaching on a similar subject, I said to myself, *For my own life and my own heart's need, I am going to take my Bible concordance and study every verse that deals with prayer.*

I found the first verse mentioned in the New Testament on prayer—Matthew 5:44: ''. . .pray for them which despitefully use you, and persecute you.'' I said, ''Lord, I am up against a stump.'' At that time wicked people were saying, ''Tom Malone steals money''; ''Tom Malone is a liar,'' and many other things. It was one of those times in my life when I was most assailed by people, and some of them, wicked people. When I came to the verse, ''. . .pray for them which despitefully use you, and persecute you,'' I drew back and said, ''Lord, I can't do it.'' God seemed to say, ''Then you can't preach on prayer. Not only that, you can't pray for anything until you can get on your knees, call by name and pray for those who despitefully use you.''

I learned a hard lesson on prayer. I learned one in travail; I learned one in tears; I learned one with a broken heart. You cannot pray unless you can pray for people who despitefully use you.

Some of you need to pray for someone you know who has wronged you. You may say, ''Well, that's hard.'' Yes, it is hard. There are many things that you have to do that are hard in order to do what God wants you to do. I had to get on my knees and weep and search my heart before I could preach on prayer. That is the first step.

In Jesus' Sermon on the Mount, He said, ''. . .pray for them

which despitefully use you, and persecute you.'' When I came
to the place that I could pray by name for those who hated me
and would love to see my name in the obituary column, then I
knew God was listening.

We are to pray for one another. What a greater church Emmanuel
Baptist Church would be if the families of God, the Lord's people, would pray for one another. James said that we should pray
one for another.

We need to learn to pray. In Luke 11:1 we read, ''And it came
to pass, that, as he was praying in a certain place, when he ceased,
one of his disciples said unto him, Lord, teach us to pray, as John
also taught his disciples.'' They saw Jesus in a certain place praying. If they looked for Jesus before daylight and found that He
was not where He lay down the night before, they knew they could
find Him out on some hillside down underneath an olive tree. In
a certain place Jesus was praying. The disciples heard Him and
watched Him and said, ''Lord, teach us to pray.'' Jesus said:

*''When ye pray, say, Our Father which art in heaven, Hallowed
be thy name. Thy kingdom come. Thy will be done, as in heaven,
so in earth. Give us day by day our daily bread. And forgive us
our sins; for we also forgive every one that is indebted to us. And
lead us not into temptation; but deliver us from evil.''*—vss. 2-4.

Friend, if you cannot look up through the blue today and call
God your Father through faith in Jesus Christ and His precious
blood, then you cannot pray, because Jesus said that relationship
is the important thing about praying. Lord, teach us to pray.

Some years ago in the hospital I called on a lady who had a
prayer book. She was religious but lost.

She said to me, ''You Baptists do not have a prayer book,
do you?''

I answered, ''Oh, yes, we do.'' I had never said that before.
But I said, ''Oh, yes, we have a prayer book.''

She said, "Well, I didn't know that!" (I didn't know it either until I had just said it!) "What kind of prayer book do you have?"

I had a little Bible in my pocket, so I pulled it out and said, "That is the prayer book of a believer." The Bible, to a large extent, is a book of prayer, a prayer book for the born-again child of God.

We need to learn to pray.

We learn to pray as we read the Bible, learn the prayer of others and learn to deal with God as an individual. You might say, "Preacher, I know all that is true, but how do we know God answers prayer?" I give seven reasons why I know God answers prayer.

I. HE HAS PROMISED IN HIS WORD TO ANSWER

In the Bible are many promises that God will answer prayer. I think of a wonderful passage in the Sermon on the Mount where Jesus spoke so simply about prayer. He did not speak simple, but He spoke simply. He was profound, but He used monosyllables. A little child could understand what He said. Jesus strove for simplicity. In this sermon, He said:

"Ask, and it shall be given you; seek, and ye shall find; knock, and it shall be opened unto you: For every one that asketh receiveth; and he that seeketh findeth; and to him that knocketh it shall be opened."—Matt. 7:7,8.

Then Jesus said:

"Or what man is there of you, whom if his son ask bread, will he give him a stone?"—vs. 9.

Jesus is saying, "If a little child asks his father for a loaf of bread, will the father give the child a stone and say, 'Here, son, eat the stone instead'?"

"Or if he ask a fish, will he give him a serpent?"—vs. 10.

Jesus is saying, "If you ask God, God will hear your prayer. God will answer you. God has promised to hear your prayer." Then Jesus went on to say:

"If ye then, being evil, know how to give good gifts unto your children, how much more shall your Father which is in heaven give good things to them that ask him?"—vs. 11.

I took a red pen and marked the word *ask* every time I found it in this passage. Prayer is asking. You can praise the Lord, yes; you can tell the Lord how you love Him, yes; but prayer is *asking* God for something. Five times in this brief passage Jesus said, "Ask." Oh, how much He said about prayer! Matthew 21:22 says, "And all things, whatsoever ye shall ask in prayer, believing, ye shall receive." Do you believe that?

Jesus talked about prayer so much. When He was on His way from the Upper Room to the bloody Garden of Gethsemane, He had a lot to say about prayer. In John 15:7 He said, "If ye abide in me, and my words abide in you, ye shall ask what ye will, and it shall be done unto you." At another time Jesus said, "Again I say unto you, That if two of you shall agree on earth as touching any thing that they shall ask, it shall be done for them of my Father which is in heaven" (Matt. 18:19).

A preacher in the South was preaching on this text years ago. While he was still preaching, a lady stood up in the audience and said, "Preacher, do you believe what you are preaching today?"

He said, "I believe it with all my heart."

She said, "Well, then, I need a prayer partner. My son, a sailor, set sail today to go out to sea. He may go out to a watery grave. I want my son saved. Do you believe, preacher, that if any two shall agree on earth as touching anything, that it shall be done?"

He said again, "I believe it with all my heart."

She said, "Will you be my partner in prayer? Will you, with me, claim the soul of my boy for God?"

He said, "I will."

After the service at an old-fashioned altar the preacher and the lady knelt and claimed this promise, "That if two of you shall agree on earth as touching any thing that they shall ask, it shall be done for them of my Father which is in heaven." Their prayer was, "O God, save this boy. He has already gone out to sea, but somehow, save him and give us the assurance that his soul is saved."

That night while sitting in the evening service, someone came and sat beside her. She turned and looked, then lost control of herself. "My son, I thought that you were gone!" She threw her arms around him.

He answered, "Mother, we started out for sea today, but something happened, and we had to turn back to harbor. I have an hour or two before we leave, and I knew I could find you in church."

That night when the invitation was given, down the aisle he came and was wonderfully saved.

God hears the prayers of His people because He has promised to do so.

One of the greatest verses on prayer in the Bible is Jeremiah 33:3: "Call unto me, and I will answer thee, and shew thee great and mighty things, which thou knowest not." God says, "I challenge you to ask Me to do something that you have never known of or have never had done before."

Psalm 91:15 says, "He shall call upon me, and I will answer him: I will be with him in trouble; I will deliver him, and honour him." God has promised to answer prayer.

In Titus 1:2 we read, "In hope of eternal life, which God, that cannot lie, promised before the world began." If God were to lie, He would cease to be God. And He said, "And all things, whatsoever ye shall ask in prayer, believing, ye shall receive" (Matt. 21:22).

You say, "Preacher, how do you know God answers prayer?" He has promised in His Word to answer.

"The effectual fervent prayer of a righteous man availeth much."

II. HE IS BOUND BY HIS NATURE
TO ANSWER PRAYER

I know God answers prayer because He is bound by His nature to answer prayer. I wish to explain to you what I mean. God must answer prayer. He is bound by His nature and His holy attributes to answer prayer.

Psalm 65:2 says, "O thou that hearest prayer, unto thee shall all flesh come." When the psalmist wanted to refer to God, he did not say "Jehovah." He did not call Him "Lord" in this instance. The psalmist referred to God as the One who answers prayer. That is God's nature and one of His attributes.

God has many attributes. There is never a conflict in the attributes of God. Every attribute agrees and harmonizes with all the others.

For instance, one of God's attributes is love. The Bible says, "He that loveth not knoweth not God; for God is love" (I John 4:8). God is love, and He has to listen to someone He loves. Can you imagine one He loves talking to Him and God saying, "I won't hear. I won't listen. I won't do anything about it. I won't pay any attention"? No, God's attribute of love demands that He listen to us when we pray.

God is almighty; that is, He is omnipotent. He is all-powerful. Genesis 17:1 tells us, "I am the Almighty God." God made this statement to Abraham who needed a prayer answered. He needed to have the promised heir to come. If God is all powerful—and that is part of His nature—then all power lies in the person of God, and God must meet our needs and supply that power. This attribute of God demands that He answer our prayer.

Jude verse 25 says, "To the only wise God our Saviour, be glory and majesty, dominion and power, both now and ever. Amen." This verse tells what we mean when we speak of the omniscience of God. If God knows everything, we don't know everything. We don't know much because God knows it all. His wisdom demands that He supply wisdom to us. So the nature of God demands that He answer prayer.

When I was first saved, I would see where one had written in another's Bible, signed his/her name and put a verse after it—his or her life's verse. I heard individuals give a testimony and say, "My life's verse is so and so."

I said to the Lord, "Lord, I want You to give me a verse that, as long as I live, I can say is my life's verse." He laid upon my heart Romans 8:32. The whole passage in that chapter and around that wonderful verse has to do in a sense with prayer. "He that spared not his own Son, but delivered him up for us all, how shall he not with him also freely give us all things?"

It is God's nature to give. This verse says that if He gave His Son, He will give us anything we need. When I come to God to ask for something, whether for healing of my body or for peace of mind or something for my dear family or for this work of God, I must remember this verse: "He that spared not his own Son, but delivered him up for us all, how shall he not with him also freely give us all things?" God has already proven that He will give His best when He gave Jesus at the cross. So Romans 8:32 became my life's verse.

I read in that same passage, in verse 31, "If God be for us, who can be against us?" God is for us—Hallelujah! The Lord is on your side—Hallelujah!

Even with a sob in it, in the darkest night and in the deepest valley, our voice is recognized by God. Jesus said, "My sheep hear my voice, and I know them, and they follow me" (John 10:27).

One time while standing at the foot of Mount Tabor, the mountain believed to be where the Lord's transfiguration took place, I saw a flock of sheep and goats. There were some beautiful little lambs and goats in that flock. About the only time goats are beautiful is when they are little. In that flock were the mothers of the lambs, the ewe lambs and others.

A boy came by with one of these little animals in his arms. The little lamb was cute but unhappy to be in some boy's arms. Somewhere out in that flock was his mother. The animals were grazing off, and the mother, too, was grazing at a distance. When the boy set the little fellow down, he let out a little call. Out in the flock the mother let out her call for her little one. Then the little lamb began to weave in and out of the flock until he found his mother.

Someone in our group said to the boy, "Go get it again." Out went the boy. He picked up the lamb and brought it back again. We held and stroked it. Then it struggled to be free. When the boy set it down on the ground, it began to call again, and out in the flock came the call of its parent. Out among the rocks and up the side of the mountain, weaving in and out of the flock it went until it found its parent again.

God recognizes your voice. God will hear you when you pray. You ask, "How do I know God answers prayer?" It is His nature to do so.

"The effectual fervent prayer of a righteous man availeth much."

III. BECAUSE OF THE EXAMPLE JESUS ESTABLISHED

There is no greater testimony to the fact that God answers prayer than the prayer life of our Lord. When I read about the prayer life of the Master, I feel so condemned. Our prayer life at its best compares weakly with His.

Luke 5:16 says, "And he withdrew himself into the wilderness, and prayed." The Lord believed in getting alone. Some Christians today want to be alone so they can get with God. So people say, "They are withdrawn." So was Jesus.

I read in Luke 6:12, "And it came to pass in those days, that he went out into a mountain to pray, and continued all night in prayer to God." Have you ever prayed all night? Jesus did.

I read in Matthew 14:23, "And when he had sent the multitudes away, he went up into a mountain apart to pray: and when the evening was come, he was there alone." Do you get alone with God in prayer?

I read in Mark 1:35, "And in the morning, rising up a great while before day, he went out, and departed into a solitary place, and there prayed." Jesus had a solitary place and before daylight He went there to pray.

I read in John 17 where Jesus prayed. He was on His way from that Upper Room to the bloody Gethsemane after He had spoken the words of John 13, 14, 15 and 16: now this statement in John 17:1: "These words spake Jesus, and lifted up his eyes to heaven, and said, Father, the hour is come; glorify thy Son, that thy Son also may glorify thee."

John 17 is really the Lord's prayer. He rendered up His life's work to God. The whole chapter is the longest recorded prayer of Jesus Christ. In this chapter He said, "Neither pray I for these alone, but for them also which shall believe on me through their word" (vs. 20). He is saying that He is praying not only for the disciples, but for all who believe on Him.

In this chapter, Jesus looked down across the centuries unborn and saw me and He said, "I am praying for you." He is praying for me, for you. The prayer life of Jesus gives us reason to believe that He answers prayer because of the example He established.

One day Jesus said to Simon Peter, "Simon, Simon, behold,

Satan hath desired to have you, that he may sift you as wheat: But I have prayed for thee, that thy faith fail not" (Luke 22:31,32). The Lord right now is at the right hand of God praying for you and me. He sees the trial of our life. He knows the burden of our heart. He knows the affliction of our body. He knows the trouble in our mind. Jesus is at God's right hand praying for us. He told Peter, "I have prayed for thee, that thy faith fail not."

Jesus must have lived in the atmosphere of prayer.

When His public ministry began, He was praying. Luke 3:21 tells us, "Now when all the people were baptized, it came to pass, that Jesus also being baptized, and praying, the heaven was opened." When Jesus got baptized, He was praying: we do not know what for.

Jesus prayed at His transfiguration when He took Peter, James and John and went to the top of that mountain. "And as he prayed, the fashion of his countenance was altered, and his raiment was white and glistering" (Luke 9:29).

Jesus prayed when He was baptized. He prayed when He was transfigured.

Then we read that He prayed in the bloody Garden of Gethsemane with the shadow of the cross hanging out upon His spotless soul. "And being in an agony he prayed more earnestly: and his sweat was as it were great drops of blood falling down to the ground" (Luke 22:44). Just before He died for you and me, Jesus prayed!

Then when they put Him on a cross and lifted Him up between Heaven and earth, He opened His mouth, and what did He say? When malefactors were crucified, they would curse those who condemned them; but what did Jesus say? Hands nailed with spikes, head crowned with thorns, body robed in blood, He was about to speak. What did He say? "Father, forgive them; for they know not what they do" (Luke 23:34). He prayed!

Jesus is a testimony that God answers prayer. On the day of Pentecost, three thousand people who were there the day of the crucifixion believed and were saved and baptized in answer to the prayer of Jesus.

I read a story about a man whom people "could never win to the Lord," they said. All of us have known someone like that. They said, "That person will never be saved." Many gave him the Gospel. Many condemned him for his sins. Many told him how he needed the Lord.

But one day a man went to him and said, "My heart is burdened for you. After a sleepless night, at three o'clock this morning my wife and I were still on our knees praying that you would be saved." Then he turned and walked away.

A few hours later there was a rap at that couple's door. There stood that crusty, hard sinner, who said to them, "I can't get those words off my mind: 'At three o'clock this morning, my wife and I were still praying to God to save you.' " He stood there trembling as he said, "God's answering your prayer. I want to be saved."

I know that God answers prayer. I know that Jesus is praying for you. Will you let the Lord have your life?

"The effectual fervent prayer of a righteous man availeth much."

IV. I KNOW BY EXPERIENCE THAT GOD ANSWERS PRAYER

By my own Christian experience I know that God answers prayer. I heard a man talking one time about the miracle of the new birth, about being born again. Another man said, "Why, there is nothing to that."

The born-again Christian said, "You shouldn't have said there is nothing to that."

"Well, then, what should I have said?"

"You should have said that, as far as you know, there is nothing to the miracle of the new birth."

Many of you could say, as could I, "I know God answers prayer because He has answered prayer for me."

Years ago I heard a great man of God whom the Lord wonderfully used. As a pastor, he was instrumental in winning thousands to Christ. God used this man, humanly speaking, to build a great church. I was in his presence when someone asked him, "Starting from nothing and with you, an untrained pastor, how was this great church built?"

I could not wait to hear his answer! He meditated a moment. Then he said, "You ask me how this church became a great church and why God has blessed it in such a miraculous way. My answer is found in John 14:13,14." Then he quoted it: "And whatsoever ye shall ask in my name, that will I do, that the Father may be glorified in the Son. If ye shall ask any thing in my name, I will do it."

I had thought that he might say, "This great church has been built by visitation work." Visitation is a vital part; but like everything else having to do with the life of a Christian, there is a combination of things. The Bible speaks about Christians working, witnessing, knocking on doors and winning the lost to Christ. But that great preacher said, "This church was built by John 14:13,14. It was built by prayer."

I happened to know for a fact that he and his workers were out on the sidewalks hour after hour, day after day, week after week; but he said, "It was built by prayer."

The Devil wants you to try to do things on your own—with your own personality, your own ingenuity, your own resources; but you cannot use them alone. God blesses that work and uses that, but God's work is accomplished by prayer and by no other way.

You will never go any deeper than you go in your prayer closet.

You will never go any farther than you move upon your knees with God. I know by experience that God hears and answers prayer. I have seen it happen many, many times.

I learned this fact as a country boy just saved, when the Lord laid it on my heart to go to school. I was absolutely penniless, a farmer boy, and God said, "I want you to go to college."

I didn't know what a college looked like. Besides, I had nothing to go on—no resources, no clothes, no one to back me, no promise of help; but I found a verse in the Bible which read, "But my God shall supply all your need according to his riches in glory by Christ Jesus" (Phil. 4:19). I learned through that verse that God answers prayer. I learned to call upon Him. I learned to depend upon Him. I learned to ask God to do the impossible, and God did it. I saw miracles happen in answer to Philippians 4:19, as I took that promise and went to prayer.

You ask me how I know God answers prayer. I know because I have had God answer many prayers in my own life.

Some years ago, after I had been saved just a short time and had been to college for a year, I had some throat problems. The doctor said, "You will have to have your tonsils out. Just come up to my office on Monday morning."

Those doctors back then didn't perform operations as they do now. That morning when I began to get ready to go to his office, which was out in the country two and a half miles away, my good, old country aunt said, "I'm not going to let you go to the doctor's by yourself." So she went with me.

The doctor told me to sit in a chair, just a plain, straight-backed chair. He got some instruments, then gave me a shot of something. He picked up his instruments, which looked as if they had not been used in a long time, looked in my throat, reached in and got hold of one tonsil and cut into it a ways. He couldn't get it cut off and couldn't get his instrument out. My aunt was having a fit! And

I was bleeding to death! I learned to pray right there.

Finally, he got both tonsils twisted out. I got up from the chair, walked down a flight of steps, got into an old Ford car, laid my head back and thought I was about to die. My aunt thought that, too. She was scared stiff!

I went home and lay down for awhile. My grandmother patted me on the head a few times, and that's about all the attention I received.

That was Monday morning. The next Friday I was to leave for North Carolina where I was to begin twelve weeks of preaching in an evangelistic campaign. So that next Friday morning I got on a bus. I would rather have walked or hitchhiked or even stayed at home, but I rode all the way to North Carolina on a bus with a sore throat. On Sunday morning I began preaching, and for twelve weeks, twice each day, I preached in evangelistic campaigns in North Carolina. That was the beginning of some serious throat problems. It was a foolish thing to do, and I did it in ignorance.

Later I had two operations on my voice. In the Emmanuel Baptist Church, week after week others preached in the pulpit because I was not able to. I was hardly able to speak distinctly, hardly able to tell people my name.

Finally one day a fine physician, a talented specialist, looked in my throat and said, "Tom, you will not be able to continue preaching. You will have to learn to write and serve the Lord in some other way."

That comment in an office building in the city of Detroit broke my heart. On the way home, with every turn of the wheel and with every throb of my heart, I prayed. When I got home, I told Mrs. Malone what the doctor had said. She replied, "There is One who knows more than all the doctors in the world." Down on our knees we went and prayed.

You know how God has answered that prayer. For many years,

many times a week, I have been preaching.

You might ask, "Do you believe in divine healing?" Yes, I believe in a miracle-working God. I believe the very fact that God has given me another privilege, another voice, means that He healed me. God spared me, and God saved my ministry.

You ask, "How do you know God answers prayer?" Because God has answered my prayers. When sorrow came and cloud after cloud came over my head, I had no way to look but up. I have gone to God and prayed. I have seen the time when, without supernatural help, I could go no farther. But God heard and answered. I have been going for thirty-five years, trusting Him one step at a time.

I have seen the time when, were it not for the power of God, this church would have been submerged in trouble, persecution and confusion. To God be the glory, the Emmanuel Baptist Church is standing in answer to prayer.

You ask, "How do you know God answers prayer?" By experience. Hallelujah! I would not want you to feel that I have apprehended in the matter of prayer. When I compare my prayer life with that of my blessed Lord, it is so insignificant. But I know God answers prayer because He has heard and answered mine according to His promise.

"The effectual fervent prayer of a righteous man availeth much."

V. GREAT EMPHASIS GIVEN TO PRAYER IN THE BIBLE

I know God answers prayer because of the great emphasis given to prayer in the Bible. Let me illustrate what I am talking about. If you could take out all the pages, all the chapters, all the verses, all the words that have to do with prayer, you would be surprised to learn how much of the Bible is taken up with prayer alone.

Back in the Old Testament God told David he was not going

to build a temple. "You are a man of war and a man of blood. You will establish a kingdom, but your son will build a house to honor My name."

It was Solomon whom God let build that great Temple, such a great house of God that it took seven years to build it. When it was finished, God put it on the heart of Solomon to dedicate it. The whole chapter of II Chronicles 6 is about the dedication of God's first permanent house. There had been the Tabernacle in the wilderness, but this was to be the more permanent house, one which was to stand for centuries.

The day of dedication had come. When you read about the dedication and think about the atmosphere on the day of the dedication of this great edifice, it was almost unbelievable.

We read where Solomon got up on a platform, spread his hands, lifted his eyes toward Heaven and began to pray. He thanked God for His blessings. Solomon dedicated that Temple to God. Again and again in this chapter Solomon said, "Now, Lord, if these people go away from You, but then turn toward this house and pray, forgive them. If we are overcome in war and defeated, but turn toward this house and pray, hear our prayer. If pestilence comes from which there is no relief, but we turn toward this house and pray, hear our prayers. If famine comes and a dearth throughout the land, but we turn toward this house and pray, hear our prayer."

God seemed to condone Solomon's words. Then Solomon said, "Now, my God, let, I beseech thee, thine eyes be open, and let thine ears be attent unto the prayer that is made in this place" (vs. 40).

Now, what was that Temple? A place of worship? In a sense, yes, a place of offering. But to know exactly what it was, we go to the New Testament.

One day when Jesus walked in that Temple He found money-changers buying and selling. Instead of bringing of their own from their flocks to be sacrificed, people came and bought at a money-changer's table. Jesus went in, upturned the tables, took a whip and drove the moneychangers from the Temple, then said, "It is written, My house shall be called the house of prayer; but ye have made it a den of thieves" (Matt. 21:13). That verse says that the first great Temple ever built in the name of the true God was a house of prayer.

No way can we determine how much of this Bible is devoted to the matter of prayer. Would God, in the only written revelation that this world has ever known about Himself, have said all this about prayer were He not a prayer-hearing and prayer-answering God?

Consider the men who have walked across the pages of the Bible. Take Abraham. Try to find the first time a man ever prayed. I do know that the first time prayer is mentioned by name, by *prayer,* is in Genesis 20, when Abraham was in the land of Abimelech. All of the people of Abimelech were a barren people. Read in Genesis 20:17, "So Abraham prayed unto God: and God healed Abimelech...."

Abraham believed that God could answer prayer. When his whole kingdom was barren and fruitless, Abraham believed God could hear prayer and work miracles, so he prayed and God heard him.

Moses twice spent forty days in the mountain with God. How Moses believed that God would answer prayer! When God said, "Moses, these people have sinned until I must destroy them," Moses pleaded with God. "O God, forgive their sins. If not, blot my name out of the Book of Life." The prayer life of Moses saved a whole godless nation.

Samuel was a great prophet or preacher, and he was godly in prayer.

Think of Daniel. When reading the book of Daniel, you are

thinking of prophecy. That book unfolds the course of the nations and the course of Gentile kingdoms. But Daniel is also a book of prayer. When people came saying, "You must eat the king's meat and drink the king's wine," Daniel had an answer: "You just give us time to pray about it." Daniel prayed to God. When the people came with their riddles unsolved, no human could tell them what the riddles meant. But Daniel went to God and prayed.

Daniel was a man of prayer, and the book of Daniel is a great book on the matter of prayer.

What shall we say about Jeremiah, that weeping prophet who prayed and prayed? One day he prayed so much that God said, "These people are so rebellious, wicked and corrupt that you need not pray for them any longer."

David was a man of prayer. David had his failure and his human weakness, but remember that no man ever knew how to pray as David did. David would go before God and pour out his heart. "As the hart panteth after the water brooks, so panteth my soul after thee, O God" (Ps. 42:1). David was a man of prayer. Many of the Psalms are nothing more or less than the prayer, word by word, that David lifted up to God.

You find also in the Psalms the prayers of Moses. The book of Psalms is largely a book of prayer. In fact, it is called by many the book of praise and prayer. Oh, the emphasis that God gives in the Bible to the matter of prayer!

You say, "Preacher, how do you know God answers prayer?" I know because of the great emphasis given to prayer in the Bible.

"The effectual fervent prayer of a righteous man availeth much."

VI. BEHAVIOR OF THE SAINTS IN TIME OF CRISIS AND NEED

I know God answers prayer because of the behavior of the saints of old in times of crisis and need. I see in the Bible what men did when they faced a great crisis in their lives. Did they scheme and plan and organize? No, not these chosen giants of the faith. They prayed.

I think of that good man Hezekiah. One day Hezekiah was sick. The prophet came to him and said, "Thus saith the Lord, Set thine house in order; for thou shalt die, and not live" (II Kings 20:1). God's Prophet Isaiah said, "Hezekiah, you are going to die, so set your house in order. Make all the arrangements, for thou shalt die and not live."

In verse 2: "Then he turned his face to the wall, and prayed unto the Lord." Hezekiah turned so that no one could see him, not even the Prophet Isaiah. Hezekiah began to pray: "I beseech thee, O Lord, remember now how I have walked before thee in truth and with a perfect heart, and have done that which is good in thy sight. And Hezekiah wept sore" (vs. 3).

Hezekiah reminded God, "Lord, I have walked in Your path; I have been Your child. Now I want You to heal me of this sickness."

God literally changed His own decree:

"And it came to pass, afore Isaiah was gone out into the middle court, that the word of the Lord came to him, saying, Turn again, and tell Hezekiah the captain of my people, Thus saith the Lord, the God of David thy father, I have heard thy prayer, I have seen thy tears: behold, I will heal thee: on the third day thou shalt go up unto the house of the Lord. And I will add unto thy days fifteen years...."—Vss. 4-6.

God said to Isaiah, "Go back and tell him [Hezekiah] that I have heard his prayer and I have seen his tears. Tell him that I am going to let him live fifteen more years."

You ask me, "How do you know God answers prayers?" I have studied the behavior of the saints of old in the Bible. What did they do when a crisis came and there was no human hope? They prayed.

The early church was loved of God and widely used. It was a fruitful church, but a hated church. The Bible says that the early church was a praying church: "And they continued stedfastly in the apostles' doctrine and fellowship, and in breaking of bread, and in prayers" (Acts 2:42). What did the people of God do when persecuted? They prayed.

I read in Acts 3:1, "Now Peter and John went up together into the temple at the hour of prayer, being the ninth hour." They believed in going to prayer meeting. Some of you do not. You don't need to be providentially hindered. Your own sorry, rotten flesh hinders you. Your unwillingness to be inconvenienced hinders you. Your desire for comfort hinders you. Not these men: these early Christians knew that prayer was important.

Peter and John were on their way to the house of God at the hour of prayer. When they went to the house of God to pray, a crippled man was there who had been that way all his life, and he had been at the Gate Beautiful for years. Along came two men of God, praying men. When he lifted up his little tin cup and expected something from them, Simon Peter gave him that classic, oft-quoted answer: "Silver and gold have I none; but such as I have give I thee: In the name of Jesus Christ of Nazareth rise up and walk" (Acts 3:6). Peter took the man by the hand and "immediately his feet and ankle bones received strength. And he leaping up stood, and walked." Praise God, a miracle was wrought!

Then the hottest persecution you can imagine set in. Peter and John were put in jail. From the content of the Scripture, it seems the people put the man who was healed in jail, too.

Isn't that something! A crippled man wound up in jail with two preachers whom he didn't even know! Maybe he asked himself, *What am I in here for? I was crippled and got healed,* so they threw me in jail! Isn't that something!

That is exactly what happened. The Devil breathed out his hot hatred against the early church.

What did they do? Acts 4:31: "And when they had prayed, the place was shaken where they were assembled together; and they were all filled with the Holy Ghost, and they spake the word of God with boldness."

Prayer is the answer. Many churches, people and preachers across this world are talking about communism, the darkness of the hour, the intensity of the work of the Devil, liberalism, ecumenicalism; but the early church shows us the answer at the prayer spot.

You say to me, "Preacher, how do you know God answers prayer?" I know because when crises came in the lives of Bible Christians, they went to their knees.

One day old Herod took a sword and cut off James' head. That act proves that Herod was not fooling around. He wanted Christianity wiped out, so he took James' head off. Then he put Peter in jail and said, "He's a little more prominent. We will save him until Easter, and then we will have another head off."

In jail Peter did the strangest thing: he lay down and went to sleep! If I thought for one moment that my head would be cut off tomorrow, I would spend a sleepless night; but not Simon Peter. With soldiers chained to either side of him, he lay down that night and went sound asleep. How could he? Peter remembered the time when, out on the shores of Galilee before the Master went away and after the resurrection, he had said, "Lord, and what shall this man [John] do?" (John 21:21).

In John 21:18 Jesus said, "Verily, verily, I say unto thee, When thou wast young, thou girdedst thyself, and walkedst whither thou wouldest: but when thou shalt be old, thou shalt stretch forth thy hands, and another shall gird thee, and carry thee whither thou wouldest not."

Jesus is saying to Peter, "Never mind about John. I will tell you about *you*. When you were young, you clothed yourself and went where you wanted to go, but when you get old, another shall bind you and make you go where you do not want to go."

Then verse 19: "This spake he, signifying by what death he should glorify God."

They put Peter in jail not long after Pentecost. Perhaps Simon Peter was middle-aged. He began thinking, "Oh, the words of Jesus have never failed. Whatever Jesus has ever said has always come to pass. His word is true, as true as His own character. His word cannot fail, and He told me that I will not die a martyr's death until I am an old man. Since I am not old yet, I think I will just lie down and go to sleep." He went so sound asleep that an angel had to awaken him.

The angel shook two people in that chapter. He shook one so hard that he has not awakened yet! That was the old, wicked Herod. The angel touched him, and he just died.

The angel woke up Simon Peter and unlocked the chained gates for him. Peter walked out between all the sleeping soldiers. Why was all of this happening? You read why in Acts 12:5: "Peter therefore was kept in prison: but prayer was made without ceasing of the church unto God for him." And God heard their prayers.

God teaches that there is a miracle-working power called prayer. Who prays? What for? Unto whom? Many people pray to be heard of men. Many quote Scripture and pray, trying to impress those who listen. God have mercy on those who pray just to be heard of men.

Sometimes when we call on a certain one to pray, he or she will answer, "May I please be excused? I am not good at it," which means, "I don't think I can pray so as to please people." We are to pray to please God, not people.

These people of the church were praying, and they kept praying. A little girl named Rhoda was peeping out through the gate. She was not even involved in the prayer meeting. As she peeped out and saw Simon Peter standing there, she ran in the house and told those praying, "Peter is at the gate."

One said, "Sit down and be quiet. We are praying for Peter's deliverance."

"But he's at the gate!"

"Listen! You are disturbing our prayer meeting. Sit down and be quiet." They even declared she was mad, or crazy.

But when she constantly affirmed, "But he is out at the gate!" they said, "It is his angel."

When Peter kept knocking, they opened the door. Now they realized that God had answered the prayers of a praying church.

Some of the great things physically that have ever happened to this world, happened in answer to prayer.

Samuel F. B. Morse invented the telegraph. When you fly an airplane, you have an instrument in it called an "omni." As you fly in a plane and look out for miles, you can see a little object that looks like an ice cream cone turned upside down and smashed against the ground. It has a little white point sticking up. As you fly and listen, you hear the Morse code. The code identifies that radio code for many, many miles. You follow the needle on the dial, and it will take you right to your destination.

People often asked Samuel F. B. Morse, "Mr. Morse, were there times when you didn't know what else to do, when it looked as if you had failed?"

He answered, "Oh, yes. Many times I was absolutely stumped. Many times I didn't know what else to do, humanly speaking."

"Well, Mr. Morse, what did you do? Why did you continue?"

He answered, "When I came to the end of my human resources, I dropped to my knees and prayed, 'O God, give further light,' and God did."

No wonder the first telegraph message ever flashed across the great ocean were these four words: "What hath God wrought!" Because he prayed, a man received wisdom from God; he prayed and God helped him to achieve his goal.

You say, "Preacher, how do you know God answers prayer?" I know because of the behavior of the saints of old in the time of crisis and need.

"The effectual fervent prayer of a righteous man availeth much."

VII. PRAYER IS HIS METHOD FOR US TO OBTAIN AND ACHIEVE

I believe God has so ordered life that one cannot obtain and achieve any other way but by prayer.

This chapter in James teaches that idea in regard to healing.

"Is any among you afflicted? let him pray. Is any merry? let him sing psalms. Is any sick among you? let him call for the elders of the church; and let them pray over him, anointing him with oil in the name of the Lord: And the prayer of faith shall save the sick...."—James 5:13-15.

"Preacher, do you believe that is for today?" you ask. Yes, just as much as I believe John 3:16 is for today.

"Do you believe oil heals?" you ask. No. Oil is a symbol of the Holy Spirit, and there is a proper order, with some guidelines to be remembered. "Is any sick among you? let him call for the elders of the church...." I don't believe anyone can say, "I am a divine healer," and go around looking for someone to lay hands on.

I heard a radio preacher say, "Lay your hands on the radio, and I will pray, and you will get thrilled and blessed." I didn't put mine there. I could have reached around behind the radio and gotten hold of the wires and received a much bigger thrill than he ever thought I could! I don't believe that.

"Is any sick among you? let him call for the elders of the church. . . ." Let the call originate with the one who needs that help. Let people anoint him with oil, praying in the name of the Lord, and the prayer of faith will heal the sick. I have seen it happen.

I remember many years ago when there were only about three members on our deacon board. One day there came an urgent call. One teenage girl had been ill so long that there was little hope of her ever getting well. The urgent call asked, "Will you do as the Bible says and come anoint her with oil and pray that God will raise her up?"

I called and was able to reach one of our deacons. We went to this home. The grandmother, who was rearing the girls, greeted us. As we walked into the room, we saw one of the girls in a wheelchair. Her tongue was out of one side of her mouth. She had an unnatural look in her eyes and was chewing on her tongue. She had no control of her hands. As she sat in the wheelchair, she looked more dead than alive.

The brokenhearted grandmother, who believed that God could answer prayer, said, "Here she is." That good deacon got down on his knees and began to pray. As he prayed, I took the oil and put it upon the girl's head and said, "O God, You are able. I know You are. Heal this girl if You can do it in Your sweet and blessed will."

Later, that girl was baptized here in the Emmanuel Baptist Church—as normal as any young woman can be.

Not long after that, while I was walking down the street an elderly lady pushed me over against a building and held me pinned there while she said, "Praise the Lord! My grandchild is well! Thank God!"

I know God answers prayer. This chapter says, "Is any sick

among you? let him call for the elders of the church....'' Don't act a fool about it. Do it in faith, do it as the Bible says, and let it work as the Bible says. That is God's way.

I thank God for doctors and medicine. The Bible talks about how God uses different means. He told a prophet to put a poultice on someone. Nothing in the Bible speaks against doctors, nurses, hospitals and medicine.

You ask, "Do you believe in divine healing?" There is no other kind of healing. If God does not want you to get well, no doctor in the world can get you off a sickbed.

This is God's method to obtain and achievé.

Prayer is most important in getting souls saved. When Jesus and the three came from the mountaintop, they found a young boy foaming at the mouth. His brokenhearted, disillusioned father said, "I brought him to Your disciples, but they couldn't cast out the demons." Jesus spoke to the boy; and with great anguish the demons came out of him, and in a moment he was well. When the disciples asked, "Why couldn't we do this?" Jesus answered them in Matthew 17:21, "Howbeit this kind goeth not out but by prayer and fasting."

We can get people saved by praying. Years ago I heard a great Bible teacher say, "It never says in the Bible to pray for lost souls." I was just a young Christian, but when I got my Bible and read what Paul said in Romans 10:1, "Brethren, my heart's desire and prayer to God for Israel is, that they might be saved," I said to myself, *That Bible teacher doesn't know what he is talking about.*

When you pray, God works. Any Christian mother or father can pray, and God will speak to a boy's heart even if he is on the other side of the world. Godly parents can pray, and God can bring a wayward child back home. Prayer is God's method to obtain and achieve.

This principle stands true when it comes to obtaining Christian workers. There is a way to get them. Matthew 9:37 says there is a problem: "The harvest truly is plenteous, but the labourers are few." But the next verse gives the solution: "Pray ye therefore the Lord of the harvest that he will send forth labourers into his harvest."

I have seen that verse in action. Years ago we used to have Monday night visitation. I told our people that we were going to pray that more people would come. Because I know that people need jobs, I went so far as to say, seriously and kindly, "If you are letting work keep you from winning souls, God may take your job away."

The next Monday night a lady came up to me with her hand shaking in my face: "Don't you ever pray that way again!"

I asked, "Why?"

She said, "I got fired. That is the only reason why I could come tonight."

I don't know whether it was because I prayed, but I do know one thing: when you pray, God puts labourers into His harvest. "Pray ye therefore the Lord of the harvest, that he will send forth labourers into his harvest."

This church ought to pray for the Lord to give us more bus workers and Sunday school teachers. This is God's method to obtain and achieve. I long to see fifty people go from this church to the mission fields in the next five years.

I know prayer is God's way to supply our needs. When they said to Jesus, "Lord, teach us to pray," Jesus said, "After this manner therefore pray ye: Our Father which art in heaven, Hallowed be thy name. Thy kingdom come. Thy will be done in earth, as it is in heaven. Give us this day our daily bread . . ." (Matt. 6:9-11).

I read a little pamphlet the other day on "Why the Lord's Prayer Should Never Be Used in Public." It was the most ridiculous thing I have ever read, yet written by a so-called fundamental Bible teacher.

The Lord is never going to let down His own who pray.

You can live one day at a time and expect God to meet your needs. Prayer is a method to obtain and achieve.

Think of those who once knew the Lord, once loved Him, once walked with Him and were close to Him. They felt His heartbeat; they worked with Him in His kingdom work: now many of them are away from God and backslidden. They are out of fellowship and have lost their joy.

You ask, "What can they do?" They can pray. One of the greatest, most wonderful, penitential prayers ever prayed is Psalm 51, where David prayed, "Restore unto me the joy of thy salvation; and uphold me with thy free spirit."

When you get away from God, the way back is on your knees. When you have lost the thrill of being a Christian, prayer is the way back. "Restore unto me the joy of thy salvation; and uphold me with thy free spirit."

We find examples of this restoration in the Bible. Jonah disobeyed God and was swallowed by a whale. "Then Jonah prayed unto the Lord his God out of the fish's belly" (2:1). Jonah said way down in the fish's stomach, "Oh, this is no place for a preacher! I'll pray and ask God to deliver me," so Jonah began praying. After awhile the whale said, "I feel rather nauseous." Jonah kept praying. After a few more minutes, that old whale said, "I just believe I'm going to throw up." He threw up a praying preacher.

Friend, the way back to God, to power, to joy, to living with your eyes upon Him is on your knees.

Prayer is God's method to obtain and achieve.

"The effectual fervent prayer of a righteous man availeth much."—James 5:16.

Chapter VI

Why I Know the Holy Spirit Is a Person

John 14:16,17,26-28; John 15:26; John 16:7-11

"And I will pray the Father, and he shall give you another Comforter, that he may abide with you for ever."—John 14:16.

As I speak on "Why I Know the Holy Spirit Is a Person," please don't immediately say, "That subject is too deep for me, and I'm not interested."

To those who believe on the Lord Jesus Christ as your personal Saviour, I doubt that you will ever hear anything more important than what I will talk about in this message. I have a deep conviction that the Lord's people need assurance.

These three chapters of John tell about a Comforter who would come. Jesus spoke these chapters the night before His crucifixion. As He left the Upper Room where the Lord's Supper was instituted, going to the bloody Garden of Gethsemane, Jesus walked with His eleven disciples. Judas had already betrayed Him at the table, had sold Him for thirty pieces of silver and had separated himself from the true believers. As Jesus walked with the eleven, He spoke to them about important matters. He talked about another Comforter who would come, and He referred to the Holy Spirit.

Many people do not believe or do not know that the Holy Spirit is a person. Some think of the Holy Spirit as a good influence; some think of the Holy Spirit as some great dynamic, impersonal force; some think of the Holy Spirit as a divine emanation or a good spirit that emanates from God. But the Bible teaches that this Comforter of whom Jesus spoke is a real and active person.

Much emphasis is given in the Bible to this person of the Trinity—the Holy Spirit. Just as much emphasis is given to this member of the Trinity as to either of the other two members.

For instance, the first New Testament book, Matthew, begins and ends with the work of the Holy Spirit. As we read of the virgin birth of our Lord Jesus Christ, we discover these words: ''...she was found with child of the Holy Ghost'' (Matt. 1:18). So the first book of the New Testament begins with the ministry of the Holy Ghost.

We read of the Holy Spirit many times in the book of Matthew. At the close of the book we read of Him again. In the Great Commission Jesus said, ''Go ye therefore, and teach all nations, baptizing them in the name of the Father, and of the Son, and of the Holy Ghost'' (Matt. 28:19).

Even the first New Testament book gives great emphasis to the Holy Spirit.

We come to the book of Acts, where we find God's great evangelistic program for the church to win people to Christ and to evangelize the world. It is impossible to overemphasize how the Holy Spirit is set forth in the book of Acts alone. In fact, *Acts of the Apostles* is not a good name for this wonderful book. Many Bible students say that it should more accurately be called the *Acts of the Holy Spirit.*

In chapter 1 the Holy Spirit is set forth four times, doing four different things. Four tremendous phases of His ministry are given in the first chapter. In Acts 1:2 is given the instruction of the Holy

Spirit: "...he through the Holy Ghost had given commandments unto the apostles whom he had chosen." God emphasizes all through His Word the personality and reality and ministry of the Holy Ghost and sets Him forth as a real person.

Acts 1:5 reads, "For John truly baptized with water; but ye shall be baptized with the Holy Ghost not many days hence," or more accurately translated, "Ye shall be baptized *in* the Holy Ghost not many days hence."

Then Acts 1:8: "But ye shall receive power, after that the Holy Ghost is come upon you: and ye shall be witnesses unto me both in Jerusalem, and in all Judaea, and in Samaria, and unto the uttermost part of the earth."

In Acts 1:16 Peter said, "Men and brethren, this scripture must needs have been fulfilled, which the Holy Ghost by the mouth of David spake before...." Four phases of His work are given in Acts, chapter 1, alone:

1. Instruction—Acts 1:2.
2. Inclusion (into the body of Christ)—Acts 1:5.
3. Induement—Acts 1:8.
4. Inspiration—Acts 1:16.

In the first chapter of Acts the Holy Spirit told the prophets and everyone else whom God used to write a book in the Bible, what to say. I say again that it is absolutely impossible to overemphasize the reality and personality of the Holy Spirit as He is set forth in the Word of God.

I would like for you to see the fourfold ministry of the Holy Spirit in the life of every child of God: His incoming, His indwelling, His uprising, His outflowing.

His Incoming. There is, first, the incoming of the Holy Spirit, which is important. See the plain and simple language of John 3, where Jesus spoke to a man about being saved. In verses 5 and 6 Jesus taught that the Holy Spirit comes into a person's life the moment he or she is saved. One need never ask for the person of the Holy Spirit after he is converted, for he receives Him, and His incoming takes place the very moment one is saved.

Remember that in this chapter Jesus is talking to Nicodemus. In verse 5 He said, "Verily, verily, I say unto thee, Except a man be born of water and of the Spirit, he cannot enter into the kingdom of God." Then in verse 6 He said, "That which is born of the flesh is flesh; and that which is born of the Spirit is spirit." So Christian, realize that what happened to you when you were saved was that the Holy Spirit of God took up His abode in your heart, in your life and in your body. The Bible plainly teaches His incoming.

His indwelling. The Bible plainly teaches His indwelling. The Holy Spirit never leaves a truly born-again child of God. You may ask, "What about Saul, the first king of Israel in the Old Testament? The Bible says God took His spirit away from him."

In the Old Testament, before Calvary, before the resurrection, before Pentecost, the Holy Spirit came and went from people as God so chose. But in the New Testament, after Calvary, after the resurrection, after the Day of Pentecost, there was never an instance when God ever took His Holy Spirit from a single child of God.

In John 14:16 Jesus said, "And I will pray the Father, and he shall give you another Comforter, that he may abide with you for ever." If you, a Christian, believe in everlasting life and in being saved through all eternity, then you are also to believe that the Holy Spirit, once He enters a person at the new birth, never leaves that child of God. He abides with him forever.

Then Romans 8:9 says, "Now if any man have not the Spirit [capital *S*, referring to the Holy Spirit] of Christ, he is none of his." God said, "If the Holy Spirit is not in you, then you are not a Christian." You cannot be saved without having Him. You cannot have Him without being eternally saved.

So His incoming and His indwelling are plainly taught in the Bible.

His uprising. The Bible speaks of what I would like to call His uprising, that is, He fills the believer. Ephesians 5:18 says, ". . .be filled with the Spirit." We need that filling. Many Baptists get a little nervous when they begin talking about the fullness of the Spirit and the fullness of the Holy Ghost and the power of the Spirit; but the Bible speaks of being "filled with the Spirit."

This experience happened to a man who one time had finished preaching. If I have ever known anyone filled with the Spirit of God, he was.

A young convert came to him at the close of the service and asked, "Do you believe you are right now filled with the Holy Spirit of God?"

This great preacher humbly, but with confidence, said, "Yes, I believe that at this very moment I am filled with the Holy Spirit of God."

What could you say if someone were to pose that question to you: "Are you this moment filled with the Holy Spirit of God?"

His outflowing. His incoming, His indwelling, His uprising— and then the teaching of His outflowing. Jesus talked of this. One of the strangest things that Jesus said, if it were not fully explained in its context, would be His words of John 7:37: "If any man thirst, let him come unto me, and drink." Then Jesus said in verse 38, "He that believeth on me, as the scripture hath said, out of his belly [his innermost being] shall flow rivers of living water."

What did Jesus mean?

Read one more verse, verse 39: "But this spake he of the Spirit, which they that believe on him should receive: for the Holy Ghost was not yet given; because that Jesus was not yet glorified."

Jesus said, "In the life of a Bible-believing, born-again Christian, there are to be rivers of living water, the constant Spirit outflow.''

It is as the dear older lady said when she talked about her cup being full, ''Lord, fill my saucer, too, and fill it until they're both running over.'' The normal Christian life, the New Testament life for the child of God, is to be so filled with the Spirit until it runs over. There are the fruits of the Spirit, the influence on other lives, the winning of souls—the outflowing of the Spirit of God from the life of a Christian.

You say to me, ''Then, Preacher, why is it that there are so many misconceptions about the Holy Spirit, so much misunderstanding and so little known of this member of the Trinity?'' I had someone ask me one time, ''How can it be that one God can be in three different personalities—God the Father, God the Son, and God the Holy Spirit?''

I answered with this illustration.

You can go to the faucet, turn it on and get water. You can go to the refrigerator and get a cube of ice. You can go to the window and wipe off a bit of vapor. One is a liquid, one is hardened, and the last is a vapor. However, all are the same substance.

God in His sovereignty has so decreed that He is to be manifest in three personalities: God the Father, God the Son, and God the Holy Spirit.

Why is there so little emphasis on the Holy Spirit of God? First, because of a lack of teaching on it. In my own ministry, where I have studied the Word of God and sought faithfully to preach it, perhaps there has been a lack of emphasis on the personality of the Holy Spirit of God. There needs to be teaching by preachers, teachers and believers on the personality of the Holy Spirit of God. You remember that Paul said to Timothy in II Timothy 2:2: ''And the things that thou hast heard of me among many witnesses, the same commit thou to faithful men, who shall be able to teach others also.''

You ask why there are so many misconceptions about Him. Many people who say they are Spirit-filled are not. I am not a judge, but I will tell you this: Spirit-filled Christians are victorious Christians; Spirit-filled Christians are soul-winning Christians; Spirit-filled Christians are faithful Christians; Spirit-filled Christians are separated Christians; Spirit-filled Christians are working Christians.

There is much misconception about what the Bible teaches about the fullness of the Spirit. Once in awhile you will get someone with a long face and a sad countenance who will feign some sort of deeper life called the "fullness of the Spirit." But when you have the fullness of the Holy Spirit, you show evidence of the power that Christians in biblical times had in their lives.

There is a lack of teaching on the Holy Spirit.

Some translations of the Bible cause misconception about His personality. For instance, we read in Romans 8:16, "The Spirit itself beareth witness with our spirit. . . ." Then verse 26: ". . .the Spirit itself maketh intercession for us with groanings which cannot be uttered." The King James is accurate when it speaks of the Holy Spirit as "itself." *Spirit* is in the neuter gender here, and the personal pronoun must always agree with its antecedent in the Greek text; hence the word *itself.* Many times He is referred to as *himself.* The Holy Spirit is not an *it*; the Holy Spirit is a *person.*

Now just suppose some lady asks another lady, "Where is your husband?"

The other lady answers, "It is standing over there."

Or if someone would ask a man, "Where is your wife?"

"Well, it just went out the door."

Suppose someone would ask you about your sweetheart, "Where is he?" or "Where is she?"

"Oh, it went away for the weekend."

It would be stupid to refer to someone dear, someone real, some personality, as an *it;* yet that is all the Holy Spirit is to many people. To many He is not the glorious, wonderful, divine personality that is set forth in the pages of the Word of God, but merely an influence or an emanation from God.

Why do people misunderstand about the Holy Spirit? Is it because of tradition, denominational slant or the substitution of other things for the real power of the Spirit? Dr. R. A. Torrey, successor to Dwight L. Moody, was a man filled with the Spirit of God and wonderfully used in a great worldwide ministry. Thousands were saved under his ministry, and thousands are still being saved under his Spirit-filled writings. Torrey was a great writer on the teachings and the ministry of the Holy Spirit.

It is said that he was speaking one time in a service on "Why I Know the Holy Spirit Is a Real Person." Following the service, his relative, who was staying with him, said, "Reuben, I never thought of it as a person before."

Dr. Torrey answered, "You still didn't get the message. 'I never thought of *it* as a person before.' The Holy Spirit is a *Him,* a real person."

The Holy Spirit is a real person who indwells every believer.

One time a lady said to a preacher, "I got the Holy Spirit last night." (Of course, that statement is wrong unless she had just been saved.)

The preacher said, "I know something better than that."

"Oh," she said, "there could be nothing better than my getting the Holy Spirit."

This preacher, a godly, wonderful man who knew the Scriptures, said, "It would be far better if the Holy Spirit could get all of you."

My friends, this is the secret. You have the Holy Spirit, but does the Holy Spirit have you? Does the Holy Spirit possess you?

Do you believe that the Holy Spirit has a hold of your life? John 14:16 states, ''And I will pray the Father, and he shall give you another Comforter, that he may abide with you for ever.''

WHY DO I BELIEVE THE HOLY SPIRIT IS A PERSON?

1. He Is Preexistent as a Personal God

Notice Genesis 1:1,2: ''In the beginning God created the heaven and the earth. And the earth was without form, and void; and darkness was upon the face of the deep. And the Spirit of God moved upon the face of the waters.''

This leads to my opening statement as to why I believe the Holy Spirit is a living person rather than just a good influence or some impersonal force. It leads me to this thought because of His pre-existence with and as a personal God.

Is it not exciting, mysterious and wonderful to find the Holy Spirit in the opening expression of the Bible?

In the Jewish Talmud this word *moved* in verse 2 is translated ''brooded.'' The words are practically synonymous. The Bible used the expression ''moved upon''—moved in the heart. It is an expression of love and emotion here. The Spirit moved or brooded upon the waters. ''And the Spirit of God **brooded** upon the face of the waters.''

We see the Spirit of God in the very opening of the Bible, leading us to know that the Holy Spirit is as preexistent as God. Before God ever made a star; before God ever made sun and moon; before the creation of this earth; before God ever made a man; we find in the beginning of time the work of the Holy Spirit of God. He was ''brooding.'' An impersonal force or mere influence could not do that.

Also, in chapter 1 of this book of Genesis, verse 26, when God was ready to make man, God said: "Let us make man in our image, after our likeness."

When God said, "Let us make man...," to whom was He speaking? No man, no woman, no intelligent being has been created; yet God is speaking to Someone. He uses the personal plural pronouns *us* and *our*. God said, using a personal pronoun, "Let us make man in our image." Bible students believe that God the Father is speaking to God the Son and God the Holy Spirit. God is a Trinity.

Man is a trinity also. The Holy Spirit is the Designer and the Creator in the beginning with God in the very creation of man. Man has a body, a living soul, a spirit—a trinity made in the image of God.

I believe that the Holy Spirit is a living person because He is preexistent with God the Father and God the Son. In John 14:16 we find, "And I will pray the Father, and he shall give you another Comforter, that he may abide with you for ever."

2. He Has All the Components of a Personality

I believe that the Holy Spirit is a person because He has all the components of a personality. Let us make this idea a little more simple. If you were to take a psychology book or any book that deals with what constitutes a personality, you would find that there are four things that constitute a personality: understanding, a will, affection and some idea as to morality. In order to have a personality, there must be these four things.

God made many things that could not be called a personality. He made many things without understanding. He made many things without a will. He made many things without affection. He made many things without morals. However, in order to have a personality, there must be these four things: understanding, will, affection and morality.

Now apply these four components of a personality to the blessed Holy Spirit of God.

In the first place, the Bible plainly teaches that He, the Holy Spirit, has complete knowledge and understanding. In I Corinthians 2:11 we read: "For what man knoweth the things of a man, save the spirit of man which is in him? even so the things of God knoweth no man, but the Spirit of God." God is saying, "The Spirit of God has understanding." In fact, God in His Book goes so far as to say that no one understands the things of God but by the Holy Spirit of God. He has complete understanding of them.

In the second place, does the Holy Spirit have a will? The Bible says that He does: "But all these worketh that one and the selfsame Spirit, dividing to every man severally as he will" (I Cor. 12:11).

"But all these"—the nine gifts of the Spirit. In spite of the fact that the church at Corinth was not the best church at all, it is the only one mentioned in the Bible that had all nine gifts of the Spirit—not the fruits of the Spirit but the gifts of the Spirit. In talking about them God said, "But all these worketh that one and the selfsame Spirit, dividing to every man severally as he will." The Holy Spirit has a will.

He not only has a will, but He also has affection. I have not heard more than a half-dozen Christians in my thirty-five years in the ministry talk about the love or the affection of the Holy Spirit; but the Bible speaks of it. Romans 15:30 says, "Now I beseech you, brethren, for the Lord Jesus Christ's sake, and for the love of the Spirit, that ye strive together with me in your prayers to God for me." The Bible is speaking of a love of the Spirit.

Christian, you need to learn that not only does God love you, and not only does Christ love you, but a living Holy Ghost loves you. He has affection. That third component of a personality the Holy Ghost of God has—love.

Then, fourth, in order for Him to have a personality, there must be some knowledge of morals or morality. It may be a low standard; a mediocre standard; a high standard; but in order to have a personality there must be some knowledge of morals.

Animals have no sense of morals; only a personality has. Does the Holy Spirit? His very name indicates it—*Holy* Spirit, not unholy, not imperfect, but *Holy* Spirit. Holy Spirit is His name, and we read that He will convict of sin because Jesus said, "They believed not on me." The Holy Spirit has the highest sense of morality, and thus, in Him, this glorious person, are all the components of a personality. Here is something that we do not understand.

You ask, "Does the Holy Spirit have a body, with hands, feet, eyes and a tongue to speak? Does He have the kind of body Jesus has?"

The Holy Spirit does not.

You then ask, "Well, how can one be a personality without a body?"

Let us notice something from the Bible. In Romans 12:1 Paul says: "I beseech you therefore, brethren, by the mercies of God, that ye present your bodies a living sacrifice, holy, acceptable unto God, which is your reasonable service."

God is asking you for your body. What for? The Bible teaches that the Holy Spirit indwells the bodies of people. When you leave this world, if the Lord tarries and death overtakes you, you will be as stated in II Corinthians 5:8, "...absent from the body, and...present with the Lord."

If Jesus tarries long enough, the hour will come when everyone shall have the separation of the spirit from the body. Will you cease to be a person when your spirit goes to meet God and you are absent from the body and present with the Lord? You will be no less a personality than you are right now, for you will still have understanding, you will still have a will and affection and a sense of morals.

It is not necessary in order to be a personality to have what might be called a "corporiety," that is, a body. Thank God, the Holy Ghost, in a sense, has one—not one but the body of every believer. He "dwelleth not in temples made with hands" (Acts 17:24). Paul said:

"What? know ye not that your body is the temple of the Holy Ghost which is in you, which ye have of God, and ye are not your own? For ye are bought with a price: therefore glorify God in your body, and in your spirit, which are God's."—I Cor. 6:19,20.

The Holy Spirit of God has all the components of a personality. So think of the Holy Spirit not as an influence, certainly not as an "it," not as an emanation from God and not as some impersonal force, but think of the Holy Spirit of God as a real person.

3. Jesus Was a Person, and the Holy Spirit Is Like Jesus

Another reason why I believe that the Holy Spirit is a living person and a reality is that the Holy Spirit is like Jesus. Remember what Jesus said in John 14:16, "And I will pray the Father, and he shall give you another Comforter, that he may abide with you for ever." Notice that Jesus said, "I am going away," "but I will pray the Father, and he shall give you *another* Comforter." In the Greek New Testament there are two words for *another.* I might say, "I will give you another book," while I have a song book in my hand. Or, I might give you a book on astronomy or astrology or sociology or some other kind of book. "I will give you another book" means that I will give you another book but not this kind of book. The word for a different kind is *eteros.*

When Jesus said, "I will pray the Father, and he shall give you another Comforter," that other word is used. I believe it is *allos* in the Greek, which means, "I will give you another Comforter just like Me." *Allos* means numerically distinct, while *eteros* means generically distinct. Jesus Christ was a person.

You ask, "How is the Holy Spirit like Jesus?"

Well, first, both came to earth. Jesus came by the lowly manger and was born in Bethlehem; the Holy Ghost came on that glorious day of Pentecost. Not only did both come to earth, but both have become incarnate: Jesus in the virgin Mary; the Holy Spirit incarnate in every born-again child of God. Both came to do a work. The work of Jesus was finished at Calvary when He cried, "It is finished" (John 19:30). The work of the Holy Spirit continued. Both are divine, and both are God and equal as members of the Trinity.

Strange as it may sound, both will have a second coming. Jesus will come to receive the church, while Ezekiel 37 teaches that the Holy Spirit will come someday back again to this earth and Israel shall be reborn in a day.

I know the Holy Spirit is a person because He is another Comforter just like Jesus.

4. He Has All the Attributes of Deity, or of a Personal God

Then I know the Holy Ghost is a real personality because He has all the attributes of deity, or of a personal God.

We think of God as being omnipotent; that is, unlimited in power; but so is the Holy Spirit. We see that in creation, for instance, in Psalm 33:6, where it says, "By the word of the Lord were the heavens made; and all the host of them by the breath of his mouth."

Breath and *Spirit* in the Bible are almost synonymous. When we read that God made man out of the dust of the ground, breathed into his nostrils the breath of life and he became a living soul, it is speaking of the spirit that God put into man. He made Him a body out of the ground and breathed into him a spirit, and man became a living soul.

We read that by the breath of His mouth we have been made a living soul, meaning that as far as man being a spiritual being, the Spirit of God has done it all. Job further clarifies this idea, in Job 33:4: "The Spirit of God hath made me, and the breath of the Almighty hath given me life." The Bible even attributes to the Holy Spirit His being the Architect, Designer and Decorator of all that has been made. What a shame that He has been relegated to some obscure place as a member of the Trinity!

Not only is He omnipotent; the Holy Spirit is also omniscient—that is, absolutely unlimited in knowledge. In Isaiah 40:13 we read, "Who hath directed the Spirit of the Lord, or being his counsellor hath taught him?" Further verses in Isaiah 40 show the Holy Spirit to be omniscient. He knows all about you. He knows your every thought. He knows every fiber of your being. The Holy Spirit is absolutely omniscient.

Not only is the Holy Spirit omnipotent and omniscient, but He is also omnipresent; that is, just as God can be everywhere at once, the Holy Spirit can be everywhere at once. He can be across the sea blessing where believers are, and He can be in this church. He is in my body, and He is in yours. He is omnipresent.

David spoke of that omnipresence in Psalm 139.

"Whither shall I go from thy spirit? or whither shall I flee from thy presence? If I ascend up into heaven, thou art there: if I make my bed in hell, behold, thou art there. If I take the wings of the morning, and dwell in the uttermost parts of the sea; Even there shall thy hand lead me, and thy right hand shall hold me."—vss. 7-10.

David said, "Where could I go from thy Spirit? To the depths of the sea or to the heights of the heavens or to the darkness of the night—nowhere could I escape from the presence of the Holy Spirit." Everywhere we go, we take Him with us. The Holy Spirit is omnipresent.

The Holy Spirit is eternal just as God is eternal. Look at Hebrews 9:14: "How much more shall the blood of Christ, who through the eternal Spirit offered himself without spot to God, purge your conscience from dead works to serve the living God?"

Just like God, He is absolutely holy. You find at least five emblems or symbols in the Bible which represent the Holy Spirit. One is a dove. To see the holiness, the absolute, divine perfection of the Holy Ghost, go back to the ark, which is a type of Christ. Noah is in the ark and has been in it for months, and the water has begun to abate. Noah has two birds, one that is unclean and one that is clean. He has a dove and a raven, also called a crow.

1. A *dove* in the Bible is a symbol of the Holy Spirit. When Jesus was baptized in the River Jordan, the Holy Spirit came in the form of a heavenly dove.

Noah released the dove from the ark, and Genesis 8:9 says, "But the dove found no rest for the sole of her foot, and she returned unto him into the ark, for the waters were on the face of the whole earth: then he put forth his hand, and took her, and pulled her in unto him into the ark." The dove went out and saw all the swollen bodies, all the putrefaction, all the decayed earth, and the dove, so clean, said, "I find no rest here," so back to the ark she went.

Noah sent out the raven and he stayed because that filth is what he wanted. But not the dove, a type of the Holy Spirit of God. The Holy Ghost never rests upon anything unclean. He is absolutely holy.

2. A second symbol of the Holy Spirit in the Bible is *fire*. He was manifest as fire on the day of Pentecost. "And there appeared unto them cloven tongues like as of fire, and it sat upon each of them" (Acts 2:3).

He was often manifest as fire in the Old Testament, as in the case of the Tabernacle in the wilderness. "So it was alway: the cloud covered it by day, and the appearance of fire by night" (Num. 9:16). Fire warms, cleanses, illuminates, energizes and attracts; so does the blessed Holy Spirit of God.

3. *Oil* is a symbol of the Holy Spirit in the Bible.

For anointing—Leviticus 8:12: "And he poured of the anointing oil upon Aaron's head, and anointed him, to sanctify him."

For light—Exodus 25:6: "Oil for the light, spices for anointing oil, and for sweet incense. . . ." And Matthew 25:3: "They · that were foolish took their lamps, and took no oil with them."

For invigoration—Psalm 23:5: "Thou preparest a table before me in the presence of mine enemies: thou anointest my head with oil; my cup runneth over."

For healing—James 5:14: "Is any sick among you? let him call for the elders of the church; and let them pray over him, anointing him with oil in the name of the Lord."

For joy: at least twenty-nine times in the Old Testament oil and wine (joy) are used in the same verse.

For energy—Zechariah 4:6: "Not by might, nor by power, but by my spirit, saith the Lord of hosts." And verses 11 and 12:

"Then answered I, and said unto him, What are these two olive trees upon the right side of the candlestick and upon the left side thereof? And I answered again, and said unto him, What be these two olive branches which through the two golden pipes empty the golden oil out of themselves?"

4. *Water* is also a symbol of the Holy Spirit in the Bible—Isaiah 44:3: "For I will pour water upon him that is thirsty, and floods upon the dry ground: I will pour my spirit upon thy seed, and my blessing upon thine offspring." And John 7:37-39:

"In the last day, that great day of the feast, Jesus stood and cried, saying, If any man thirst, let him come unto me, and drink. He that believeth on me, as the scripture hath said, out of his

belly shall flow rivers of living water. (But this spake he of the Spirit, which they that believe on him should receive: for the Holy Ghost was not yet given; because that Jesus was not yet glorified.)"

5. *Wind* is a type or symbol of the Holy Spirit—Acts 2:2: "And suddenly there came a sound from heaven as of a rushing mighty wind, and it filled all the house where they were sitting." And Ezekiel 37:9,10:

"Then said he unto me, Prophesy unto the wind, prophesy, son of man, say to the wind, Thus saith the Lord God; Come from the four winds, O breath, and breathe upon these slain, that they may live. So I prophesied as he commanded me, and the breath came into them, and they lived, and stood up upon their feet, an exceeding great army."

5. He Can Be Mistreated as a Person

Then I know the Holy Spirit of God is a person because He can be mistreated as a person.

First, the Bible plainly teaches that He can be lied to. In chapter 5 of Acts is the record of Ananias and his wife, Sapphira, who sold a certain piece of property for so much money and came with a portion of the money and said, "This is all we have; we are giving it all to God." Peter said to Ananias: "Ananias, why hath Satan filled thine heart to lie to the Holy Ghost, and to keep back part of the price of the land?" (Acts 5:3). The Holy Ghost can be lied to.

I wonder how many believers have lied to the Holy Ghost. I wonder how many promises have been made to Him and have not been kept. "Oh, I will be for You what You want me to be, if You will do for me what I want You to do." I wonder how many believers have promised the Holy Spirit to read their Bibles, promised the Holy Spirit that they would serve the Lord, promised the Holy Spirit that they would tithe their income, promised the Holy

Spirit that they would win souls; yet they have not done these things.

Oh yes, He can be mistreated as a person. He can be lied to. He can be resisted, as Stephen said in Acts 7:51, "Ye stiffnecked and uncircumcised in heart and ears, ye do always resist the Holy Ghost: as your fathers did, so do ye."

If God is speaking to your heart and you are not a child of God, if you do not know that you are born again and if you do not yield to God, you are resisting the Holy Ghost. Some of you may say, "Well, I'm not going to do what that preacher says. I'm not going to walk down that aisle." It is not so important that you do what this preacher says, but it is most important that you not resist the Holy Spirit of God.

The Holy Spirit can be mistreated as a person; He can be lied to; He can be resisted; and the Bible says that He can be grieved— Ephesians 4:30: "And grieve not the Holy Spirit of God, whereby ye are sealed unto the day of redemption."

You cannot grieve an influence. You cannot grieve an impersonal force. You cannot grieve a mere emanation from God. You can only grieve a person. You can only grieve someone who loves you and whom you love.

If a total stranger goes down the street and does not speak to me, I am not grieved. I don't know him; there is no special affinity between the two of us. If someone I know well passes me on the street and ignores me, I am grieved.

You can grieve the Holy Spirit because He loves you. He is as sensitive as a dove, that mournful little bird. He can be resisted and grieved.

And He can even be despised—Hebrews 10:29: "Of how much sorer punishment, suppose ye, shall he be thought worthy, who hath trodden under foot the Son of God, and hath counted the blood of the covenant, wherewith he was sanctified, an unholy thing, and hath done despite unto the Spirit of grace?''

The Holy Spirit can be quenched—I Thessalonians 5:19: ''Quench not the Spirit.''

The Holy Ghost can be mistreated as a person because He can be blasphemed.

In Matthew 12:31,32 Jesus spoke of a particular sin for which there is no forgiveness. Jesus was careful to say no forgiveness in this life and no forgiveness in the world to come. What is that sin? Jesus said:

"Wherefore I say unto you, All manner of sin and blasphemy shall be forgiven unto men: but the blasphemy against the Holy Ghost shall not be forgiven unto men. And whosoever speaketh a word against the Son of man, it shall be forgiven him: but whosoever speaketh against the Holy Ghost, it shall not be forgiven him, neither in this world, neither in the world to come."

What is the blasphemy against the Holy Ghost? What is the sin called the ''unpardonable sin''? What is the sin that Jesus Christ, the Son of God, said, ''For this sin there is no forgiveness''? Blasphemy against the Holy Ghost—what is it? It is attributing the work and power of the Holy Spirit to the Devil. If you ever see someone with the Spirit of God and some blasphemer says, ''That is the work of Satan,'' remember that Jesus said, ''That sin will never be forgiven.''

You say, ''I thought we could be saved from anything!'' Take Jesus at His Word: ''And whosoever speaketh a word against the Son of man, it shall be forgiven him: but whosoever speaketh against the Holy Ghost, it shall not be forgiven him, neither in this world, neither in the world to come.'' So He can be mistreated as a person.

6. He Acts Like a Person

I know that the Holy Spirit is a person because He acts like one.

He speaks. I read in II Peter 1:21, "For the prophecy came not in old time by the will of man: but holy men of God spake as they were moved by the Holy Ghost." That is why we have this Bible. This Bible is the speaking of a personal Holy Ghost: "...holy men of God spake as they were moved by the Holy Ghost." The word *moved* can be translated *borne*—borne along or carried along. "...holy men of God spake as they were carried along by the Holy Ghost."

Only a person speaks. Influences do not speak. In Acts 8:29 we read how deacon Philip led the Ethiopian eunuch to Christ. "Then the Spirit said unto Philip, Go near, and join thyself to this chariot."

The Holy Spirit is a person because He speaks and because He loves—Romans 15:30: "Now I beseech you, brethren, for the Lord Jesus Christ's sake, and for the love of the Spirit, that ye strive together with me in your prayers to God for me."

The Holy Spirit guides—John 16:13: "Howbeit when he, the Spirit of truth, is come, he will guide you into all truth: for he shall not speak of himself; but whatsoever he shall hear, that shall he speak: and he will shew you things to come." Here in this verse we find four times the personal pronoun *he*. The Holy Spirit guides us.

The Holy Spirit restrains. Talking about Paul's second journey, Acts 16:6,7 says:

"Now when they had gone throughout Phrygia and the region of Galatia, and were forbidden of the Holy Ghost to preach the word in Asia, After they were come to Mysia, they assayed to go into Bithynia: but the Spirit suffered them not."

The Holy Spirit fellowships—II Corinthians 13:14: "The grace of the Lord Jesus Christ, and the love of God, and the communion of the Holy Ghost, be with you all. Amen." The Bible here mentions that we have fellowship with the Holy Spirit.

7. He Should Be Treated as a Person

Finally, the Holy Ghost should be treated as a person. How should the Holy Spirit be treated? He should be given complete access to your body. He should possess every fiber of your being. If it be true—and it is—that our body is the only body that the Holy Spirit will ever have, He should have complete access to all of it. That is the way the Holy Spirit should be treated.

I have had the privilege in Athens, Greece, to see beautiful buildings erected hundreds of years before Christ. On a little mountain called Mars' Hill Paul stood looking at all that antiquity and said: "God that made the world and all things therein, seeing that he is Lord of heaven and earth, dwelleth not in temples made with hands" (Acts 17:24). He meant by that that God does not dwell in all these religious buildings but in the person of the Holy Spirit in the bodies of believers.

A fine Christian writer was once being entertained in a home. The hostess showed her to her bedroom and said, "Now we do not allow visitors to have access to our kitchen. You are welcome here, and we are happy to have you spend your time here as one of the servants of the Lord, but you do not have access to the kitchen." As the hostess was about to leave the house to go shopping, she turned again and said, "Also, we would appreciate it if you would not use the living room, where our family meets. This bedroom will be your room."

This fine Christian writer sat down on the bed in her room and thought, *I really am not a guest in this home, just a guest in a tiny part of it. I am not welcome in the kitchen nor in the living room. I am welcome only back here in this little corner called a bedroom.*

I wonder if the Holy Spirit of God, that living Person who indwells every believer, has not often said, "I am a restricted Guest in this house, in this person. I occupy only a little corner of the mind, the heart and body."

The Holy Spirit—a living Person—wants to fill us with His fullness. The blessed Holy Spirit is a Person.

"And I will pray the Father, and he shall give you another Comforter, that he may abide with you for ever."—John 14:16.

Chapter VII

Why I Know There Is a God

"In the beginning God...."—Gen. 1:1.

All of us believe there is a God, but if someone asked me, "How do you know there is a God?" what would my answer be? Where would I start? I think I would start where the Bible starts:

"In the beginning God created the heaven and the earth. And the earth was without form, and void; and darkness was upon the face of the deep. And the Spirit of God moved upon the face of the waters. And God said, Let there be light: and there was light."—Gen 1:1-3.

In the beginning of the Bible we read three tremendous statements about God. We read, first, that there is a God: "In the beginning God...." We read, second, that God loves people: "And the Spirit of God moved [brooded] upon the face of the waters." This is a picture of God brooding over souls. Third, we read that God has spoken: "And God said...."

The Bible starts with God. "In the beginning God created the heaven and the earth."

A young man came to me not long ago who was what we would call a "hippie." He had the long hair, the faded sweat shirt, the blue jeans and all that goes with that crowd. He was not a very tidy-looking young man, and not even very clean. He had gone to his so-called preacher who had said, "It is Sunday, and I am busy, and I don't have time to talk to you." Someone said to the young man, "I know a preacher who will talk to you."

My telephone rang in the afternoon, and this young hippie said, "Someone told me you are a preacher who talks to peope in need of help. I need help. Would you talk to me?" I answered, "Yes, I will."

That Sunday afternoon he came to my office. Naturally, as any Christian would do, I began talking to him about the Lord Jesus Christ and what God could do for his life. He said to me, "Now wait just a minute, Preacher. First of all, there are two things that I don't believe in or am not sure of. First, I don't believe the Bible is the Word of God. Second, I'm not even sure there is such a thing as a God."

I said to that young man, "If there is no God, then you have no reason for living. If there is no God, then there is no hope for the future. If there is no God, there is no hereafter. And if there is no God, there are no answers to all of the questions on your mind."

"In the begining God...."

The atheist says, "There is no God."

The agnostic says, "I cannot tell whether there is a God or not."

The materialist says, "It doesn't make any difference anyway. We can rule the world as it is now. What difference does it make whether there is a God or not?"

The man whom the Bible calls a fool says, "I don't want there to be a god." Read it in Psalm 14:1, "The fool hath said in his heart, There is no God."

We Christians say, "I cannot do without God."

I know there is a God, but not only that, I know He is a God without whom I cannot survive.

We have those who call themselves atheists. The situation has changed in the last fifty years, but there was a time when the atheists were blatant and outspoken. They stood on the street corners and cried out to the crowds, "I don't believe there is a God!" But the atheists of today is far more subtle. He stands in the classroom, educated, polished and refined. Quietly he says, "That is an antiquated belief; no longer do people believe there is a God."

Bob Ingersoll, of a few decades ago, used to draw great crowds. He said, "There is no God. It is a myth, a fallacy of man's mind, a figment of the imagination. There is no such thing as God." He used to take out his wach, stand on the platform and say, "I will put the time watch on God and find out if there is a God. If there is, I challenge Him to kill me in sixty seconds."

There would come a breathless stillness over the audience. In thirty seconds he would say, "God has thirty seconds to prove Himself." Then he would count, "Ten seconds, nine seconds... four seconds, three seconds, two seconds, one second," and with a satanic look on his face, he would put his watch back in his vest pocket and say, "See; I told you there is no God."

What Bob Ingersoll did not know is that God is a God of grace, a God of love, a God of infinite mercy and a God who sometimes permits people to speak as Bob Ingersoll spoke, and yet have another chance to be saved. God is "not willing that any should perish, but that all should come to repentance" (II Pet. 3:9).

The atheist says, "There is no God."

In this country is a woman by the name of Madalyn Murray O'Hair. This woman has had as much influence on the Supreme Court of our land as any other one individual who has ever lived. She is as much responsible for the Bible no longer being allowed in the public school systems of America as any other person in our nation. It does not speak well of our Supreme Court that one infidel woman could have such influence. She says, "There is no God." I don't know if she is sincere in her belief or not, but I have often heard veterans of the Bible and veterans of the ministry say, "Many infidels are nothing more than 'in-for-hells' and really do not know what they are talking about."

No doubt that statement is true of Madalyn Murray O'Hair. She seems to be an embittered woman, one who has had some unpleasant experiences in her life, so she is fighting against a God whom she knows exists. When she says, "There is no God," she is just an embittered lost sinner. When she stands in the white light of His holiness, her hands dripping with the red blood of His Son spilled at Calvary, she will then know there is a God.

You say to me, "Preacher, that is preaching and talking, but prove how you know there is a God." I have infallible proofs. Any intelligent mind, any open mind, can prove there is a God.

I. BECAUSE OF THE SUPERNATURAL REVELATION OF HIMSELF

I know there is a God because there is a supernatural revelation of Himself. I speak, of course, of the Bible.

I do believe the Bible. The Bible is not on trial; the Bible puts men on trial! The Bible has proved itself. No one has ever found an error in it. No prophecy of the Bible has ever failed to come to pass in God's time. No promise in the Word of God has ever fallen under.

The Bible begins with and ends with God. It begins, "In the beginning God...." And the closing statement of all this great and wonderful miracle Book is this: "The grace of our Lord Jesus Christ be with you all. Amen" (Rev. 22:21).

Almost in the middle of the Bible, you read this statement in Psalm 14:1: "The fool hath said in his heart, There is no God." God did not say the fool said it in his head. God said he said it in his heart. The fool did not reason out this idea. He did not come to an intelligent conclusion. Rather, out of the depravity of his black and sinful heart, which he would not bring to God for cleansing and salvation; out of his depraved, rebellious, sinful and fallen nature, he said, "There is no God." He said it because he did not want to face God.

One cannot, with one stroke of his hand, remove from his mind the truth of God.

All through the Bible we read, "There is a God." In I Timothy 2:5 we read, "For there is one God, and one mediator between God and men, the man Christ Jesus." Hebrews is another book which starts with the greatest Name in all human language:

"God, who at sundry times and in divers manners spake in time past unto the fathers by the prophets, Hath in these last days spoken unto us by his Son, whom he hath appointed heir of all things, by whom also he made the worlds."—Heb. 1:1,2.

The Bible says that there is a God. Then Hebrews 11:6 says, ". . .he that cometh to God must believe that he is. . . ." You cannot come to God unless you believe He is God, a personal God.

You may say there are two general views about what this Bible is. One group of people say that the Bible is man's effort to create a God. Man wanted a God so much that he just wrote a Bible that describes a God whom he would like to have. The other view, the one you and I take, is that there is a God who wanted to be known to man so much that He wrote the Bible, which is a perfect description of Himself.

I know there is a God because of the supernatural revelation of Himself in the Bible.

This story may sound funny to you, but in most instances, a young lady has the choice to pick out her own husband and see him before she marries him; likewise, a man has the choice to pick the young lady he wants to marry. In the old days, and I guess to some extent now, there have been in this country what people call "mail-order marriages." When transportation was a problem and communication was difficult, people would advertise in a magazine, "An eligible man wants to correspond with an eligible lady, with a view to marriage."

I read of one of these mail-order marriages. For two years two people who had never seen each other wrote to each other. They exchanged pictures and gave a description of what they were like. The lady told how much she weighed, how tall she was, what color hair she had and the color of her eyes. She gave a whole description of her life and what she was like. The man did the same thing. They told each other about their background and manner of dress. Before they ever saw each other, they had come to love one another.

At the end of the two years of revealing by communication what each was like, they were to meet. The train was to stop, this lady was to step off the train and meet her would-be husband.

When the train pulled to a stop, there was a throbbing heart in the breast of that woman on the train and a throbbing heart in the man out there waiting. There were multitudes of people, for the train was filled. Although hundreds came to meet the train, the two saw each other and came together as if they had known each other for many years. They embraced and were soon married.

I have a Bible that tells me what God is like. When I met God thirty-five years ago, I found Him to be just exactly what this Bible describes Him.

You ask, "Preacher, how do you know there is a God?"

I know because of His supernatural revelation of Himself in a Book called the Bible.

II. BECAUSE OF THE MIRACLE OF CREATION

I know there is a God because of the miracle of creation. The Bible leaves no ground for argument about the existence of all things. The Bible leaves no ground for confusion as to the source of all things. The Bible leaves no ground for argument as to where we came from.

We read in the Bible about this wonderful creation. Psalm 19 is a most beautiful passage about the miracle of nature and creation. In Psalm 19:1, "The heavens declare the glory of God; and the firmament sheweth his handywork."

Step out at night and with the natural eye we see the moon shining in the sky. That moon says, "Yes, there is a God." Take a telescope and look beyond the moon into the star-studded sky of God: look at the worlds yonder in the sky. The Bible says, "The heavens declare the glory of God; and the firmament sheweth his handywork." Then look again at what the Bible says in verse 2: "Day unto day uttereth speech, and night unto night sheweth knowledge." Ponder that statement for a moment. Picture the things God has made and placed yonder in the sky—the planets and galaxies and stars and constellations which have never been explored to their fullest extent by human science.

Yonder in the dark continent of Africa man walks out of the jungle and sees a blinking star and a shining moon, and the star-studded heavens, and that man says, "I don't know Him. I don't know what He is like. I have never heard the story of His love. But there must be a God."

The man yonder in India stands alone on India's dark land and at night looks yonder into the heavens. By day he sees that shining sun running its orbit, just as God made it to do. That man says, "There is a God."

Standing yonder on the frozen wastelands of Iceland, a man goes out and waits for the sun to come upon those frozen regions. Looking yonder into God's sky, he says, "I may not know Him, nor have I ever heard of His love, but I know there is a God."

That is what the Bible is talking about when it says:

"The heavens declare the glory of God; and the firmament

sheweth his handywork. Day unto day uttereth speech, and night unto night sheweth knowledge. There is no speech nor language, where their voice is not heard.''

Notice again: ''There is no speech nor language, where their voice is not heard.'' There are languages in which this biblical truth has never been heard, and that is a heartbreaking thing. Think of the tribes and nations of the world that never one time have had the privilege to hear about Jesus, His cleansing blood and His saving grace. God's Word says, ''There is no speech nor language, where their voice is not heard.'' There is no language, no voice in which God's creation has not spoken to man.

Then verse 4 says, ''Their line is gone out through all the earth, and their words to the end of the world. In them hath he set a tabernacle for the sun.''

''Preacher, why do you believe there is a God?'' Because of the miracle of creation—Hebrews 11:3: ''Through faith we understand that the worlds were framed by the word of God, so that things which are seen were not made of things which do appear.''

I don't want to be technical, but four ideas, down through the ages of human history, have come into being about where we have come from. You have never heard anything more foolish. What is the cause of nature? Who made man, and how was he made? Where does all this material, the cosmos, originate? Where did it come from? There are four general ideas.

There are those who say that the constitution of nature is eternal and its forms have existed forever—that is, that there always have been material things. There always has been the atom. There always have been the tangible things. Of course that thought is not true. ''In the beginning God created....'' would deny that material things have always existed.

There is the theory that matter has existed forever, but that its present arrangement is of God. They say that matter always has existed, but one day God arranged it as it is today. That is not what Genesis 1:1,2 teaches.

A third theory exists, which is that matter has existed forever and was created by God and has undergone self-development. This self-development idea is unscriptural and unscientific.

Finally there is a fourth theory, the one we take, that everything that is was made by the omnipotent, creative hand of a supernatural, personal God and that the present order of things is just as God made it. The Bible teaches that Satan was cast out of Heaven and darkness fell upon all of God's creation, and then God rearranged it. And that is what believers believe. We cannot believe in the so-called unscientific theory of evolution.

The silliest thing I have ever heard is someone with a Ph.D. degree trying to come up with the missing links. There are no links; all are missing. There has never been one found.

I got the shock of my life when I saw the replicas of the Heidelburg Man, the Piltdown Man, the Java Man, etc. Someone took a handful of bones and a wheelbarrow full of plaster of Paris and made a man with a long jaw, stooped shoulders, a humped-up back and said, "This is what man looked like." No truly intelligent man or woman can believe in the theory of evolution. It is a Devil's lie to raise a question as the one Satan raised in the Garden of Eden about the truth of God's Holy Word.

I know there is a God because of a supernatural creation. You cannot explain it any other way. I would like for someone to explain to me, if there is no God, where all this world came from. Recently I was amused and shocked when, in large, block letters in the newspaper, an Associated Press article said that scientists now accept the "Bang Theory." That is one of the funniest things I have ever read—that scientists have accepted the "Bang Theory," that is, that one time there were only great areas of unconfined gases, then, all of a sudden, for some unexplainable reason, there was an explosion. After this explosion, Bang! Here we are! That is the "bang" theory! Do they expect intelligent people to believe that sort of foolishness? No matter how many degrees the educated have, they have no wisdom who say that.

Just suppose I show you a watch and ask you, "Have you ever made a watch?" Most people would say, "No, I have never made a watch."

Then suppose I say to you, "Did you ever see a watch made?" Most people would have to answer, "No, I never saw a watch made."

Then I start to explain to you about this watch: "There are three hands. One makes a complete revolution every 60 seconds. One makes a complete revolution every 60 minutes. One makes a complete revolution every 12 hours. This watch will tell you what time it is, day and night. This wonderful thing has many intricate wheels, pieces of machinery and jewels in it."

You say, "I have never seen a watch before. Explain to me where the watch came from. I have never seen one made, have never helped make one. I never knew that it has three hands, one which makes a revolution every 60 seconds, another one which makes a revolution every 60 minutes, and the third one which makes a revolution every 12 hours. Explain to me where this watch came from."

Now, I might explain it this way. "I am a scientist, a learned person with university degrees. So having gone beyond the average intelligence of man, I can explain where this watch came from. At one time there were some unconfined gases and, for some unexplainable reason, all of a sudden, there was an explosion, and there it was!" With such an explanation I would soon be taken to the State Institution, and that is where I ought to be taken. Any person who would say that this watch does not have a mastermind, a master designer, a master architect, is a fool.

"The fool hath said in his heart, There is no God."

You ask me why I know there is a God. I know because of a supernatural creation. This Bible is not a book on science, but whenever it speaks of science, it has never been proven incorrect. How do we know there is a God? We know because of a supernatural creation.

III. BECAUSE OF SUPERNATURAL ANSWERS TO PRAYER

Third, I know there is a God because of the supernatural answers to prayer. To the unconverted, natural mind, that statement would sound simple or very elementary, but when you ask, "How do you know there is a God?" I can answer that I know because of answers to prayer.

The Bible has a lot to say about prayer and miraculous answers to prayer. Jeremiah 33:3 promises, "Call unto me, and I will answer thee, and shew thee great and mighty things, which thou knowest not." I have thought of that promise many times. I say to the glory of God that I have had the Lord do things for me which never had been done for me before.

We read in John 14:13,14:

"And whatsoever ye shall ask in my name, that will I do, that the Father may be glorified in the Son. If ye shall ask any thing in my name, I will do it."

God said, "No matter what you ask, if it is in My name and is that the Father may be glorified in the Son, I will do it." God promises to answer prayer.

Jesus said,

"Ask, and it shall be given you; seek, and ye shall find; knock, and it shall be opened unto you: For every one that asketh receiveth;

and he that seeketh findeth; and to him that knocketh it shall be opened.''—Matt. 7:7,8.

Five times in this same passage one finds, ''Ask God for things, and you will get them!''

I have tried that.

Once, in Kingsport, Tennessee, God wrought a wonderful miracle for me, a poor preacher with an old automobile, just my wife and me with no dwelling place or furniture. Everything we owned we kept in the car, and it was by no means filled. We traveled up and down the country by faith.

A man had asked me to come to a rescue mission to preach. I have never once asked how big any place is; I have never asked how much money I would get. I went to that rescue mission. In the mission my wife and I lived with the men and women off the streets. We ate what they ate, and ate at the table with them. For a week we lived as if we were on welfare in the rescue mission. Crowds would come in off the streets—the derelicts, the lost, the gamblers, the drunkards, the harlots—and I would preach at night.

One night the preacher took up an offering, a love offering. You know, there can be a lot of love in some little things, and I guess this fact is true of this place. There were a few pennies, a few little pieces of silver, and maybe two or three dollars at the most.

My next meeting was to be in Cincinnati, Ohio, while the meeting in the rescue mission was down in the mountains of Kingsport, Tennessee. I thought to myself, *How in the world will I get gasoline and food?* At that time the journey on a little two-lane mountain road was long. How would I ever get from Kingsport, Tennessee, to Cincinnati, Ohio? I had driven from North Alabama to Kingsport, Tennessee, and I had not put a drop of gas in the tank. I had been in Kingsport, Tennessee, for one week, and that tank was empty.

I drove to a filling station and said, ''Fill it up.''

The man put the nozzle into the tank and turned the gasoline on. In less time than it takes to tell the story, the gasoline was running everywhere. Almost with a curse word, he pulled the nozzle out, put the cap on and said, "You didn't need gas in the first place!"

You ask, "Where did it come from?" Who cares about where it came from? I know it came as an answer to prayer.

One Wednesday night in 1935, I got down on my knees and told the Lord, "Unless I have $70.00 before Friday, I must leave school and cease my preparation for the ministry."

While I was on my knees praying, a man stood up in a little church down in North Alabama who knew not one thing about my problem and said, "I feel a burden on my heart. A few weeks ago there walked out of these red-clay hills from that farm down yonder in the country, a young man who went up to study for the ministry. He is a poor boy, raised on a little farm in overalls and tennis shoes. I feel burdened for him tonight. I am not well-to-do, but I have a little of the Lord's money, and I will give some."

Another stood up and said, "So will I." Then another stood and said, "So will I."

While these decisions were going on, I was in Cleveland, Tennessee, down on my knees praying. With God as my witness, not one living soul knew my needs but Him.

Two days later I received a large brown envelope. I tore the end of that envelope off and emptied it down on the little bed where I had knelt that Wednesday night and prayed. In that envelope were small checks and dollar bills. When I counted them all, there was a total of just exactly $70.00—not $69.98 nor $70.23, but just exactly $70.00!

Two nights before, down on my knees, I told a God who answers prayer, "I have to have $70.00." God said to a man sitting in church that Wednesday night, "Stand up and say something." That man stood up and said, "I feel a burden to help."

Don't tell me God does not answer prayer!

I am willing to do whatever God says, but I have often said to the Lord, ''I would rather go Home than to ever quit preaching.'' Preaching is my life. For thirteen weeks, after two operations on my throat, I could not preach. One day down in an office in Detroit, one of the finest, most learned physicians in the Midwest said, ''Tom, you will probably never preach again, so you had better learn to write and learn to serve without a voice.''

When I got out of that chair, looked through the window and saw Woodward Avenue with the cars coming and going and the multitudes of people, I said to myself, *Never preach again while there are multitudes lost and without God and without hope? Never preach again?*

When I got home, my wife and I got on our knees. She said, ''There is Someone who knows more than doctors.'' So down on our knees we wept, prayed and cried out to God.

A day or two later I was sitting up in my office when there came a rap at the door. I opened it, and there stood a short man with hair as white as snow, holding his hat in his hands. He said to me, ''Brother Malone, I never saw you before, and I have never met you, but I was near here—about thirty miles away—and God laid a burden on my heart to come and see you.'' He walked in, laid his hat on the floor and got on his knees. I can see that white hair now. He lifted one hand toward Heaven and began to pray, ''O God, restore to this preacher his voice.''

In less time than it takes to tell it, I knew that I would soon be preaching. To God be the eternal glory, in a few days God restored my voice, and I have been preaching ever since.

Now you come to me and say that there is no God! If there is a God, how do I know there is a God? I will tell you how I know. He looks over the battlements of Heaven and does what no one but God can do.

Thank God, I not only know there is a God, but I know Him better than I know my own family.

IV. BECAUSE OF SUPERNATURAL SALVATION

In the next place, I know there is a God because of a supernatural salvation. This matter of being saved cannot be explained apart from the presence of a personal God in the life of a true believer. In II Corinthians 5:17 we find these words: "Therefore if any man be in Christ, he is a new creature: old things are passed away; behold, all things are become new."

Think for a moment about some of the great Bible verses dealing with salvation.

There is Romans 6:23:

"For the wages of sin is death; but the gift of God is eternal life through Jesus Christ our Lord."

In Romans 10:9,10 God says:

"That if thou shalt confess with thy mouth the Lord Jesus, and shalt believe in thine heart that God hath raised him from the dead, thou shalt be saved. For with the heart man believeth unto righteousness; and with the mouth confession is made unto salvation."

In John 1:11,12 we read:

"He came unto his own, and his own received him not. But as many as received him, to them gave he power to become the sons of God, even to them that believe on his name."

God has said that He would save those who believe in the Lord Jesus Christ. That fact is a reality. God does save people. God has saved people. There is the miracle of salvation that, unless there is a God, has no explanation whatsoever.

A man at one time, when asked, "Do you believe that Jesus

actually turned water into wine?'' gave this answer: ''There is no doubt that Jesus turned water into wine, for in my own life, He turned wine into bread. I, a drunkard, an alcoholic, could find no deliverance, no relief though I sought it and hungered for it and wanted it with all of my heart.

''We were in poverty. My home was ruined and destitute. Then one day Jesus walked across the threshold of my heart and came into my life. You ask me if I believe Jesus could turn water into wine. Yes, I believe in the miracle that Jesus could turn water into wine because Jesus wrought a miracle in my life and saved me.''

You see many miracles in the Bible. There was a man for whom society could do nothing. He was called the maniac of Gadara. The Bible says they would bind him with chains, but the chains could not hold him. Perhaps they would imprison him, but the prisons could not hold him nor change him. His behavior pattern was unaffected by all men did to him.

But one day there came the Man of Galilee. This man of Gadara looked at Jesus, and Jesus looked at him. He believed in Christ, and Christ worked in him.

Here is this man, demon-possessed and so satanically powerful that no man could affect him. But when Jesus came into his life, the Bible said that he was sitting clothed and in his right mind, and he desired to follow Jesus. When the people saw this change, we read in Mark 5:20: ''...and all men did marvel.''

One of the greatest marvels, one of the greatest miracles, one of the greatest wonders I have ever known, is that miracle that takes place when by faith a person claims the Son of God and is miraculously changed and made a new creature in Christ Jesus.

How would you explain, apart from God, such happenings as an old drunkard in the gutter in the city of Grand Rapids, Michigan, by the name of Mel Trotter who became a mighty witness for Christ after Christ touched his life?

How would you explain the miraculous change in the life of a drunkard lawyer by the name of Sam Jones, who was kicked out of the saloons and rolled into the streets many a night? One night he turned to Christ and was gloriously saved and became one of the greatest preachers of many generations.

How would you explain how one day a young Jew, breathing hatred against the church of our Lord, met on the Damascus Road the Lord, the Son of God? Christ turned him around and made him the greatest preacher and the greatest Christian the world has ever known.

You see, there is the miracle of supernatural salvation. No man can explain it. Every Christian brought out of darkness into light, every one delivered from sin into the freedom that is in Christ Jesus, is a miracle. You cannot explain it apart from the fact that there is a God.

I know there is a God because of supernatural salvation.

V. BECAUSE OF A UNIVERSAL INTUITION OF MEN

I believe there is a God because of a universal intuition of men. I am not a Bible scholar, but I have read books of scholars on why they believe there is a God. But I have yet to read one in which it was not mentioned that there is a universal intuition in the hearts of men of every race, of every color, of every kind, that says there is a God. There are examples of this intuition in the Bible.

The Apostle Paul went to Athens. All the philosophers and all the religions were represented on Mars' Hill where Paul preached. Someone must have said one day, "There is a God, a God we do not know, but there is a God—a God not made with hands, a God not carved of wood and stone—a real God, a living God, an eternal God." Out there on that hillside they erected a monument and inscribed on it, "To the Unknown God." They said,

"We do not know Him, but we know there is One."

My friends, a universal intuition in the hearts of men says there is a God, whether they know Him or not. You read about it a number of times in the Bible.

One day when men turned from God, the whole human race seemed to have turned from God. In Genesis 11:4 we read, "And they said, Go to, let us build us a city and a tower, whose top may reach unto heaven; and let us make us a name...." Here is a group of men who, contrary to the truth of God, contrary to the will of God and contrary to the Word of God, said, "Let us build us a tower that may reach unto Heaven." Why? They knew there is a God: "We are not coming to Him as He said to come. We are not acknowledging Him as He taught us to. We are not in His truth, but we know there is a God." So they said, "Go to, let us build us a city and a tower, whose top may reach unto heaven; and let us make us a name...."

Of course, men cannot do that. But even men in unbelief acknowledged there was a God and a place called Heaven. This universal intuition in man that says there is a God has always been in existence.

I have had the privilege to visit the antiquity of Egypt. From 400 miles south of the city of Cairo, up the River Nile to a place called Luxor, where we saw ancient Egypt, there were literally stone gods by the thousands dating back to 3500 years before Christ ever walked this earth. Even in those days in that heathen land, man in his ignorance said, "There is a God. We do not know what He is like, and we do not know the truth about Him. We do not know that He is a Person, and we do not know how to come to Him, but we do know there is a God."

In the hearts of every race, of every color and of every kind, there is a natural intuition that there is a God.

VI. BECAUSE OF THE COURSE OF HISTORY

I believe there is a God because of the course of history. No man, regardless of how brilliant he may be, can explain history apart from God.

Go back to the book of Genesis, chapter 12. One day God said to Abraham:

"Get thee out of thy country, and from thy kindred, and from thy father's house, unto a land that I will shew thee: And I will make of thee a great nation, and I will bless thee, and make thy name great; and thou shalt be a blessing: And I will bless them that bless thee, and curse him that curseth thee: and in thee shall all families of the earth be blessed."

There you find the beginning of the history of the Jewish nation. It has come to pass exactly as God said it would. He has blessed every nation that has blessed the Jew; He has cursed every nation that has cursed the Jew.

Over in Germany, where it is said that six million Jews were slaughtered, is a dividing wall [written before the Berlin Wall came down] and a torn nation because of this truth of God's Word. Man does not make history; God makes history. You cannot explain the course of history for the nation of Israel without the admission of a personal, living God.

Think for a moment about the book of Daniel. This book gives a picture of a great image and explains that image. Hundreds of years before Christ ever came, God said that there would be four great Gentile nations: the nation of Babylon, the nation of Persia, the nation of Greece and the Roman Empire.

History throws truth and testimony upon the Word of God and the fact that God rules history. You cannot explain history without admitting there is a God. When looking back in the course of history, we find that Proverbs 14:34 has always been true:

"Righteousness exalteth a nation: but sin is a reproach to any people." God has blessed the nation that has honored the Lord; God
has cursed the nation that has dishonored Him.

Daniel Webster once said:

> If we abide by the principles taught in the Bible, our country
> will go on prospering and to prosper, but if we and our posteri-
> ty neglect its instruction and authority, no man can tell how sud-
> den a catastrophe may overwhelm us and bury our glory in pro-
> found obscurity.

Let me say that this nation has about come to that crucial point.
Twenty-five or thirty years ago, who would have dared even in-
timate there is no living God? Today people are debating, "Is there
a God?" You find bumper stickers that say, "God lives," and
"There is a God." My friends, the very fact that in this country
in the last twenty-five or thirty years the existence of God has been
brought into question proves that this nation is on its way down.

You cannot explain history without the admission of God. Look
at the trouble America is in right now: torn with racial strife and
social problems for which no one has the answer. Here is the reason
for the problems: "Righteousness exalteth a nation: but sin is a
reproach to any people."

VII. BECAUSE OF THE MIRACLE OF JESUS CHRIST

I believe there is a God because of the Miracle Man, Jesus Christ.
Think with me about the Lord Jesus Christ. First, think of His
miracle birth. The Bible says that His mother Mary was with child
of the Holy Ghost.

There are four ways in which people come into this world. First,
they come as Adam came—created without father and mother,
under the direct hand of God; second, as Eve came—from the side
of man, made of a rib of a man; third, as every one of us came—
by the natural birth of a father and a mother; fourth, as Jesus

came—with an earthly mother and a heavenly Father.

Jesus not only had a miracle birth, but He also died and lived a supernatural life. One time He stood before a crowd of people and said, ''I do always those things that please the Father,'' then added, ''Who convinceth me of sin?''

Suppose some woman stood up before an audience and said, ''Who convinceth me of sin?'' Someone could. Suppose one of the best men in the church stood to say, ''Who convinceth me of sin?'' Someone could. Jesus one time stepped out across the stage of human history and said, ''Who convinceth me of sin?'' No one ever has, for God's Son is a perfect Son.

He lived a miracle life and died a supernatural death. When Jesus died, the sun refused to shine; darkness covered the earth; God rent the rocks with an earthquake; God rent the veil of the Temple and brought the dead out of the grave.

Jesus not only had a miracle birth and lived a perfect life and died a supernatural death, but He had a visible, physical, bodily resurrection. Not only that, He had a miraculous ministry. Think of how the teaching of Jesus has spread throughout every generation and down across the centuries. He has reached to the far corners of the world. There is more said about Jesus than about any other person of all time.

Think not only of His miraculous ministry, His teachings, His miracles, His healings, but of His unparalleled influence. Jesus has had more influence on literature, on music, on people, on history, than any other person who has ever lived.

Think of His undeniable presence. Jesus said in Matthew 18:20, ''For where two or three are gathered together in my name, there am I in the midst of them.'' There are not enough witnesses of Satan to make me believe that Christ is not with us. The undeniable presence of Christ in our midst is a proof there is a God.

Thank God for His presence! I have enjoyed His presence in

the dark hours of life. I have known His presence in the deep valleys of experience. I have felt His presence in the greatest hours of victory and in the hours of indescribable loneliness. I have been conscious of His presence in the midst of heartache and sorrow.

This Jesus, who has conquered and has gained more followers and for whom more people have gladly died, cannot be explained apart from the actual existence of a living God. One not only must admit that there is a God, but he must face the truth that he is to meet God. The Bible says that every man must give an account of himself to God.

I know there is a God because of a Miracle Man named Jesus.

"In the beginning God...."

Chapter VIII

How I Know God Is Alive

(Preached in the Emmanuel Baptist Church on Sunday, February 7, 1971)

READ: Hebrews 3

"Take heed, brethren, lest there be in any of you an evil heart of unbelief, in departing from the living God."—vs. 12.

I speak to you on the subject, "How I Know God Is Alive."

You say to me, "Preacher, you are talking to people who know God is alive."

Did you ever think we would come to a place, in our country, especially, where there would be a great discussion about whether or not God is alive? Did you ever think you would live to see the day come in theological circles when that question would be discussed?

When I first began to think on the subject, I was almost prone to feel that people would think that was a foolish subject to discuss, but not at all. Bumper stickers on cars all over this country say, "God Is Alive." I always felt that was a foregone conclusion. "Is God Alive?" is not a foolish question.

Many times in the Bible God is referred to as "the living God." Again and again the Bible refers to God as the God who is alive. He is not a god made with hands. God is not a concoction of man.

God is preexistent and eternal and the Originator of all things. He is the living God. Four times in the book of Hebrews alone God is referred to as "the living God," and our attention is called to the fact that He is alive. The fact that God in His Word emphasized this truth over and over again shows that it is an important matter.

The book of Hebrews speaks of departing from the living God. My text says, "Take heed, brethren, lest there be in any of you an evil heart of unbelief, in departing from the living God."

We have come to the day where the teaching of evolution and other philosophies of men have caused many to wonder, "Is there a personal God who is alive?" So even the text of this message is a warning about people departing from the living God.

The book of Hebrews talks about serving the living God: "How much more shall the blood of Christ, who through the eternal Spirit offered himself without spot to God, purge your conscience from dead works to serve the living God?" (9:14).

The book of Hebrews talks about falling into the hands of the living God: "It is a fearful thing to fall into the hands of the living God" (10:31).

Hebrews 12:22 speaks of the city of the living God: "But ye are come unto mount Sion, and unto the city of the living God, the heavenly Jerusalem, and to an innumerable company of angels."

Seven statements in the Pauline epistles declare that God is alive or the "living God."

1. "...the children of the living God" (Rom. 9:26).
2. "...the Spirit of the living God" (II Cor. 3:3).
3. "...the temple of the living God" (II Cor. 6:16).
4. "...to serve the living...God" (I Thess. 1:9).
5. "...the church of the living God" (I Tim. 3:15).
6. "...trust in the living God" (I Tim. 4:10).
7. "...the living God, who giveth us richly all things" (I Tim. 6:17).

At least ten times in the Old Testament He is referred to as the living God:

1. "...the voice of the living God" (Deut. 5:26).
2. "...the living God is among you" (Josh. 3:10).
3. "...the armies of the living God" (I Sam. 17:26).
4. "...to reproach the living God" (II Kings 19:4).
5. "...thirsteth for...the living God" (Ps. 42:2).
6. "...my heart and flesh crieth out for the living God" (Ps. 84:2).
7. "...he is the living God" (Jer. 10:10).
8. "...the words of the living God" (Jer. 23:36).
9. "...servant of the living God" (Dan. 6:20,26).
10. "...sons of the living God" (Hosea 1:10).

I mention these numerous statements where our God is referred to as the "living God" in order to show you that my subject is not an insignificant or irrelevant subject. Being a living God, He manifests all of the attributes of a person. Because He speaks, I have His Word. Because He hears, He answers my prayers. Because He sees, He watches over me day and night. Because He feels, He knows my every spiritual and physical need. Because He knows, all of my ways are constantly before Him. Because He lives, I too shall live forever with Him.

You say to me, "Preacher, how do you know God is alive?"

I have never made claim to scholarship, but for thirty-five years I have been a student of one Book. For thirty-five years I have read it every day of my life. I have read it from beginning to end. I have read it from end to beginning. I have read it seated. I have read it standing. I have read it lying on my face on the floor, pleading with God to show me His wonderful truth. I am a preacher who believes the Bible. You call me an ignoramus if you want to, but I believe the Bible and for thirty-five years I have studied it and have never found an error.

Now other people say they have. People who have never read it through one time have found errors, they say. I never have. I know the Author of the Book, and He is my Teacher, and I believe whatever this Bible says.

You say, "Preacher, why do you believe God is a living God?" For a number of reasons.

I. GOD IS ALIVE BECAUSE HE STILL HEARS
AND ANSWERS PRAYER

I have seen people pray all over this country and over much of the world, people who believe they can lift their voice toward the throne of grace, call upon God and He will hear them when they pray.

I have called upon God a few times to do something impossible and impractical and, humanly speaking, something that could never come to pass. But God has done it! Do you blame me for believing God answers prayer when my very existence behind a pulpit and the very voice with which I preach is because God is still able to hear and answer prayer? I once completely lost my voice and then God performed a miracle and gave it back to me.

In the Old Testament the great high priest went once a year into what was called the Holy of Holies. There was the ark of the covenant, about the size of a communion table, overlaid with gold inside and out. It was a sacred thing and a type of Christ. Then there was the heavy veil that shut the Holy of Holies and ark of the covenant off from other people. No one was allowed to go beyond that veil except the high priest and he only once a year. He could never go without a basin of blood in his hands to sprinkle it on the mercy seat of that ark.

God wanted that high priest to wear a certain kind of garment. There is a complete description of the kind of garments. God told them to put around the bottom of the robe that the priest wore a little golden bell and a pomegranate, a golden bell and a pomegranate, a golden bell and a pomegranate, a golden bell and a pomegranate.

Whenever that priest, not seen by human eye and with blood in his hands to sprinkle on the altar, went beyond that veil, the people stood outside and listened. They heard the little golden bells ringing and when they heard it, they said, "The high priest lives and ministers for us to God."

When we as believers come in the privacy of the prayer closet and go yonder to the Holy of Holies, we too can hear the bells of Heaven ring.

I know God answers prayer. God, in a miraculous way, hears and answers the prayer of the humble saint.

Someone asked a sweet saint who had read the Bible and loved the Lord and lived that pure, clean life of a dedicated Christian, one who had raised her family and had her health sustained through prayer, and in her old age, her needs met through prayer, "Is God alive?" She said, "Well, if God has died, He has done it in the last fifteen minutes because I was just talking with Him."

You ask me how I know God is alive. I know because He still answers prayer.

Another dear old Christian lady said, "My God is alive; I am sorry about yours!"

Mine is alive. I thank God that there is One who "rules over the affairs of men": this world today is still in the sovereign hands of an omnipotent God whose power has no limitations, and that God answers prayer.

An arrogant, bigoted, egotistical, young rabbi, religious but lost, had just been saved. He was seeking to kill all Christians who didn't believe just as he did. One day the Lord wonderfully saved him. That fellow could have easily been a member of the Emmanuel Baptist Church. Ananias was a fundamentalist right down the line. He believed it all, but he wasn't doing anything about it.

One day God said, "Ananias."

"Here I am!" Ananias answered. He thought to himself, *I imagine the Lord wants me to be the chairman of the Board, or they are having a building program, and He wants me to head up the building committee. He probably wants me to sit on the platform every Sunday and have a few words to say.*

The Lord said, "Ananias."

"Here I am!"

God said, "I want you to go make a visit for Me."

That is not very dramatic, is it, to go down to someone's house where there are people for whom no one cares? They have no church home; they are living a mediocre life, living in a void, with no happiness, no purpose in life; and they know not where they will spend eternity. "Make a visit. Knock on their door. Minister to them."

Listen! The curse of the church in America is that it doesn't go. God's church is to be a going church. Many people criticize our church. How do I know? Because they criticize it right to me.

They call me on the phone and say, "What about this literature you left on my porch?"

You don't know how dumb I can be when I try! I say, "Literature?" You see, I didn't put it there in the first place!

They say, "I don't want that trash left on my doorstep!"

I say, "I don't know who left it," and I don't. It could have been one of many people.

They call me up and say, "Now, listen! I work Saturday nights, and I need to sleep Sunday morning. That Sunday school bus comes down the street, 'Beep! beep! beep!' Tell that fellow to quit blowing that horn!"

That fellow is blowing that horn because he doesn't want little boys and girls to turn out to be draft-dodgers, card-burners and dope-addicts. He doesn't want them to be lost and go to Hell. "Tell them to quit blowing that horn, and keep that bus off this street!"

I know folks criticize, but we are going to keep knocking on doors. People come to my door who are not invited. It is their right to come. We have a responsibility to God, a divine compunction to move out into our community.

Ananias was a Bible-believer, a fundamentalist right down the line.

God said, "Ananias."

"Here I am, Lord!" Ananias reasons: *I bet the Lord wants me to sing the leading part in the Christmas cantata this year.*

The Lord said, "On this street called Strait lives a man named Judas. Go to his house. You will find a fellow there that I want you to talk to."

"Who is it, Lord?"

"Saul of Tarsus."

Ananias got scared. I don't blame him. Don't criticize him. One of the best men that ever lived was Stephen, a deacon in the church. Stephen went out telling people about the Lord, how God could save people and how God loved people. This fellow the Lord told Ananias to go see was one of the men standing near telling people he would hold their coats while they stoned to death that deacon. Saul was the instigator of the whole thing.

The Lord said to Ananias, "Go talk to Saul."

Ananias said, "Who? Me?"

"Yes, he is the one I want you to talk to."

The Lord knew Ananias was scared. I would have been, too. So the Lord said, "Ananias, you go talk to him, for behold, he prayeth" (Acts 9:11).

It doesn't say so in the Bible, but I imagine Ananias said, "If he is praying, that is all right."

One of the greatest signs of life in the Lord is that people pray. And when people pray, the answer comes.

You say, "Preacher, I don't get any answers."

Listen! The Christian who knows the Lord and believes His promises can pray and get answers.

My wife and I can testify how God has answered prayer in our more than thirty-five years of serving the Lord. Sometimes it looked as if everything on earth was against us and what we needed to get done, but God intervened and answered our prayer.

I never will forget one man coming to me one time. First Corinthians 10:13 always meant a lot to me, but it meant a lot more after that: "There hath no temptation taken you but such as is common to man: but God is faithful, who will not suffer you to be tempted above that ye are able; but will with the temptation also make a way to escape, that ye may be able to bear it."

This fellow, who worked for a large international company, came to me and said, "My whole life is subject to one awful habit that binds me, chains me, and I am a slave to it. I don't belong to myself nor to my family nor to my company. I belong to a habit. I have no way to be free."

I asked, "Are you a Christian?"

"Yes, I made a profession of faith in your church."

"Then there is a way to be free," I said. I opened my Bible to I Corinthians 10:13 and read that verse just quoted: "There hath no temptation taken you but such as is common to man: but God is faithful, who will not suffer you to be tempted above that ye are able; but will with the temptation also make a way to escape, that ye may be able to bear it."

I said, "God can liberate you."

He said, "How? I have promised myself, my wife, my company and I have told my friends, but I am still chained. How will it ever happen?"

"Have you ever promised God?" I asked.

"No."

"Then tell Him that you want to be free."

Down on our knees we went and prayed with an open Bible and I Corinthians 10:13. And when we got up off our knees, he dried his tears and said, "I'm a changed man! I don't believe I'll ever be again as I was."

I had the privilege to observe him for many years before his company transferred him to North Carolina, and I can testify that he was never the same. I can think of business people he would go out and get and bring to me and say, "Preacher, this fellow needs what happened to me when we prayed that night"; he would then help to see that the same would happen to them as happened to him.

All this in answer to prayer.

I am preaching to people whose home is on the rocks. I am preaching to people whose life is a failure. I am preaching to people whose life has no purpose. Prayer is the answer! Thousands, millions of church members all over America have a life without meaning, but when you pray to a living God, He hears and answers your prayers.

It is like a man who said to a little boy on the street, "Son, I lost a piece of my camera somewhere in this large area. My camera is worthless without it. Son, will you help me find it? If you will, I'll give you $10.00."

The little boy disappeared. Then he came back. The man asked, "Have you found it yet?"

The little boy said, "Not yet."

He said, "Why aren't you looking? What are you waiting on?"

The little boy answered, "I'm a Christian; and when there's something that I don't know how to do, I go get on my knees and I ask the Lord to show me. I asked the Lord to help me find the piece of camera that you lost." Then the little boy began looking around, and in a minute he bent over and picked up something and said, "Sir, is this it?"

The man said, "That's it! I have been over that place I don't know how many times."

The little boy said, "Well, here it is." The man pulled out a $10.00 reward, but the little boy said, "I don't want $10.00; just give me $5.00."

The man asked, "Son, why don't you want $10.00?"

The little boy said, "Well, only half of it belongs to me. Give the Lord the other $5.00. When I went in there and prayed, the Lord told me He would help me find it."

You don't believe in that, do you? Then you ought to try it! Try it when you feel, *What a failure I am in life! Is life not worth living?* Pray; then you will know!

I believe God answers prayer. He says, "And call upon me in the day of trouble: I will deliver thee..." (Ps. 50:15), and, "Take heed, brethren, lest there be in any of you an evil heart of unbelief, in departing from the living God" (Heb. 3:12).

II. GOD IS ALIVE BECAUSE HE STILL SAVES PEOPLE

I know God is alive because He still saves people. I have had people say to me, "Preacher, what do you mean by 'saved'?" Sometimes they ask because they really want to know. Then sometimes they ask because they are being critical. I always answer, "I mean whatever the Bible means when it says, 'Believe on the Lord Jesus Christ, and thou shalt be saved, and thy house.'"

We read in I Timothy 4:10, "For therefore we both labour and suffer reproach, because we trust in the living God, who is the Saviour of all men, specially of those that believe." You will be surprised at how many times the Bible doesn't just say God, but "the living God." The living God is still saving people.

People say, "Well, some have an emotional experience." Listen! Can you imagine an emotional experience lasting for thirty-seven years? (I was saved in 1935.) Can you imagine that emotional experience becoming more precious every day of those years? Can you imagine it becoming more real every day for thirty-seven years?

Someone says, "You just had an emotional experience and got all stirred up and got to crying." I sure did! I cried! I had lived with a vacuum and a void, and I had found a Friend. I was so thrilled that I wept.

Someone says, "Well, it was mob hysteria." I get so tired of these Ph.D.'s who think they know everything. Talking about mob hysteria: there were about sixty people there, a handful of people in a little old country church. Mob hysteria! No, it wasn't mob hysteria; it was God saving my soul.

The Lord not only saved me, but for thirty-seven years He has kept me. Listen, friends! Saving someone like me was a problem, but keeping someone like me is a bigger problem. For thirty-seven years the Lord has kept me.

You ask, "How do you know the Lord is alive?" He was alive the second week of August in 1935, and He has been alive every day since, because He has kept me. In I Timothy 1:15 Paul says, "This is a faithful saying, and worthy of all acceptation, that Christ Jesus came into the world to save sinners; of whom I am chief."

Paul is not the only one who ever felt that way. When I came to the Lord in 1935, I felt I was the dirtiest young man, the most wicked sinner there was. I felt I was the chief of sinners. Yet God saved me just like Paul said.

Folks say, "Preacher, if I believed I could hold out, I would be a Christian." Bless your heart! You don't have to hold out. Let me illustrate.

If I were going to cross the main road with one of my little grandsons, one two years of age and the other four, and I were crossing that road in traffic, would I stick out one finger and say, "Now, Tommy, hold on. If you lose your grip and a car hits you, it's your fault. If you get killed, it's no problem of mine. It's your life; hold on''?

No granddaddy holds onto little children like that. I wouldn't even get him by the hand: I'd grab him by the arm and squeeze him so tight he would say, "Grandpa, you're hurting my arm." I'd say, "I will let up when we cross the road." My grandson doesn't have to hold on. If he tried to get loose, he couldn't.

It is not a matter of your holding on. The Lord gets a grip on you. "For whosoever shall call upon the name of the Lord shall be saved" (Rom. 10:13).

Some years ago two brilliant young attorneys in England said, "If we could just disprove two things in the New Testament, we could knock the whole arc stone out from under Christianity. If we could just prove that Jesus never came out of the grave and if we could disprove that the Apostle Paul was ever really saved, we could defeat Christianity."

Each agreed to study a year, then meet together and share their findings.

When these two lawyers had given one year's study to those two questions, at the end of that year they met again.

One asked, "What did you find about the resurrection?"

The other said, "As an attorney studying all the facts of the case, I am convinced beyond any shadow of doubt that Jesus Christ arose from the dead. What did you find?"

The other said, "I find that the Apostle Paul was saved on the Damascus Road just like the Bible said. And not only that, I have found in studying about it that I have been saved."

The Lord saves people. It is a reality. You can't explain God taking a libertine and cleaning him up and taking a drunkard and making him honest—you can't explain it apart from the reality of the Christian experience called in the Bible the new birth.

I know God is alive because He still saves. And He will save you if you are not saved.

When the *Titanic* went down, it hit an iceberg that God put there. The *Titanic* was unsinkable, they said. On that ship was John Harper, a wonderful Christian. He loved the Lord. This business-man used every opportunity to talk to people about Christianity and being saved and the happiness it could bring to a person's life. John Harper drowned at the sinking of the *Titanic*.

Some years later up in Ontario, Canada, at a church meeting, a man stood up and said:

> I met a man once by the name of John Harper. I am his last convert. When the *Titanic* struck the iceberg and the ship was filled with the frozen water, I was riding on the piece of broken spar and holding on for my life.
>
> A man floating near me asked, "Are you saved?" I told him no, but I would love to be. The man said, "Do you know where you are going when you leave this world?" Then he drifted off. I hoped he would drift closer again.
>
> John Harper did drift closer again, and he said, "Believe on the Lord Jesus Christ, and thou shalt be saved—Acts 16." Then he said, "For God so loved the world, that he gave his only begotten Son, that whosoever believeth in him should not perish, but have everlasting life—John 3:16."
>
> Then he again drifted away. I never saw him again. Then I saw his name listed among the dead. I was rescued. And I was John Harper's last convert. I was saved that day in those icy waters by believing on the Lord Jesus Christ.

I know God is alive. God shows that He is alive every Sunday of the world in the Emmanuel Baptist Church by saving people, forgiving them of their sins, coming into their lives and giving them peace and happiness.

"Take heed, brethren, lest there be in any of you an evil heart of unbelief, in departing from the living God."—Heb. 3:12.

III. GOD IS ALIVE BECAUSE HE GAVE HIS SON

I know God is alive because He gave His Son. Jesus is the proof that God is a living God. I am not talking about gods carved out of stone—and I have seen them literally by the hundreds. In Egypt, four hundred miles south of the city of Cairo, they are lined up, those relics of antiquity that man has made out of stone. They cannot speak, they do not hear, they have no warmth, they do not move, they have no power, they are not able to save people.

But we have a personal God manifest in three different glorious personalities. And God gave His Son. He walked out of the infinitudes of God and over the battlements of Heaven, came down, lived among men, walked in a human body like yours and mine, died suspended between two thieves on a bloody cross, then came out of the grave with the keys of death dangling at His side and said, "Behold, I am alive for evermore" (Rev. 1:18).

I know God lives because He gave His Son. There is a wonderful illustration of this in the Old Testament, in the book of Joshua. Remember that for more than four hundred long, laborious years God's captive people had served under the severe taskmasters of Egypt. Then one night God delivered them with the blood of a lamb.

God said, "There are seven nations in this land, all more powerful than you, but I will give you this land." The people said, "How will we know God is with us? How will we know there is a living God amongst us?"

God said in the book of Joshua 3:10, "Hereby ye shall know that the living God is among you, and that he will without fail drive out from before you the Canaanites, and the Hittites, and the Hivites, and the Perizzites, and the Girgashites, and the Amorites, and the Jebusites."

Then in Joshua 3:11 God said, "Behold, the ark of the covenant of the Lord of all the earth passeth over before you into Jordan." God was saying, "When you take the ark of the covenant, borne by the priest, and touch your feet to the waters of Jordan, the waters will roll back and you shall go across that Jordan; and the ark of the covenant among you, that instrument of power, that mysterious type of Christ, shall show you that God is a living God and that He is among you.''

Just that little part of the covenant, no larger than a communion table, the top of which was called the Mercy Seat, overlaid and inlaid with pure gold, had three things in it: ''Put these things in it, and they will be in it all the time,'' God said, speaking to the people of God.

1. When Moses came from smoking Sinai and threw down those tablets of stone and broke them because the sins of God's people angered him, the Lord told them to put those broken pieces of stone in the ark of the covenant.

2. When manna came daily from Heaven in that wilderness as God wrought a miracle and rained bread from Heaven, that little white flake, which lay like the hoary frost upon the ground, spoke of the Bread, the Son of God, Heaven's true Bread. God said, ''Take a golden pot, fill it with manna, and put it in that ark of the covenant.''

3. Then one day in the contest as it were between God's men, Moses and Aaron, and the enchanters and magicians of Egypt, those Satan-inspired charlatans, God said to Moses, ''Throw down that shepherd's crook in your hands.'' He did, and it turned into a snake. God said, ''Take it up.'' He did, and it turned back into a shepherd's crook. Then God said to Aaron, ''Throw down that shepherd's crook.'' He did, and it became life, it became an almond limb with almonds on it, and it bloomed and budded. God said, ''Put it in that ark of the covenant.''

There we have one of the greatest types of Christ in the Bible. Thank God, He satisfied that broken law, which everyone in this world has broken. Thank God, He is the eternal, the daily, the perpetual Bread from the ovens of Heaven to meet the hunger of human souls. Thank God, just as a dead stick bloomed and budded, He walked out of the grave in wonderful life and said, ". . .because I live, ye shall live also" (John 14:19).

God said, "If you want to know whether God is alive or not, take that ark of the covenant." (Just the top was called the Mercy Seat. The blood was sprinkled seven times, once a year behind the holy veil in the Holy of Holies which spoke of Jesus.) God said, "I want to show you that Christ is among you, and that there is a living God who brought you out of Egypt and put you into Canaan."

Listen! God is just the same today. God is alive today. My friends, we serve a living God. We not only serve Him, but He is among us, in us, right now. Yes, God is alive.

I know He is alive because He gave His Son.

I think of that wonderful conversation between Jesus and the disciples in Matthew 16; when Jesus asked them the all-important question upon which hangs the eternal destiny of all our souls: "Whom do men say that I the Son of man am?" they answered, "Some say that thou art Jeremias [Jeremiah]." Why would anyone say, "Why, you are Jeremiah"? Jeremiah was the weeping prophet who said, "Oh that my head were waters, and mine eyes a fountain of tears, that I might weep day and night for the slain of the daughter of my people!" (Jer. 9:1).

Jesus was a weeping Man. He was acquainted with sorrows. Grief was His constant companion. He wept at the gravesides, wept in the garden, wept over the city, wept over the lost; so someone said, "This must be Jeremiah reincarnated."

Jesus again asked, "Whom do men say that I the Son of man am?"

"Some say that thou art John the Baptist."

John the Baptist, who preached with such power and people were saved and miracles were wrought. Someone said, "Why, He must be John the Baptist!"

Jesus turned to that little circle of twelve and said, "But whom say ye that I am?"

Oh, God bless that one who gave this answer, for he speaks my heart: "Thou art the Christ, the Son of the living God."

Then Jesus said, "Blessed art thou, Simon Bar-jona: for flesh and blood hath not revealed it unto thee, but my Father which is in heaven."

When Peter looked at Jesus, he said, "He fulfills all the description. Every Old Testament type and shadow and prophecy that points to the coming One is fulfilled in this one glorious Man."

Peter said, "Thou art the Christ, the Son of the living God."

Peter watched what Jesus did for three and a half years; he followed in His footsteps, slept with Jesus under the stars at night, saw Him perform His miracles, heard Him teach His parables, saw Him raise the dead, heal the sick and save the lost. For three and a half years he studied Him and never found any wrong in Him. When Jesus said, "But whom say ye that I am?" Peter was quick to answer, "Thou art the Christ, the Son of the living God."

Only a living God could give His Son as God gave Jesus. Peter watched Him live, Peter watched Him die. Peter watched Him arise from the grave, and he knew He was the living God.

I know that God lives today because He gave His Son. Jesus referred to this in His ministry. John 6:57 says, "As the living Father hath sent me, and I live by the Father: so he that eateth me, even he shall live by me." Jesus is saying, 'Except you partake of my flesh and drink of my blood, you have no life.' That is called by a large religious group the doctrine of transubstantiation, meaning when one partakes of the elements, they actually turn to the body of Christ and actually turn to the blood of Christ. But we know they are symbols of the greatest truths that you and I will ever know.

Jesus said, "A living Father hath sent Me, and unless you partake of Me, you have no life." That means acceptance; that means a vital, personal participation in Christ.

I know God lives because He gave His Son. When His Son came and walked among men, this world was not impressed, except for a little handful. Some historians have even tried to say that there was no such man as Jesus; but how foolish they are! He has left His mark on the annals of time. History revolves around His coming, His death, His resurrection. It dates either before or after. His existence on earth is the focal point of all time, around which everything revolves. God, a living God, gave His Son. History is "His Story." Seven hundred years before Christ was even born, Isaiah said, "For he shall grow up before him as a tender plant, and as a root out of a dry ground: he hath no form nor comeliness; and when we shall see him, there is no beauty that we should desire him" (53:2). Then says verse 7, "...he is brought as a lamb...."

Isaiah not only saw Him come as a Man; He saw Him come as a Lamb. Isaiah said, "He will be so marred and scarred that he will not even resemble a human being." Yes, that was God, a living God!

I was reminded of a story I heard one time when I visited the city of Vienna, the home and heart of great classical music. Some of the most famous musicians of all times either were born there or studied there or wrote some of their greatest compositions there.

One of these great men was Mozart. Mozart was little of stature, but he was a great genius. It is said that Mozart was deeply in love with a young lady, but he was small, so diminutive to look at, that she broke off their relationship and their engagement. This broke his heart.

Then as the years went by and Mozart became known as a genius in the field of classical music, she then made this statement: "When I looked at him, I just saw a little man; I did not see his genius."

This old world didn't see all there was to that Man. There is a lot more. He was the One who stood on the horizon of eternity and flung all worlds into space. They did not see His deity as you and I know it to be true today.

I know God lives because He gave His Son.

"Take heed, brethren, lest there be in any of you an evil heart of unbelief, in departing from the living God."

IV. GOD IS ALIVE BECAUSE OF THE TESTIMONY OF HIS SAINTS

Stop and think of the believers. I know we are in the minority. God said we would be.

One day Jesus looked at His disciples and said, "Fear not, little flock; for it is your Father's good pleasure to give you the kingdom" (Luke 12:32).

God's people have always been in the minority. It doesn't mean that we are losers. Just as sure as God is on His throne, just as sure as you live and breathe, we are on the winning side and always will be.

Think of the multitudes around this encircled globe who believe that the Bible is the Word of God, who believe that Jesus is God's Son, who believe that the blood cleanseth from all sin, and who believe just exactly like you do. Is someone going to say that all these around the world who believe, all the millions who believed who are now absent from the body and present with the Lord, were all deluded and deceived and didn't know what it was all about? No one could do that.

Thank God for the multiplicity of millions of witnesses, both with the Lord and still on this earth, who say, "God is alive."

This is the way it has always been. I remember when little David's father said to him, "Your big brothers are up there in the army fighting; take them something to eat." So David took them some bags of parched corn and left his flock in the field.

The little ruddy-faced David went on up there toward the place where they were fighting, and there was this giant, a Philistine, nine feet tall. He would come out every day and say, "Someone come out and fight me." But no one would come out and fight him.

David got up there, and when he saw what was going on, this little stripling of a lad said, "Who is this uncircumcised Philistine, that he should defy the armies of the living God?" (I Sam. 17:26).

God has always had His people. I don't care how dark this world gets, nor how much communism engulfs the countries of this earth, nor how strong liberalism and infidelity are, according to the Bible God will always have His remnant. God has always had His saints—from Adam in the Garden of Eden, to this hour.

The psalmist believed it, for he said in Psalm 84:2, "My soul longeth, yea, even fainteth for the courts of the Lord: my heart and my flesh crieth out for the living God."

They saw the stones, the carving of wood. They saw Dagon, the Philistine god. They saw Baal, that hideous-looking half-bull, half-man-headed monster, but David said, "...my heart and my flesh crieth out for the living God."

Hallelujah! God is alive!

It says in II Corinthians 6:16, "And what agreement hath the temple of God with idols? for ye are the temple of the living God; as God hath said, I will dwell in them, and walk in them; and I will be their God, and they shall be my people." Our bodies are the temple of the living God.

Some foolish person comes along and says, "Why, God is not alive." I say He is.

"How do you know?" I ought to know who lives in my body.

"How do you know God is alive?" I ought to know who my Tenant is. I know who has been in my heart for thirty-seven years.

God is a living God. You ask me how I know He lives. Because He lives in my heart.

In I Timothy 3:15 we read, "But if I tarry long, that thou mayest know how thou oughtest to behave thyself in the house of God, which is the church of the living God, the pillar and ground of the truth." God lives in His church. God is alive. God is with us. Jesus said, "For where two or three are gathered together in my name, there am I in the midst of them."

I know God lives because of the testimony of His saints.

V. GOD IS ALIVE BECAUSE HIS VOICE IS STILL HEARD

Our God speaks and, when He speaks, He says something. A lot of religious people do a lot of talking, but they haven't said anything yet. God has something to say, and God has said it. Our God has a voice. Deuteronomy 5:26 says, "For who is there of all flesh, that hath heard the voice of the living God speaking out of the midst of the fire, as we have, and lived?"

God spoke through types. The smitten rock, the blood on the lintel, the ark of the covenant, the ark in the Flood, the brazen serpent, every lamb on a Jewish altar slain, said, "There is a living God."

The prophets were the voice of God. God even spoke audibly, as He did when Jesus was baptized: "This is my beloved Son, in whom I am well pleased" (Matt. 3:17).

God has spoken through nature: "The heavens declare the glory of God; and the firmament sheweth his handywork. Day unto day uttereth speech, and night unto night sheweth knowledge. There is no speech nor language, where their voice is not heard" (Ps. 19:1-3).

God has spoken through His Son: "God, who at sundry times and in divers manners spake in time past unto the fathers by the prophets, Hath in these last days spoken unto us by his Son, whom he hath appointed heir of all things, by whom also he made the worlds" (Heb. 1:1,2).

God has spoken through the Bible; this perfect revelation of God is His voice: "Bless the Lord, ye his angels, that excel in strength, that do his commandments, hearkening unto the voice of his word" (Ps. 103:20).

God spoke, and God still speaks. He may be speaking to you right now. God spoke to this country boy in 1935. He said, "Tom, you are a sinner. Tom, you are lost. Tom, you are going to Hell. Tom, Jesus is your only hope." Then God said, "Tom, I want you to preach." My whole life is based on the fact that God spoke to me and saved me.

I know God is a living God because His voice is still heard.

"Take heed, brethren, lest there be in any of you an evil heart of unbelief, in departing from the living God."

VI. GOD IS ALIVE BECAUSE OF CREATION

Paul went to Lystra, where he was stoned. The people thought they had killed him. The Bible doesn't make it clear whether they did or not. Paul didn't mention it for fourteen years, then referred to it only one time. Then he said, "I knew a man in Christ above fourteen years ago, (whether in the body, I cannot tell; or whether out of the body, I cannot tell: God knoweth;) such an one caught up to the third heaven . . . and heard unspeakable words, which it is not lawful for a man to utter" (II Cor. 12:2-4).

Before that happened to him at Lystra, Paul, with the power of God, wrought miracles. They came and put garlands around his neck, started to worship him, declared him to be a god and gave him the name of a heathen god. But Paul refused worship. No man in the Bible ever accepted worship. Peter never did. Paul never did. To worship man is of the Devil. Paul warned about this: "Sirs, why do ye these things? We also are men of like passions with you, and preach unto you that ye should turn from these vanities unto the living God, which made heaven, and earth, and the sea, and all things that are therein'' (Acts 14:15).

Listen! The Bible doesn't stop there. We read in Hebrews 1:2,3: ''...by whom also he made the worlds; Who being the brightness of his glory, and the express image of his person, and upholding all things by the word of his power, when he had by himself purged our sins, sat down on the right hand of the Majesty on high.''

Think of the miracle of creation and how God operates it all. Just suppose the waters in the oceans would spill out. Remember, this earth travels 1,050 miles an hour. What keeps everything from being all mixed up? What keeps the waters from running out of the oceans? What is to keep the stars and planets and constellations and countless galaxies of worlds from colliding and from falling to earth? The Bible says God not only made it, but He upholds it ''by the word of his power.''

So I know there is a God because of the beautiful order of God's creation. The Bible says that God is the ''maker'' of all things: ''Thus saith the Lord the maker thereof, the Lord that formed it, to establish it; the Lord is his name'' (Jer. 33:2). Only a living God could make the world and all things therein.

VII. GOD IS ALIVE BECAUSE OF HIS CONSTANT AND DAILY GIFTS

Paul gave one of the greatest verses in I Timothy 6:17 where he said, ''Charge them that are rich in this world, that they be not highminded, nor trust in uncertain riches, but in the living God, who giveth us richly all things to enjoy.''

My life's verse is Romans 8:32: ''He that spared not his own Son, but delivered him up for us all, how shall he not with him also freely give us all things?''

The Lord has been giving and giving and giving to me for thirty-seven years. ''...who giveth us richly all things to enjoy.'' I know God is alive because His gifts keep coming.

He gives us air to breathe, water to drink, sunshine to sustain life. He gives us family, food and love. He gives us salvation and with that, joy, peace and fellowship. He is not some god of wood and stone, of silver and gold who cannot give. God is a giving God.

I know He lives today because He is a God who gives.

Some years ago I read a story about a little boy with a drunkard father. He never knew God in his home or heard the word of Jesus unless it was taken in profanity.

One Sunday morning his father sent the boy to the grocery store with a dollar bill. A note was attached to bring back a beer.

But while he was on his way, the dollar bill blew out of his hand. The little boy was brokenhearted. He had often been beaten by his godless father. There he was on a cold, winter morning, back in the entrance of a closed store out of the wind, standing there shuttering and crying.

A man of God was on his way down the street with his Bible under his arm, going to the house of the Lord. As he neared the entrance of the closed store, he heard sobs of a broken heart. Turning into the entrance of the closed store he said, ''Little man, why do you weep?''

The boy said, ''My father sent me to the store for some things, including a beer, and I have lost the dollar, and I'm scared to go home. My father is a drunkard, and he beats us up. I dread to go home to another beating.''

As the Christian man dried the child's tears, he said, ''Son, I'm a Christian. God gave His Son for me, and I love Jesus. And Jesus loves you, and He wants you to be saved and be a happy boy.'' He said, ''I don't believe in buying anything wrong,'' but he said, ''I'm going to give you a dollar, and I want you to go on to the store and buy what you were sent for, then go back home remembering that Jesus died for you.''

It is said that the little boy, with quivering lips, looked up into the face of that dear man and said, "Sir, I wish you were my daddy."

How I thank God today that I can look up through the blue and say, "He is my Father, and I would rather have Him for my Father than to own worlds." My heavenly Father giveth to me everything that has ever been worthwhile in life. "Every good gift and every perfect gift is from above, and cometh down from the Father of lights, with whom is no variableness, neither shadow of turning" (James 1:17).

God is alive because He keeps giving.

"Take heed, brethren, lest there be in any of you an evil heart of unbelief, in departing from the living God."—Heb. 3:12.

Chapter IX

Why I Know Trouble Can Never Destroy a Christian

Acts 27:13-44

*"And now I exhort you to be of good cheer: for there shall be no loss of any man's life among you, but of the ship. . . . Wherefore, sirs, be of good cheer: for I believe God, that it shall be even as it was told me."—*Vss. 22,25.

Notice especially this part of verse 25: ". . . for I believe God, that it shall be even as it was told me."

In this chapter of Acts, Paul is continuing on his journey to the imperial city, the city built on seven hills, the city called Rome, whose empire at this time ruled all the known world. Paul had a burning in his heart and an absorbing passion in his soul to get the Gospel to this great world-known city, the imperial city, the city of Rome, the headquarters for the world-dominating empire. In Acts 19:21 Paul said, "I must also see Rome," to get the Gospel to them.

When Paul wrote the letter, the epistle, to the church of Rome, he said, in Romans 1:13, "Now I would not have you ignorant, brethren, that oftentimes I purposed to come unto you. . . ." Many times Paul expressed his desire to go to Rome, to take the Gospel to that city. Paul wrote to them, "Now I would not have you ignorant, brethren, that oftentimes I purposed to come unto you, (but was let hitherto,) that I might have some fruit among you also, even as among other Gentiles.''

So, we see here that Paul had a burden for the city of Rome.

We read in the book of Acts where Paul was in Jerusalem and left for Caesarea. His every step, his every prayer, his every move, his every desire, was to take the Gospel to Rome.

One day God spoke to Paul: ''Be of good cheer, Paul: for as thou hast testified of me in Jerusalem, so must thou bear witness also at Rome'' (Acts 23:11). God told Paul that nothing would keep him from getting there.

Paul is on his way.

In the midst of the journey, a great storm arose. When the ship was broken into many pieces and all these people's lives were in danger, deep down in his heart Paul knew he was going to get where he started out to go, because God had told him that he would reach that place.

Friends, when the Lord saved us, He started us to a place that is fairer than day and where the sun never sets. I believe we are going to reach that place. There will not always be the ''soft winds'' from the south. There will often be the winds like the Euroclydon wind, that cold, stormy, violent wind from the northeast that whips up the high waves and dashes the ships against the rocks; but we are going to reach Heaven. That is what the journey of life is all about for the Christian.

We have many illustrations of how the Lord leads people to set out on a certain course; then opposition comes. Storms arise. I think of the time when Jesus said to the disciples ''to get into the ship, and to go to the other side...'' (Mark 6:45).

One of the greatest miracles Jesus ever wrought was the feeding of the five thousand. As people pressed upon Jesus, He, leaving Tiberia on one side of the Sea of Galilee, said to His disciples,

"...go to the other side," while He sent away the people.

They crossed the Sea of Galilee and went over to a little community called Bethsaida, while Jesus went up to the top of a mountain. On that mountaintop, all alone with God, He began to pray.

Now the disciples are in the midst of the sea. Out in the midst of the sea, dashing down over the high rocks of the east side of the Sea of Galilee, a storm arises. Their boat is tossed. The waves are high. It looks as if they are going to go down. Jesus had said, "...go to the other side." He did not say, "You are going out in the lake. A storm will come, and your boat will sink."

When it seems as if all hope is gone, they look out on the stormy waters that night and see the form of One walking upon the waves. At first they think it is a spirit, and they are afraid. But it was Jesus, and He said, "Be of good cheer: it is I; be not afraid" (Mark 6:50). Jesus gets into the disciples' boat, and they go to the other side.

The Lord says to you and me who are saved, "Go to the other side, out of this world and into the presence of God, in a city called Heaven." That is where we are going. There will be many storms along the way. We may never know where they come from nor from what direction they will blow. Yes, there will be many storms along the way.

Sometimes they will look like the storm which came to Peter. When put in jail, Peter did the strangest thing: he lay down and went sound asleep. He didn't worry about whether he would be martyred or not. Do you know why? The Lord had told Peter he would die when he was "old."

"Verily, verily, I say unto thee [Peter], *When thou wast young, thou girdest thyself, and walkedst whither thou wouldest: but when thou shalt be OLD, thou shalt stretch forth thy hands, and another shall gird thee, and carry thee whither thou wouldest not. This spake he, signifying by what death he should glorify God."*—John 21:18,19.

So knowing that, in prison Peter went to sleep. The prison officials had told Peter they were going to cut off his head, but he knew that would not happen. The Lord had told Peter he would live a full life.

God will give that same confidence to the Christian today. Trouble cannot destroy you; adversities cannot thwart the will of God for your life.

Another reason I know trouble cannot destroy a Christian is that Jesus prayed to this end. That great, high priestly prayer of our Lord Jesus Christ is found in John 17:24: "Father, I will that they also, whom thou hast given me, be with me where I am; that they may behold my glory, which thou hast given me: for thou lovedst me before the foundation of the world."

The Lord has prayed, "I want these people with Me who are saved." And with Him is where we are going to be.

Now some things we can expect on the journey of life. We are going to have some contrary winds. Everything is not going to go the way to suit us. We are not always going to have it easy. Even if you have everything this world has to offer, you will not always have the south winds. The contrary winds—hatred, persecution, frailty of your own flesh—will be your enemy. So expect on the journey of life some contrary winds.

Then everyone must expect along the journey of life some hopeless situations. This chapter says that all hope—human hope—that they should be saved was gone. You are going to have some hopeless situations yourself. A loved one in your family will become ill, and the doctors will say, "There is nothing more we can do. Unless God intervenes, this person will not survive."

Things will come into your life that you would have never dreamed would come, things to break your heart and make you weep, things to embarrass you before your friends and people who know you. These hopeless situations will indeed come. They are a part of life.

Along the journey of life, you can expect temptations to come, causing you to want to give up. Recently I said to someone, "If it weren't for the grace of God, I would have given up many times." God gives more grace. He gives power when it is needed. He manifests His presence in the midst of hopeless situations.

Those in this hopeless situation said, "We'd better get out of this ship." But Paul said, "Stay inside." They insisted: "There is no hope of our being saved unless we desert the ship, the company and the fellowship."

Some times along the journey of life we are to expect storms. Then is when you are going to want to give up. I am preaching to someone right now who is thinking, *What's the use? What does this life have? What is the use of serving the Lord and going to church and trying to do right?* You are going to be tempted to give up.

Another thing we will face along the journey of life—and it is in this chapter—is, we are going to receive some ill advice. Expect people to advise you to do things that could be disastrous to your life.

Paul said to these people, "It is not time to set out on this journey." The same old story. "Preachers don't know much of anything" is in the minds of some people. We may know a little bit about the Lord, a little bit about the Bible and the Gospel, but nothing more. It was the same in Paul's day. Knowing they should not make this journey just yet, Paul gave them that advice. But Acts 27:11 says, "Nevertheless the centurion believed the master and the owner of the ship, more than those things which were spoken by Paul."

A Christian can learn some things from God that he or she will not learn anywhere else. God had told Paul, "Don't let them go. Advise them not to go." That advice was the right advice.

But you can expect along the journey of life some wrong advice.

"Do not go to this school"; "Do not attend that church"; "Do not give your money to the Lord"; "Do not associate with those fundamental Christians." You will get some wrong advice. The same is true in this chapter.

Something else you can expect is that in the darkest hour, daylight will finally come. In this chapter daylight came. I read twice in this chapter that they wished for the day. For many days, neither sun, moon, nor stars appeared. "Then fearing lest we should have fallen upon rocks, they cast four anchors out of the stern, and wished for the day" (Acts 27:29).

As we have so often said in our family, "It is a long road that never turns." You must keep looking in His face, and finally the daylight will come. The dark shadows of night will not last forever. The morning will come when God will throw sunshine on your situation.

I heard a preacher one time who had been frightfully burned when he was young. This young man, who later became a great preacher, was burned so badly that there was no human hope for him to live. His godly mother sat by his bed the first few nights. There was that awful odor of burned flesh. There was that helplessness, that fever, that awful delirium, and that charred body, barely alive. In the dark hours, while all the world was asleep, she hovered over that body of her boy and prayed, "O God, if You will spare his life, I will give him to You."

God did spare his life, and he did become a great preacher, winning literally thousands to the Lord. Now he has gone to Heaven. I heard him tell that story. He said that one night when his life was held by a brittle thread between life and death, he awoke for a moment. His mind was clear. It was dark, but there was the shadowy form of his mother by his bed. He looked at her and said, "Mother, will daylight never come? Will daylight never come?"

She answered through the darkness of that room, "Son, yes,

you wait. Daylight will come. Daylight will come.''

Let me say to you: maybe you are with a broken heart, maybe you are in some crisis in your life; but daylight will come. The sun will rise someday, and God will clear everything. Hallelujah!

You can expect many of these things on the journey of life, but trouble and adversity can never destroy a Christian.

WHAT ARE WE TO DO IN TIMES OF TROUBLE?

What are we to do in times of trouble? What are we to do when storms come against us, over which we are absolutely helpless? I believe this chapter teaches a number of things that Christians can do. May God burn them into our hearts.

I. RECONCILE GOD'S PROVIDENCE WITH OUR RESPONSIBILITY

I believe God teaches us to reconcile God's providence with our responsibility. What do I mean by that statement? When things happen to many people, they say, ''Well, I didn't expect that and didn't invite it, but it has happened, and I can't do anything about it.'' So they fold their hands and either give up or wait until it passes by.

That attitude is not the attitude of a Christian in the will of God. I want you to see something in this chapter that is not technical or difficult to see. Notice that verse 22 says, ''And now I exhort you to be of good cheer: for there shall be no loss of any man's life among you, but of the ship.''

When those on board said, ''We'd better give up. We'd better jump from the ship,'' Paul said to the centurion and to the soldiers, ''Except these abide in the ship, ye cannot be saved'' (vs. 31).

God said, ''There shall be no loss of life among you.'' Paul said, ''Except these abide in the ship, ye cannot be saved.''

Here is the unalterable will of God. And here is human responsibility. God said, "No one will be lost," but He also said, "Stay in the ship. Stay where I tell you."

You have a responsibility.

Someone has said, "When situations come, if you can change them, change them; if you can't, commit them to God."

In this chapter, you must reconcile God's providence with human responsibility. Verse 16 says, "...we had much work to come by the boat."

Do you know what some people in Emmanuel Baptist Church might have done if faced with this situation? Some would have said, "Now listen! The Lord said that no one would be lost, so everyone relax. Don't lift a muscle. Let's just sing, preach and fellowship; everything will work out all right." No, that is not the way.

Someone said to me recently, "When you pray for something, like dollars for missions and souls to reach, if God answers prayer, why do you do things to make your prayer request come to pass?"

You know, there is no conflict in doing what you can do and in trusting God to do what you cannot do. A person must reconcile God's providence with human responsibility. That happens here.

God said, "No one is going to be lost." Paul said, "You will drown if you don't stay in the ship."

A Christian should never give in to situations. The Christian who folds his hands and does not work, does not reap the great blessings of God. When you read the Bible, it makes so many things beautiful that would not ordinarily be so.

When Paul was put in jail, he might have said, "Well, I needed a rest anyway."

I have often thought how nice it would be to be put in jail for a couple weeks. No one could call you because there are no private telephones. You would have no responsibilities. Someone would bring you some beans, a dry crust of bread and some weak coffee. Then you could lie down and rest. I have often thought that jail might not be too bad.

Paul spent much time in jail. When he went into a town, he never asked, "Where is the nearest hotel?" but, "Where is the jail?" He knew before long he would be in it. Many of these great books in the Bible were written while Paul was a prisoner. Paul was a prisoner in jail, but he said, "I have a responsibility."

We have to reconcile things in life—God's providence with our responsibility.

A young man, a few years ago, was called to preach. He is a great soul winner, a godly man. When this young man realized that he was beginning to lose his eyesight, he said, "I must get to the Scriptures as quickly as I can." So what time he had left, he spent reading and memorizing the Word of God. Then he asked his wife to read it while he listened. It seemed that, since God was taking one of his senses, He quickened the others. He had a great memory of the Word of God and became like a walking Bible, although nearly blind.

The providence of God was to lose his eyesight, but his responsibility was to fill his soul with the Word of God during the tragedy.

I was reared in northern Alabama. Twenty-five miles from my home, a baby named Helen Keller was born. Helen Keller, at best, had only two of her five senses. She could not hear, she could not see, and she could not speak. With only two of the five normal senses, Helen Keller became one of the great women of the world because she would not give up.

The providence of God was that she be born without eyes, without speech and without hearing; but Helen Keller became a brilliant woman when a godly person began to press her fingers into the palms of Helen Keller's hands in order to teach her.

I have seen people argue with God. "O God, why did You let

this happen to me? Why did You put me here?'' We must reconcile the providence of God with human responsibility, as it happened in this chapter.

"And now I exhort you to be of good cheer: for there shall be no loss of any man's life among you, but of the ship. . . . Wherefore, sirs, be of good cheer: for I believe God, that it shall be even as it was told me."—Acts 27:22,25.

II. RETIRE TO THE SECRET PLACE, ALONE WITH GOD

In the journey of life, not only must you reconcile God's providence with your responsibility, but you must also learn to retire to the secret place alone with God. ''He that dwelleth in the secret place of the most High shall abide under the shadow of the Almighty'' (Ps. 91:1).

When the storm was at its fiercest and people were doing everything they knew to do with human hands to recover the situation, Paul disappeared. ''But after long abstinence Paul stood forth in the midst of them...'' (vs. 21).

While tossed upon the stormy sea, down in some small corner of the bottom of this vessel Paul was talking to God. The Bible says:

"But after long abstinence Paul stood forth in the midst of them, and said, Sirs, ye should have hearkened unto me, and not have loosed from Crete, and to have gained this harm and loss. And now I exhort you to be of good cheer: for there shall be no loss of any man's life among you, but of the ship."—Vss. 21,22.

Paul said, ''For there stood by me this night the angel of God'' (vs. 23).

Paul would have never seen the angel of God had he not been in that secret place. Angels do not appear to people in the busy rush and race of life but in the secret places. Unless you learn to retire and be alone with God, life will always be a stormy voyage. Paul learned that.

Other men in the Bible had to learn that. Not only did Paul learn it, but Isaiah learned it: "But they that wait upon the Lord shall renew their strength; they shall mount up with wings as eagles; they shall run, and not be weary; and they shall walk, and not faint" (Isa. 40:31). Who? "They that wait upon the Lord shall. . .mount up with wings as eagles." Something to lift us above the care, sorrows and disappointments of this world is what we need. God gives eagle's wings to those who wait upon the Lord.

I read a true story one time about a mountain boy who went out hunting with his old-fashioned rifle, which had a mini-ball in it. When he heard an eagle soaring around overhead, he lifted that rifle and with dead aim, put a bullet in the wing. The eagle came tumbling down into the dirty barnyard. He bound the eagle's feet with a chain that was connected to a stake driven in the ground in the middle of the barnyard. That bird, that goes higher than any other bird, that mountaintop bird, that bird that could go beyond the clouds, was down there in a barnyard with a broken wing.

It is said that the boy fed the eagle, and the wing began to mend. The wing, now dragging in the dirt and filth of the barnyard, would come closer to his body as it healed. The eagle then would try to fly, but the chain would hold him. The old eagle would hear another eagle flying overhead and would hear the call of the sky, but he could not go to it.

One day the boy came out, took the fetters off the eagle's leg and set him loose. As he stretched his wings and looked toward the sky, he seemed to say, "I was not made to live in this filth. I was made for yonder heavens." And with an eagle call, he stretched his wings and began to fly, soaring higher and higher until he was above the highest mountain.

Listen again to Isaiah 40:31: "But they that wait upon the Lord shall renew their strength; they shall mount up with wings as eagles; they shall run, and not be weary; and they shall walk, and not faint.'' No one has to live the mundane, mediocre life: all can fly like an eagle. But there must be that aloneness with God. A bumper sticker I saw said: IF YOU WOULD FLY LIKE AN EAGLE, YOU CANNOT RUN WITH THE TURKEYS.

Jacob was subtle and scheming. He wanted a birthright, and he got it. But after twenty years he decided to go back home. Now he has to ''face up'' and meet Esau. With twelve boys to rear, Jacob has had much responsibility. One day the responsibility suddenly hit Jacob, and out to the Brook Jabbok he went and got down on his knees. All night long he wrestled with God. An angel came, and he wrestled with that angel. Finally, when daylight was about to come, the angel said, ''Let me go, for the day breaketh.'' But Jacob answered, ''I will not let thee go. I have to meet my brother, and he vows he is going to kill me. I have twelve boys to rear. I must have the power of God in my life. I can't let you go.''

The angel touched him on the hollow part of his thigh, and Jacob walked with a limp the rest of his life. God said, ''Jacob, thou hast prevailed. You will have power with God and with men.'' Let's read it in Genesis 32:28: ''. . .for as a prince hast thou power with God and with men, and hast prevailed.'' That order is correct—with God, then with men; never with men, then with God.

Do you know that prevailing power? It comes when you learn to retire alone to that secret place.

Some years ago a man wrote this poem:

> **I met God in the morning**
> **When my day was at its best,**
> **And His presence came like sunrise—**
> **Like a glory in my breast.**
> **All day long this Presence lingered;**
> **All day long He stayed with me,**
> **And we sailed in perfect calmness,**

> O'er a very troubled sea.
> Other ships were torn and battered;
> Other ships were sore distressed,
> But the winds that seemed to drive them
> Brought to me a peace and rest.
> Then I thought of other mornings
> With a keen remorse of mind,
> When I, too, had loosed the moorings
> With this Presence left behind.
> So I think I've found the secret,
> Learned through many a troubled way:
> You must meet God in the morning
> If you want Him through the day.

When the storms of life come, God expects a Christian to retire to a secret place of holy communion and prayer, as Paul did.

Several years ago a young man came to Midwestern Baptist College, as young folks have come from all over the United States for several years. He was married and had some children. One day God took one of them. As I watched that young man, I wondered what this trouble would mean to him. Will it defeat him in his purpose for studying for the ministry, or will it make a better man of God out of him?

A few months went by, then a year or so. Then another little child lay in a hospital bed. I went late one evening, looked through the large window glass and saw that beautiful baby lying there in a crib. I saw the nurses come and bend over the child and give it artificial respiration. I saw them stand at that crib and give their best effort to save that little life.

But in a while, the little face became pale and the body became still. The couple once again faced the lonely grave in the cemetery. I wondered what they would do, what this would mean to them. Will it mean defeat? Will it mean a stumbling block or a stepping stone in the lives of these Christians?

Thank God, it was a stepping stone! They are still in the ministry.

Their faces are bright; their countenance is radiant with the glow of God, because trouble can never defeat a truly born-again child of God who will let God calm the stormy sea.

III. RECKON UPON THE UNFAILING PRESENCE OF GOD

Many of the Lord's people are not conscious of the presence of God. As a Christian, I should always be conscious of the fact that God is with me.

In the midst of this storm, which lasted for several days, Paul said, "For there stood by me this night the angel of God, whose I am, and whom I serve." Paul was conscious of the presence of God.

You may be saved and lose the consciousness of the presence of God. To lose that means losing the most wonderful thing in all the world.

When Moses seemed to be at the most crucial time of all his forty years of leadership, he had to reckon upon the unfailing presence of God. Down at the foot of the mountain when the people of Israel had engaged in that lascivious dance of idolatry, Moses had broken the tablets of Law and had come in anger against sin. God said, "Let Me destroy this nation and begin again." But Moses sobbingly cried, "O God, forgive their sins."

God answered, "I will, and I will lead you and these people on." Then Moses said something that expresses the heart of anyone who has ever known any leadership in the work of the Lord: 'God, You have been saying You will send someone. Whom are You going to send with me?' God answered, "My presence shall go with thee." Then Moses said, "If thy presence go not with me, carry us not up hence" (Exod. 33:14,15).

Friend, you don't want to live without that sensitivity of the presence of God. If you do not know that God is with you, you are missing the sweetest thing in all this world. There is no companionship like that unfailing presence of God in the life of a Christian. God said, "My presence shall go with thee, and I will give thee rest."

After the bloody cross, the victory over the grave, when Jesus walked out of the tomb and appeared to His own, one of the last things He ever said is found in Matthew 28:20: "Teaching them to observe all things whatsoever I have commanded you: and, lo, I am with you alway, even unto the end of the world."

Do you sometimes feel as if God is not even with you? Yes, He is. All you need is the consciousness of His presence.

I read a story years ago of a man who knew that he was going to die. A Christian physician came to see him and ministered to him daily.

One day the dying man said, "Doctor, I know that soon I will cross over the river, for death is going to come. I know that I'm saved. I feel good when you are sitting in that chair, because I know someone is with me. But how do I know but that some dark night, when no one is in this room, I will have to cross the river alone?"

Friends, many people are alone when they die. If you are about to die and your family is with you, and you can speak to your sons and daughters and loved ones and tell them how you feel and say a good-by, remember that most people do not often die like that. They die with a little curtain around the bed. They die with only a nurse or a doctor on the floor. They die in the wee hours of the night.

Be sure in such an hour that you have the presence of God.

That doctor said, "Friend, there is Someone sitting in this chair all the time. If when you wake up at night and I am not here, nor any of your family, I want you to lay your hand on the chair. Lay it on the chair now." The doctor reached over and gripped his hand as he did so and said, "I want you to know that sitting by your bed hour after hour, unfailing, is the presence of the Son of God. And when that hour comes, reach out to Him. He will be there."

One morning when the family came to the sickroom, they found the man had gone to be with the Lord. But he was in a strange position. His arm was lying on the arm of the chair and his hand as if in a grip in the midst of the chair.

When the doctor was called, they said, "This is how we found him." The doctor smiled and said, "He died with his hand in the nail-scarred hand of the Son of God."

Friends, what a wonderful way to die! But it is also a wonderful way to live—with the presence of God in your life. Paul said, "For there stood by me this night the angel of God, whose I am, and whom I serve" (Acts 27:23).

Reckon upon the presence of God in your life.

IV. RELY ON THE PROMISES OF GOD

I believe you have to rely on the promises of God. Paul did in this instance. God had said to Paul, "Thou must be brought before Caesar" (Acts 27:24), who was in Rome. You find in the Bible that God told Paul he was going to Rome, and nothing would stop him—Acts 27:24: "Fear not, Paul; thou must be brought before Caesar: and, lo, God hath given thee all them that sail with thee." Paul took God at His Word. He did not sit down and fold his hands, but he prayed and worked and did everything he knew to do, believing that God meant what He said. Paul said, "Wherefore, sirs, be of good cheer: for I believe God, that it shall be even as it was told me" (Acts 27:25).

A Christian ought literally to live in the promises of God. Paul believed it would be just as God said it would be. That is the way a Christian ought to live—with the promises of God in his life.

What do the promises of God mean to you? Are they just words in black and white in this wonderful Book, or are they experiences in your life as you walk with God?

Oh, the promises! Someone has said there are four thousand of them in the Bible. Someone else has said that there are five thousand in the Book of God. Well, every promise in the Book is mine. There is never a moment but what God has a promise for you. You can pillow your head upon the promises of God and be like Paul who said, "I believe God, that it shall be even as it was told me." And Numbers 23:19 reminds us, "God is not a man, that he should lie; neither the son of man, that he should repent: hath he said, and shall he not do it? or hath he spoken, and shall he not make it good?" God will make good every promise in this Book that He has spoken.

I have had a little taste of this, for I have lived with some of the promises of the Word of God. When I walked out of the red clay hills of Alabama as a country boy thirty-seven years ago to study for the ministry, living in absolute poverty, I found Philippians 4:19 in the Bible: "But my God shall supply all your need according to his riches in glory by Christ Jesus." Many times I have opened my Bible to that promise and said, "Lord, You said it and I believe it. Now I claim it."

Some eighteen years ago, Mrs. Malone and I boarded a plane to go across the ocean. We were to be thirteen hours in flight from New York City to a little island, just a little dot in the Azores, called the island of Saint Helena. As I walked out of the hotel room going to the plane leaving New York City, big, block headlines said, "PLANE DOWN IN ATLANTIC!" God gave me a promise in Deuteronomy 33:27: "The eternal God is thy refuge, and underneath are the everlasting arms." So I said, "Lord, I am not riding in an airplane; I am being rocked in the arms of God."

I believe that every step I take, I have the eternal God as my refuge. And every breath that I breathe, I breathe locked in the arms of the eternal God.

My friends, rely on the promises of God.

When Adoniram Judson went to Burma to take the Gospel, he was put in jail. One day people looked through those bars in that rat-infested cell and said, "Now, what about your future?" Adoniram Judson, with the sunshine of God in his soul, said, "My future is as bright as the promises of God."

Yours is, too. Your present and your future are as bright as the promises of God right now. How good are the promises of God? They are as good as the character of God.

One time people asked an older lady, "Suppose the Bible is not true and you lose your soul."

She answered, "God will lose more."

"How will God lose more?"

She answered, "I will lose my soul, and God will lose His honor and integrity."

What God has promised you, He will do. There will not always be that soft south wind, for the storms will come. There will not always be that balmy breeze like the one in Acts 27. The breeze that makes the flowers grow and makes you feel happy will not always be there. That other wind mentioned in this chapter is going to come, the Euroclydon, a northeastern wind. It whips up the storms, and the sailors fear it. What are you going to do when it comes? Will you rely on the promises of God?

V. RECOUNT THE BLESSINGS OF GOD

I believe we ought to recount the blessings of God. When someone asks me, "How do you know what to preach?" I tell him I just pray about what I need, and I preach that. If others get blessed, well and good, but I preach to myself.

How wonderful it is to recount the blessings of God, as Paul did. In verse 35 of Acts 27 we read: ''And when he had thus spoken, he took bread, and gave thanks to God in presence of them all: and when he had broken it, he began to eat.'' This was before the ship broke up. For fourteen days he and the others on board had fasted and prayed that somehow God would deliver them from this awful storm. Fourteen days they fasted.

Then one day Paul said, ''Now that is enough. We are going to believe God. Let us take bread and give thanks in the presence of everyone.'' When he broke the bread and began to eat, he praised the Lord.

Just to praise the Lord is the best medicine in the world. It is good to smile and to be happy, to be relaxed in the Lord, to have peace, and to be conscious of the blessings of God. It is good for a Christian to laugh. There is no piety in trying to see how ill you can look. You may be just bilious and need some medicine!

The people of God ought to be happy. Some people have not let out a ''holy grunt'' in ten years. With a long, sad face, they go around asking, ''Have you got the joy, brother?'' I don't want that kind of joy. There is a rest, a peace, a happiness that comes from counting God's blessings. Try it sometimes when the storm comes. There is always something for which to praise the Lord. God told Paul, ''Wherefore I pray you to take some meat: for this is for your health: for there shall not an hair fall from the head of any of you'' (Acts 27:34). In Matthew 10:30 the Lord tells us that the very hairs of our head are all numbered.

Paul got happy. I can see him now. He broke that bread and walked up and down the deck of that boat praising the Lord and saying, ''The old boat is still under us. The promises of God are real. We are going to be saved!'' No doubt he began counting His blessings—a contagious thing to do. If someone gets happy in the Lord, someone else will get happy in the Lord. The opposite is contagious, too. When you find someone with that bilious look, the first thing you know, everyone will be looking sick. A most wonderful thing is a happy Christian who knows the Lord and is enjoying it. God never told us to endure Christianity: He told us to enjoy it. Paul was giving thanks.

I am sometimes a little disappointed in the disciple I was named after. Evidently Thomas was a twin because he was called Thomas Didymus. *Didymus* means twin. I guess the Lord thought one of them would be enough, so He got just one in the apostolate, Thomas.

Read the words of the twelve apostles and their dialogues from time to time. Jesus talked much with Peter, and John spoke to Him often. But when you read what Thomas said, you find it was always something discouraging. He was a pessimist. He wore a belt and suspenders at the same time! He was always afraid that he was going to lose something. Every time he opened his mouth, he said something pessimistic. He was a crepe hanger, hanging crepe on every door.

In John 11, the news came that Lazarus, whom Jesus loved, was sick. Jesus waited four days before saying, "Lazarus is dead. Let's go to Bethany."

Thomas, out of a clear sky, said, "Let us also go, that we may die with him" (John 11:16). Where in the world did he get that idea? Jesus had said Lazarus was dead, and here were twelve men in good health—but Thomas says, "...Let us also go, that we may die with him."

I would not want him in the Emmanuel Baptist Church, even though he was an apostle. We don't need anyone hanging crepe on our door. We don't need someone throwing cold water on every meeting we hold. "I don't believe it can be done." "Well, I would tell you one thing. If I were up there, I would not have said that." "Well, I would have done it some other way. I just would not have spent all that money." Crepe-hangers are everywhere. There are always some who never count their blessings.

I read again of Thomas in John 14:4 where Jesus says, "And whither I go ye know, and the way ye know."

Thomas said, "Lord, we don't know the way. We don't know where You are going."

Many people are like this. They cannot hear. I do not mean they are deaf; they are tuned out to everything God has to say. Thomas wasn't listening. He came to church, folded his arms and said, "I have been listening to Jesus preach now for three years. He couldn't say anything I haven't heard. So what's the use having my ears all pricked up listening?" Thomas did not hear.

Jesus said: "I am the way, the truth and the life. You know where I am going."

Thomas said, "Lord, we know not whither thou goest; and how can we know the way?" O Lord, save us from that kind of people!

When Jesus arose from the grave, walked through an unopened door and appeared on that first Lord's day to the disciples, Thomas was absent from church. He was not there the first Sunday. He missed the whole occasion when Jesus appeared to the disciples. The large stone door of that Upper Room was locked for fear of the Jews. Then, all of a sudden, without the creak of a hinge or the opening of a door or the turn of a knob, in walked the Son of God.

Someone went out, found Thomas and brought him in. Then do you know what Thomas said when the disciples told him about Jesus? "Except I shall see in his hands the print of the nails, and put my finger into the print of the nails, and thrust my hand into his side, I will not believe" (John 20:25). Thomas said in effect: "I'm going to throw a bucket of cold water on this resurrection scene."

Listen! Count your blessings today. I will never get through counting mine. I would have to start from down in the red clay hills of Alabama, when I was nineteen years old and without God, on my way to Hell. I would have to start with that old preacher who led me to Christ that glorious moment when I walked out of darkness into light. I would have to go back to that glorious hour when I was translated out of the kingdom of darkness into the kingdom of God's dear Son. I have been riding in the chariot with the King ever since. Thank God for the privilege of being a Christian! Count your blessings.

One time a one-legged man said, "I complained about losing a limb until I saw a man who had neither." Listen, you can always find something to thank the Lord for. You can find some blessing to thank the Lord for. Everyone can count his or her blessings.

VI. REFUSE THE HINDRANCES TO GOD'S WILL

Paul did something else. He refused the hindrances to God's will. When the storms come, sometimes they help rid you of some things.

There is an interesting thing in this chapter. We read in verse 38 of Acts 27: "And when they had eaten enough, they lightened the ship, and cast out the wheat into the sea." The boat started in Alexandria, Egypt. Egypt raised wheat, so no doubt that boat was literally loaded with wheat destined for a certain place. They kept saying, "Don't lose the wheat," but finally they said, "The wheat has to go."

Wheat was valuable cargo; it meant money. You will come to a place in life when money doesn't mean a thing. You would throw it in the gutter in order to have God meet the need of your life.

I read another interesting thing in verse 18: "And we being exceedingly tossed with a tempest, the next day they lightened the ship." Then verse 19: "And the third day we cast out with our own hands the tackling of the ship."

When they started out on this voyage, they had all the tackling, the rope and all that had to do with the sailing of this ocean-going vessel. They wouldn't dare start on the journey without all this.

But they came to a time when they said, "There is something a lot more important than this. Throw all the ropes overboard. Throw all the cargo overboard. Everything that we can do without, throw overboard." You are going to have that storm sometime. God lets the storm come so we can get rid of something.

I have often said that there are a lot of things worse than smoking. I have also said there are some things better! I don't believe in condemning one for smoking a cigarette when someone else in the church is tearing down God's people in a mean, hateful spirit and is lacking the joy of the Lord and the fullness of the Spirit of God, things which are just as harmful.

A fellow in the Emmanuel Baptist Church years ago used tobacco. One day the Lord talked to him about it and convicted him. The only thing that will ever get anyone to quit is the Lord's conviction. Sometimes when the Lord is dealing with a person about something, he gets grouchy while he is going through this time. It is like the time when the Lord cast out demons from a boy who was foaming at the mouth and rolling on the ground. It looked as if the boy were going to die. Many times when the Lord is dealing with us about some things, we go through an awful grouchy period.

This fellow went to a certain place and began talking to a fellow, also a member of this church. The man sat there with a grouchy look on his face, and the other man from the church, a godly man, said, "What's wrong with you, Joe?"

Joe did not answer. He was sitting there with his head down. The man said, "Come on. What's wrong?"

Joe said, "You know, Dr. Malone had better be right about something."

The godly man said, "Joe, what's that?"

"He had better be right about this thing about tobacco. If I get to Heaven and find out that Paul, Peter, James and John used tobacco, I'm going to look up Dr. Malone and kick him right down the streets of Glory."

The other man said, "Why?"

Joe said, "Because I have given it up, and I want to know that I am doing the right thing. I am telling you that that preacher had better know what he is talking about."

I know what I am talking about. Sometimes God lets the storms come so that you will throw something overboard that God knows is not good for you. God lets the storms come so that you will get rid of some cargo that God never meant for you to carry. Paul refused the hindrances to the will of God.

I am reminded of a young woman who came to church years ago in a similar situation. I was preaching, and at the invitation she came with her godly aunt and knelt at the altar. Others were being saved. The aunt motioned for me to come.

I knelt down beside the girl. The aunt said, "She is under conviction and needs the Lord, but she won't be saved."

I said to the girl, "You came to the altar with your aunt, and you know that you need the Lord. Why not be saved?"

She said, "I love to dance, and I can't give it up."

I said to her, and her aunt looked shocked, "Well, if the dance floor means more to you than the gates of Heaven, then go back to your seat."

She got up and went back to her seat.

A few nights later she came again, brokenhearted and weeping, and said, "Nothing in this world is worth missing the gates of Heaven. God being my helper, I will give up anything to be saved." The Lord saved her before she could even get the words out of her mouth. Sometimes the storms come.

VII. REMEMBER THE SOULS OF MEN

When the storms come, remember the souls of men. God said in Acts 27:37, through Luke who wrote it, "And we were in all in the ship two hundred threescore and sixteen souls." There were 276 souls on that ship. Notice that the Bible says "souls"—not bodies, not people, but "souls."

You say to me, "Preacher, do you believe I have a living soul?" I believe you *are* a living soul. Here were 276 souls for whom Jesus died. Remember all the time that every experience of life is that souls might be saved through you. Sometimes these experiences are strange.

I have mentioned before how much I love little children. I love them when they are right, and I love them when they are wrong. I love my little grandchildren. I love all children.

One day God brought one to our home and left it for awhile. She was a beautiful baby. Then God took her away. The night our baby died, I preached while Mrs. Malone led the singing. Her body lay in the funeral home.

People said, "I don't see how you can do it." One man said to his wife, "I am going to watch. If they can do that, there is something real to salvation." Not long after that, he was saved at the age of 54. Not long ago, he died and went to Heaven. He had said, "If they can keep their heads up and bury their little baby and still keep preaching and singing, then I am going to become a Christian." He was saved and baptized in Emmanuel Baptist Church.

Listen! Whatever God brings your way, it is that more souls might be saved. If it takes a storm to make you a soul winner, pray that God will send the storm.

"And now I exhort you to be of good cheer: for there shall be no loss of any man's life among you, but of the ship. . . . Wherefore,

sirs, be of good cheer: for I believe God, that it shall be even as it was told me.''—Acts 27:22,25.

Chapter X

Why I Know There Is a Place Called Heaven

John 14:1-6

"And if I go and prepare a place for you, I will come again, and receive you unto myself; that where I am, there ye may be also."—John 14:3.

Many times people have asked me, "Preacher, do you know beyond any doubt that, when that dark hour comes and a loved one is taken and hearts are broken and people walk in the deepest valley, there is a Heaven?"

Thank God, I know there is a Heaven!

I want you to notice this passage of Scripture in John. If you could see the setting, it would make the passage even sweeter. In John, chapter 13, Jesus is in the Upper Room. In the Upper Room that night, He observed the Passover Supper and instituted the Lord's Supper. The hand of Judas is on the table to betray Him. Everyone left that room singing a hymn.

Jesus starts to the Garden of Gethsemane where He will sweat great drops of blood and wrestle with the darkness of this world for your soul and mine. On His way from the Upper Room singing a hymn, to a bloody garden, Jesus speaks John, chapter 14,

John, chapter 15, John, chapter 16; then He kneels in prayer to God and prays John, chapter 17.

This passage of Scripture in John 14 was spoken by Jesus from the Upper Room to the bloody garden. But in this pilgrim journey through life, we people of God are not on our way from the Upper Room to the bloody garden: we are on our way from the bloody garden to the Upper Room. On our way to the Upper Room, that heavenly Home, we can have assurance.

"How do you know there is a place called Heaven? How do you know it is real?" Many folks have asked these questions about Heaven. I do not claim to have all the answers.

I have had people ask, "Preacher, will we know our loved ones over there?" I believe we will. In this message I will show you how you will know your loved ones in Heaven. I will know in Heaven those whom I have known and loved here in this life. Will we know our loved ones in Heaven? The Bible has an answer.

People have come to me and asked, "Preacher, is it a real place?" Yes, Heaven is real.

Others have asked, "Preacher, how big is it? Will there be room for everyone?" Heaven is foursquare, like a cube. You could set one corner of it on the city of New York. Another corner would reach to Denver, Colorado. From New York City one would reach down to Miami. And the other would go on down across the Gulf of Mexico. Then, it is just as high as it is wide. God said that it is a city foursquare.

Jesus said, "In my Father's house are many compartments or mansions." Heaven is going to be a large complex. I am going to figure out sometime how high the ceilings are going to be. They will have to be higher than usual because of all the jumping and shouting and praising the Lord! I am going to figure out how many stories Heaven is going to have. But there will be room for everyone.

I have had people ask, "Will people show their age in Heaven? That is, if they have passed on to be with the Lord as infants, will there be infants in Heaven?" No, thank God. Heaven knows no time.

I have had people ask if Heaven is real, how large it is and who will be there. I have also had them ask, "Will we eat in Heaven?" A lot of folks hope so!

They ask, "Will we work in Heaven?" An interesting question. Others ask, "Will we sleep when we get to Heaven?"

There are many questions asked about Heaven.

In the Bible the terms *"heaven," "heavens," or "heavenlies"* are used approximately 600 times, but the terms are not always talking about the same thing. Actually, there are three heavens mentioned.

First, there is what I would call the first heaven, the one we see when we look out our window and see the light of day; the one the psalmist spoke of in Psalm 19:

"The heavens declare the glory of God; and the firmament sheweth his handywork. Day unto day uttereth speech, and night unto night sheweth knowledge. There is no speech nor language, where their voice is not heard. Their line is gone out through all the earth, and their words to the end of the world. In them hath he set a tabernacle for the sun."—Vss. 1-4.

That is the heaven that the Bible speaks of as the first heaven, the one we see.

Then there is the second heaven, one that cannot be seen with the naked eye. The scientist must take his most expensive telescope and gaze yonder to the heavens that you and I have never seen with the naked eye. Even then, he sees only a small part of what God has made. These planetary heavens have their millions of worlds of which this one is only a small part. But that second heaven is not the one that I am talking about.

When you ask me, ''Preacher, do you know beyond a shadow of doubt that there is a Heaven?'' you are referring to what the Bible calls the third Heaven, the Home of God, the Home of the Saviour, that land of which our loved ones have sung:

There's a land that is fairer than day,
And by faith we can see it afar....

The Bible talks of that land as the third Heaven.

After Jesus was crucified and arose from the grave, He appeared to His own, His disciples, during the forty-day period after His resurrection. We read in Luke 24:51: ''And it came to pass, while he blessed them, he was parted from them, and carried up into heaven.''

Jesus wasn't taken to that first heaven, neither to the second, but all the way to the throne of God. Jesus went back to Heaven. Four times the first chapter of the book of Acts mentions that He was taken up into Heaven. That is the Heaven that you are asking about—that third Heaven, that Paradise of God.

The Bible tells us that there is a Paradise. Paul had an experience that God does not want me to be able to explain. Paul couldn't explain it either. At Lystra they stoned Paul until they were positive they had killed him; but God's time was not yet up for Paul. They had dragged him on the ground by the feet like a dead dog, and out to the place of refuge in the city dump they left him as dead. The disciples gathered and wept over what they thought was Paul's dead body; then all of a sudden Paul stood to his feet. He never mentioned this experience again for fourteen years.

When Paul wrote the letter to the church at Corinth, he said:

''I knew a man in Christ above fourteen years ago, (whether in the body, I cannot tell; or whether out of the body, I cannot tell: God knoweth;) such an one caught up to the third heaven. And I knew such a man, (whether in the body, or out of the body,

I cannot tell: God knoweth;) How that he was caught up into paradise, and heard unspeakable words, which it is not lawful for a man to utter.''—II Cor. 12:2-4.

Paradise—that is what I am talking about.

You may ask, ''Preacher, do you believe there is a Heaven?'' I cannot believe the Bible without believing there is a Home for the saved called Paradise.

Now that Heaven is the Home of God. Again and again in the Bible we read that fact.

In I Kings 8 the first Temple was dedicated. When Solomon prayed that great prayer, God heard him and filled all that house with such glory of God that they were interrupted in the dedication. One thing Solomon said in I Kings 8:30 was this: ''. . . when they [the people of God] shall pray toward this place: and hear thou in heaven thy dwelling place: and when thou hearest, forgive.'' Solomon said, ''O God, You live in Heaven. That is Your dwelling place.''

Psalm 2:4 says that when it speaks of the angry nations of the world who have sought to break the cords of God from them and set at naught God in this world: ''He that sitteth in the heavens shall laugh: the Lord shall have them in derision.''

Heaven is where God lives. In praying, the psalmist said, ''Unto thee lift I up mine eyes, O thou that dwellest in the heavens'' (Ps. 123:1).

Heaven, the Home of God, is the Heaven I am talking about. I am not talking about the stars, the sun, the moon or planets or galaxies and universes which we have never seen, but about the place where God lives, the Home of the saved.

Every time people pray what is commonly called The Lord's Prayer (but what should be called The Christian's Prayer), they begin, ''Our Father which art in heaven, Hallowed be thy name.'' That is the Heaven we are talking about, the Home of God, the Home of angels, who are there without number.

When Jesus was in the Garden that night and Judas came with the multitude, Peter drew his sword and struck a servant of the high priest and cut off his ear.

Jesus said to Peter,

"Put up again thy sword into his place: for all they that take the sword shall perish with the sword. Thinkest thou that I cannot now pray to my Father, and he shall presently give me more than twelve legions of angels?"—Matt. 26:52,53.

When Jesus told the story of the lost sheep, the lost coin and the wayward boy, people criticized Him. "He is interested in publicans and sinners instead of us Pharisees and religious people." Jesus said, "I say unto you, that likewise joy shall be in heaven over one sinner that repenteth, more than over ninety and nine just persons, which need no repentance" (Luke 15:7). Again in Luke 15:10 Jesus said, "Likewise, I say unto you, there is joy in the presence of the angels of God over one sinner that repenteth."

One of the most wicked things in fundamentalism today is that there are ninety-nine Christians sitting doing nothing about the lost out in the world, without hope and without God. Jesus said that the thing that makes the angels of God shout in Heaven is to see someone saved. The angels! Heaven is the Home of the angels.

Heaven is the Home of the saved. One of the greatest questions that you will ever ponder is answered in II Corinthians 5. Many have asked me, when a loved one has died and we have gathered at the funeral home or church or in the home, "Where is my daddy?" or, "Where is my dear wife?" I have had them look at that little white box and say, "O Preacher, will I ever see my baby again? Where is my little one?"

In II Corinthians 5:8 the Bible says that those who die in the Lord are "absent from the body...present with the Lord."

You ask, "Preacher, do you believe there is a Heaven?" I know there is a Heaven. It is the Home of the saved people: "absent from the body...present with the Lord."

Dwight L. Moody one time said, "Someday you will read where Dwight L. Moody is dead, but don't believe it. People will pass by my casket and say, 'Here lies Dwight L. Moody,' but don't believe it. I will not be there. You can say when you pass the casket that holds my body, 'Here is the old house where Dwight L. Moody used to live,' for I will have a new address."

Every Christian can look forward to a moving day. Death is no enemy that comes and overthrows you. Death is God's way to get you into His presence. "...absent from the body, and to be present with the Lord."

John 14:3 says, "And if I go and prepare a place for you, I will come again, and receive you unto myself; that where I am, there ye may be also." Where Jesus is—that is my Home. I am a citizen of that country.

You ask, "Well, Preacher, why do you know there is a Heaven?" In the plan and purpose of God, it has been ordained and decreed by Almighty God, who is sovereign in His purpose, that where Christ is, we are to be also. That is established.

You ask, "Where is Heaven?" They talk about the vacuum in the North, and the Bible speaks of something mysterious about the North of the heavens. I don't know where it is. I don't care whether it is north, south, east or west—just so Jesus is there. The main thing is that the Lord has said that we will be with Him. Thank God for that!

There are seven reasons why I believe there is a place called Heaven.

I. WE ARE TO SPEND ETERNITY WITH HIM—WHERE HE IS

I believe there is a place called Heaven because we are to spend eternity with Him and be where He is. Hebrews 8:1 says, "Now of the things which we have spoken this is the sum: We have such an high priest, who is set on the right hand of the throne of the Majesty in the heavens." Now remember that Jesus had said, "...that where I am, there ye may be also" (John 14:3). Where is He? On the right hand of the throne of the Majesty in the heavens. And He has said, "...where I am, there ye may be also."

When Jesus was caught up, as Acts, chapter 1, describes, two men in white apparel came down. In Acts 1:11 they said, "Ye men of Galilee, why stand ye gazing up into heaven? this same Jesus, which is taken up from you into heaven, shall so come in like manner as ye have seen him go into heaven." He has gone up into Heaven; and remember that Jesus said, "...where I am, there ye may be also."

Do you believe God would answer the prayer of Jesus? I do. I believe that all you have to do to get a prayer answered is to pray something in the will of God and pray it with the right motive and pray it with the right heart.

Just before Calvary—just before that blood-thirsty mob took Him and accused Him and beat Him and persecuted Him and finally put Him on the cross and killed Him—Jesus prayed, "Father, I will that they also, whom thou hast given me, be with me where I am; that they may behold my glory, which thou hast given me...." Then He continued: "...for thou lovedst me before the foundation of the world" (John 17:24).

The blessed Son said, "O Father, if You love Me, then My request is that these whom Thou hast given Me be with Me to behold My glory...."

If you were to ask me how I know there is a Heaven, I would

answer: I know it because it is an answer to the holy, fervent prayer of the Son of God and the last great prayer that He ever prayed this side of Calvary.

Thank God for Heaven! Some of you have loved ones over there, there where Jesus is.

A famous man years ago had a Christian boy by the name of Charlie who died. The years came and went, just as they come and go for you and me, and more quickly than we can possibly imagine. One day on his deathbed, with his family gathered around, the famous man was shouting the praises of God. The old saint was about to go Home, and the family wanted to say something to comfort him. So one of his daughters said, "Dad, in a little while you are going to see Charlie." He raised his head as high as he could from his pillow and said, "In a little while I will see Jesus, the One who means the most to me."

Oh, yes, we love our loved ones. We weep when they are ill, and we weep when God takes them. How it breaks our hearts when death comes to our home. Death breaks the family circle and leaves an empty chair and an empty heart. Oh, yes, we love them; but the main thing is that we are going to be where Jesus is.

II. OLD TESTAMENT SAINTS LONGED
FOR HEAVEN AND BELIEVED

I believe there is a Heaven because Old Testament saints of God longed for Heaven and believed in it long before Jesus ever came to this world.

One of the most wonderful verses is found in Hebrews 11, the great faith chapter of the Bible. It tells that the people believed in God in spite of the circumstances, environment, obstacles, problems and in spite of the work of the Devil.

Abraham believed God. One day God said to him, "Get thee out of thy country, and from thy kindred, and from thy father's house, unto a land that I will shew thee'' (Gen. 12:1).

Now listen! Abraham left Ur of the Chaldees. Go to the place Abraham left, and you will find more stable ruins there than anywhere else in the world, from that period of time. When the people built something in Ur of Chaldees, they thought they had built something to last for eternity. The stones are so large that no man knows how they could have been moved. The place Abraham left was solidly built.

But notice Hebrews 11:10: ''For he looked for a city which hath foundations, whose builder and maker is God.'' He is talking about foundations. He is not looking for some city that will crumble, but one that will last forever.

The word *builder* here could be translated *architect*. God said, ''I will design it and build it, and it will last forever.''

Even the New Testament saints looked for it. As the thief on the cross was dying, he said, ''Lord, remember me when thou comest into thy kingdom'' (Luke 23:42). (Remember, this is before the resurrection, before the day of Pentecost.) Jesus answered, ''Verily I say unto thee, To day shalt thou be with me in paradise'' (vs. 43).

Paradise once was down, but now it is up. It has been moved, the Bible teaches us, but that is a technical and lengthy subject within itself.

Jesus said to the thief that day before His own resurrection, before the day of Pentecost, before, officially, the age in which you and I live, ''Verily I say unto thee, To day shalt thou be with me in paradise.''

One day a man came up missing, and to this day he has never been found. His name was Enoch. Do you know why people have never found him? Because ''Enoch walked with God: and he was not; for God took him'' (Gen. 5:24).

I have often imagined that the Lord and Enoch walked together every day and talked. Enoch would say, "You know, Lord, this earth that You have made is great. It is so productive, plentiful, so magnificent and gigantic." As they walked on, Enoch would add, "You know, Lord, I surely do love You."

Then God would say, "Enoch, I love you, too."

Enoch would say, "Lord, I would rather be Your child than anything else in the world. This world You made for me and all that You have done for me are not the main things. Lord, it is You. I love You."

They would continue walking and talking. After a bit God would say, "It is getting nighttime, so you go back to your family, and I will see you another day."

Another day would come, and Enoch would walk with God. Maybe they would hold hands and Enoch would say, "I love You more today than I did yesterday."

God would answer, "I love you with a perfect, eternal love."

One day Enoch said, "Lord, I love You so much that I wish I could walk with You forever and ever, never having to be separated from You."

God said, "Enoch, I will tell you what I will do. I will take you Home with Me tonight."

Then Enoch and God walked along together; then they walked up an invisible stairway back into Glory, and Enoch never died. "And Enoch walked with God: and he was not; for God took him."

I have often wished that could happen to me. I hope the Lord will come soon and take all of us up to be with Him.

You have heard the expression, "As sure as death and taxes." Taxes are pretty sure, but death isn't. When the Lord comes, I am going up without dying. I don't have claustrophobia, but I don't like being confined. I never have been put in a box, and I don't want to be put in one. Before going to bed at night, I loosen the covers. I don't want anything binding my feet. Just to think of being in a box with my body confined—I would kick the lid off! I am not looking forward to getting in one: I am looking forward to being with the Lord. Enoch went to Heaven without dying. Paul said:

"Behold, I shew you a mystery; We shall not all sleep, but we shall all be changed, In a moment, in the twinkling of an eye, at the last trump: for the trumpet shall sound, and the dead shall be raised incorruptible, and we shall be changed."—I Cor. 15:51,52.

A generation of Christians will go to Heaven without dying, just as Enoch did. Heaven is real, and the people there are real.

In Matthew 17 when Jesus was transfigured, a wonderful thing took place: "And, behold, there appeared unto them Moses and Elias talking with him" (vs. 3).

Moses did die. Angels had charge of his funeral. No one has ever known where Moses was buried. People have known the mountain, but no one has known the exact place. If anyone had known, someone would have built a church over the place and charged admission to see it. Moses lived to be 120 years old.

Elijah didn't die. One day the Lord came, caught Elijah away, and he went to Heaven without dying.

Many centuries later, Jesus took Peter, James and John up to the mountaintop. The heavens parted, and the glory of God came, and God said, "This is my beloved Son, in whom I am well pleased; hear ye him."

There appeared at that time two men who talked with Jesus about His decease, which the Bible says He would accomplish at Jerusalem. That is the only reason anyone can ever go to Heaven.

There were Moses and Elijah. One died—which speaks of the saints who will precede the coming of the Lord in death. Elijah was caught up without dying—a picture of the rapture.

These two men talked with Jesus and Peter. James and John

found out that they were Moses and Elijah. They were visible; they talked; they worshiped Christ on that mountaintop.

Saints of God of all ages—Moses, Elijah, Abraham and others—have believed there is a place called Heaven.

Luke 16:23 says, "And in hell he [the rich man] lift up his eyes, being in torments, and seeth Abraham afar off, and Lazarus in his bosom." The rich man died without God and without hope. He looked across the great gulf fixed which no one can cross between the abode of the lost and that of the saved; he looked across that gulf fixed which God put there and saw Abraham and Lazarus, who had just died, in the Home of the saved.

Saints of God through all ages have believed that there is a place called Heaven.

A dear lady used to do a little work for us years ago. She had raised a large family and was a sacrificial woman. She was not really a godly woman, but she was a Christian, and her big goal in life was to see her children receive an education so that they wouldn't be poor as she had been. Her husband was dead. She took in washing and scrubbed floors and literally worked herself to death.

One day the Lord took her Home. She was not a member of my church, and she lived in a poor section of the city; but when I heard that she had died, I went to her home and met her children. A big boy of about seventeen years of age was weeping.

I said, "Son, your mother has gone to be with the Lord." I had talked to her many times. I said, "Your mother worked hard. She loved you so much. She worked to the midnight hour. She ironed clothes until one or two o'clock in the morning." I told him, "Your mother loved you. She worked to send you to school. She wanted you to have an education. She wanted you to have advantages. Your mother is in Heaven."

He said, "Preacher, I want to ask you something. Do you suppose that in Heaven my mother will have to scrub floors and stand over a hot iron ten or twelve hours a day?''

I said, ''No, Son, she won't. Nothing ever hurts or tires one in that land over there.''

He wiped the tears from his eyes as he said, ''Thank God for Heaven!''

Oh, listen, friends! Heaven is a wonderful place. One of the most wonderful things about Heaven will be making sure that every member of your family is there. The prime responsibility of every man who is head of his home is to see that every member of his family is saved. God's ordained duty to every mother is to see that the children are saved and that the circle is unbroken over there.

A Christian man was an engineer. He used to drive his engine past an old farm home where he was reared. I saw almost this same story enacted with my uncle who was a conductor on a passenger train that went within fifty yards of his parents' home, my grandparents' home, where I lived most of my boyhood.

This fellow was an engineer, and when he would get near the farm home, he would blow the whistle as he was leaving on his run. Two old people would come, one tottering on a cane, the other holding onto his arm. When they came out on the porch, he would blow the whistle and wave out the window of the train. They would comment, ''Willie is going out on his run.''

He would be gone forty-eight hours; then late in the evening, he would come back and blow that whistle. Out they would come, one tottering on a cane, the other holding onto his arm. As Willie blew that whistle and waved that hand, they would wave their wrinkled hands and say, ''Thank God, Willie is home now!''

One day when he blew the whistle, only one came out. One had graduated. The tottering old woman who lived alone said, ''Willie is going out.''

Two days later when Willie blew the whistle, the old, gray-haired, stooped lady said, "Thank God, Willie is home!"

Then one day when he blew the whistle, the door never opened. He knew that both Mom and Dad had gone to Heaven.

The years came and went. One day after he had retired, he was giving his testimony. He told this story and added, "Up yonder in Heaven are two wonderful people who are looking over the battlements saying, 'One of these days Willie is coming Home. When Willie gets here, all of our family will be united.' " He wept as he said, "Thank God, I am going Home!"

Friends, that is the eternal Home of all who are saved. That is where I am going. I am one day closer Home right now than I have ever been. Heaven—how wonderful to know that you have a home in Heaven!

III. WE ARE TO BE UNITED WITH LOVED ONES

I believe there is a Heaven because the Bible plainly teaches we are to be united with our loved ones. Death comes. That is something no one can avoid. You may try to get it out of your mind, but the hearse comes down the street in a funeral procession just the same. You may try not to think about death, but you will pass a cemetery along the way. Every tombstone in it is a silent testimony to the frailty of life and the fact that people die.

The Bible teaches that we are to be united again with our loved ones. In the Old Testament were many great men, but three, in a sense, stood for the people of God. When their names are mentioned, God is speaking of all the Old Testament saints of God.

For example: Jesus said, 'Abraham, Isaac, and Jacob will come from the north, south, east, and west, and sit down in the kingdom of God with them.' These three symbolized the Old Testament people of God. All three went the way of the earth. All three died. Abraham lived to be 175. His son Isaac lived to be 180. Isaac's son Jacob lived to be 147. When we read the obituary of each of these three, who symbolized the Old Testament people of God, we always read the same identical statement, the same identical words:

"Then Abraham gave up the ghost, and died in a good old age, an old man, and full of years; and was gathered to his people."— Gen. 25:8.

"And Isaac gave up the ghost, and died, and was gathered unto his people, being old and full of days...."—Gen. 35:29.

"And when Jacob had made an end of commanding his sons, he gathered up his feet into the bed, and yielded up the ghost, and was gathered unto his people."—Gen. 49:33.

When Abraham died, God said, "...gathered to his people."
When Isaac died, God said, "...gathered to his people."
When Jacob died, God said, "...gathered to his people."

The Old Testament saints had been taught from God and from His truth that Christians are to be united in the world beyond the grave, in the eternity. People who are saved are to be together. God has taught His Old Testament people that, when they died with faith in Jesus Christ, they were gathered to their people. Thank God for that hope!

When you come to the New Testament description of that hope, it is most beautifully worded in I Thessalonians 4, beginning with verse 13. Paul used an expression that he often used in writing the truth of the Word of God to the people:

"But I would not have you to be ignorant, brethren, concerning them which are asleep, that ye sorrow not, even as others which have no hope. For if we believe that Jesus died and rose again, even so them also which sleep in Jesus will God bring with him."—I Thess. 4:13,14.

The word *if* is a poor translation, not found in the original Greek

New Testament, and should read: "For *since* we believe that Jesus died and rose again. . . ."

There is no question about whether we believe that Jesus died and rose again. Paul said:

"For if [since] *we believe that Jesus died and rose again, even so them also which sleep in Jesus will God bring with him. For this we say unto you by the word of the Lord, that we which are alive and remain unto the coming of the Lord shall not prevent* [precede] *them which are asleep. For the Lord himself shall descend from heaven with a shout, with the voice of the archangel, and with the trump of God: and the dead in Christ shall rise first: Then we which are alive and remain shall be caught up together with them in the clouds, to meet the Lord in the air: and so shall we ever be with the Lord.*"—I Thess. 4:14-17.

". . .so shall we ever be with the Lord." *We* is plural. Who is that? Our loved ones, our Christian family—everyone who is saved.

In the dark hour of the funeral, when people's hearts are broken, I have often said that one of the most beautiful words in the Bible is *together*. This Bible plainly promises that beyond the grave, God's people are to be united again.

I believe there is a Heaven because God promises that loved ones are to be united on the other side of the grave throughout all the endless ages of eternity.

Years ago I heard of a godly woman who took in washing and scrubbed and worked and taught her boy, her only boy, to love Jesus. One day she called him to her side and said, "Son, your mother is not well. I may not be with you long. After I am gone, God will some way provide for you. God will take care of you."

Then one day she slipped out of that little frail body and moved into the presence of Christ. Her last words were, "Son, I am going to Heaven because of the blood of Jesus and my faith in Him.

I want to meet you there. Son, I will be waiting there for you.''

It is said that after her death the little boy again and again kept repeating, ''She said that she would be waiting for me.''

He would often go to the newly made grave, which had no monument on it. One day the boy went to a place where monuments are made and inscriptions put on them, wanting to buy a marker to put on his mother's grave. He had taken his wagon and hauled papers and saved his nickels and pennies: now he said to the man, ''I want to buy a monument for my mother's grave.''

The man said, ''Son, these monuments cost $100, $200, $500 or $1,000. How much money do you have?''

The little boy answered, ''Only $2.58.''

The good man said, ''Son, I would like to see you put a marker on your mother's grave, but your money won't buy much of a marker. There is a broken piece of stone over there, with no inscription on it—you can have that for that amount.''

The young boy hauled it in his wagon back home. Day after day he would go out and inscribe on it with a hammer and chisel.

But one day while hurrying home after selling his papers, a runaway team ran over him. He lived but a day or two. People said he seemed to be thinking only of that until he died, for he kept saying, ''I didn't get it done, but she'll know I meant to finish it, won't she? I'll tell her so, for she'll be waiting for me.''

When the people found the stone, they saw that the little man had tried to keep the lines straight, and evidently thought that capitals would make it look better and bigger, for nearly every letter was a capital:

MY MOTHER SHEE DIED LAST WEAK SHEE WAS ALL I HAD. SHEE SED SHEAD Bee WAITING FUR—

and here the lettering stopped.

When the men in the cutter's yard heard the story of the boy, they got a good stone, inscribed upon it the name of the newsboy, and underneath it the touching words:

HE LOVED HIS MOTHER

The Christian has beating in his heart the hope of Heaven. God's holy Word plainly teaches that we will be united again on the other shore.

A Christian said to me one time, ''Brother Tom, I used to think I had a lot in this world, but as the years have come and gone and I have come to the shady side of the hill, all of a sudden, I have realized that I am far richer on the other side. One by one my loved ones have gone; the chairs are empty in the home here. There are more filled across the river.''

Thank God for that Home over there! Thank God for the hope of a reunion for the people of God! I believe in a real, literal Heaven where people with real, literal, visible bodies will enjoy their loved ones, their united families, their saved friends and the presence of the King of kings and the Lord of lords. After every mountain has crumbled to dust and every star has fallen, there will be a Heaven come down out of the sky for the people of God.

I believe there is a Heaven because we are to be united with the Lord and our loved ones.

IV. THE BIBLE AND REASON TEACH SEPARATION FROM EVIL, FROM SINNERS AND HELL

I believe there is a Heaven because the Bible and reason teach us that there is a separation from evil and from sinners and from Hell. The Bible and reason teach, secondly, that God is going to separate the good from the bad. There are no good people, but saved people. God has promised a separation from evil, from sinners and from Hell. Revelation 21:8: ''But the fearful, and unbelieving, and the abominable, and murderers, and whoremongers, and sorcerers, and idolaters, and all liars, shall have their part in the lake which burneth with fire and brimstone: which is the second death."

God has said that He will put the lost in Hell—the unbeliever, the Christ-rejecter, the one who has not been cleansed with the blood of the Son of God, the one who has done despite to His grace, the one who has scorned His Holy Spirit, the one who has turned a deaf ear to God's Word.

You might say, "Preacher, I don't believe in Hell-fire." You talk to God about that, not me.

You say, "Preacher, I don't believe God is going to separate all the people who are lost." You talk to God about that. I didn't write the Bible. But it plainly says that God is going to put them in Hell—Revelation 20:15: "And whosoever was not found written in the book of life was cast into the lake of fire." God said that.

God has promised that there is to be a separation. Jesus talked about it—Matthew 7:13,14:

"Enter ye in at the strait gate: for wide is the gate, and broad is the way, that leadeth to destruction, and many there be which go in thereat: Because strait is the gate, and narrow is the way, which leadeth unto life, and few there be that find it."

Jesus said there are two roads, just two: one leads to Hell and the other to Heaven. There are more people following the road to destruction than there are following the road that leads to eternal life.

God has promised His people that there will be a separation from all evil and from sinners and from Hell. How wonderful that is!

I hear people take God's name in vain. Late one evening a man called me on the telephone. Among other things he said, he took the name of God in vain.

I responded by saying, "Someday you will know there is a God. When God gets through with you, you will know there is a God.

You can't do that to God and get by. God will make people know there is a God."

The man said, "I am never going to acknowledge there is a God."

I said, "Yes, you will. The Bible says that every knee shall bow and every tongue shall confess that Jesus is Lord to the glory of God the Father. Someday you will bow your knee to God."

God is going to have a separation day. I think of these liberalists and modernists who deny the Bible and deny the deity of Jesus, the power of the blood and the reality of the new birth. God is going to put them all in Hell. I want to be separated from that bunch. I have heard them ridicule my Jesus, talk about His Bible and downgrade His truth. I don't want to spend eternity with that crowd. I believe that God, if I may say it, owes it to a born-again Christian to separate him from that crowd throughout eternity.

I believe there is a Heaven because God is going to take us out of all that.

I called on a lady with several little children, but I never got into the house. I asked her if she knew the Lord.

She said, "No, I don't."

As we kept talking, she told me her husband was a drunkard. "Look at these blue marks on my arm. He has beat me, and the kids hate him. I can't go to church because I don't have anything to wear. At the beer garden he drinks up his paycheck. My children don't have shoes or clothes, and they are hungry."

I said, "But, lady, wouldn't it be a shame to have to live like that, then finally to miss Heaven and spend eternity in the same Hell with that fellow?"

She answered, "God is letting me have my hell right here."

I said, "Lady, God bless you. My heart goes out to you for what you have suffered, but you are not saved, and you are going to spend eternity in the same place as that other crowd."

In Heaven we won't have to hear anyone take the name of God in vain.

I was in a restaurant with one of our deacons. A fellow was blaspheming the name of God, so I said to him, "You know, that is a mighty dirty way to talk about Jesus."

He said, "You want to change it?"

I said, "I think the Lord can change it. He changed mine."

He said, "You want to change it?"

I said, "I think I could, but I know the Lord can change it."

I don't like to hear the name of the Lord taken in vain. Anytime you don't mind people taking the name of the Lord in vain, you wouldn't mind their slandering your wife or your daughter.

Thank God, there is a land fairer than day where that will never be! God's people are going to be separated from sin and from Hell and from all eternity with them. God has promised us that fact. There has to be a Heaven if that is true.

I believe there is a Heaven because the Bible and reason teach that we will be united with our loved ones, and we will be separated from all evil.

V. THE BIBLE AND REASON TEACH
A PLACE OF REWARDS

I believe there is a Heaven because the Bible and reason teach a place of rewards. God has promised to reward us. While the Lord Jesus was on this earth, He said, "Lay not up for yourselves treasures upon earth, where moth and rust doth corrupt, and where thieves break through and steal."

I know what that means, because recently while my family and I were at the church, thieves broke through our window and stole twelve or thirteen hundred dollars' worth. They had done that before. Thieves like to break into preachers' homes, tear up things and desecrate his house. I know what the Lord is talking about, for they broke into ours.

Then we read on:

"But lay up for yourselves treasures in heaven, where neither moth nor rust doth corrupt, and where thieves do not break through nor steal: For where your treasure is, there will your heart be also."—Matt. 6:20,21.

Here you have a great contrast: treasures in Heaven, treasures on earth. When the unsaved leave this world, they leave everything they have; but when Christians leave this world, they go to their riches, for their treasure is in Heaven. More especially is this fact true for the child of God who lays up treasure in Heaven.

It is a wonderful and sweet thought that there are treasures in Heaven for the people of God.

Down in Corpus Christi, Texas, where I was preaching years ago, I heard of a rich man who used to get a handful of silver, silver dollars and half-dollars, back when they were more plentiful, and throw them on the street and watch people make fools of themselves. Folks would start scrabbling on the curbs. Women would get down on their knees and ruin their nylons and dresses and get their faces dirty—just running over one another to pick up the silver. This rich man would stand back and laugh.

It was said that there was an old pit down there which was part of an oil refinery, waist deep with slimy looking stuff. Every once in awhile he would throw a handful of silver dollars down in there just to see people wade through that slime for that money. Then he would throw back his head and laugh.

When people talked to him about God, he would say, "All you want is my money." That is one of the most stupid things I have ever heard.

A fellow said to me recently, "All you folks want is our money." I don't mean this wrong, but he didn't have enough to buy a $2.50 steak. I couldn't be after his money because he didn't have any. "Why, all you preachers want is my money," he would say every time anyone talked to him. He loved his money. Just like the Texan, this fellow loved to see people make fools of themselves.

But one day he died. There was not enough money on earth to keep him from dying.

As he was wheeled away, one man standing by said, "I wonder how much he left." Another man said soberly, "He left it all." Everyone is going to leave it all.

But, thank God, we never leave that which is in the Glory! I thank God that I have some treasure in Heaven. Every time I put money in the offering plate and every time I say a word for Jesus, that is treasure in Heaven. And if the treasure is in the bank of Heaven, no one is going to break in and steal it, for the Lord has the greatest burglary system in the universe. Jesus said our treasure is "where neither moth nor rust doth corrupt, and where thieves do not break through nor steal" (Matt. 6:20).

There has to be a Heaven, because God has promised that in eternity Christians will enjoy their rewards forever.

There is a Heaven where there will be rewards.

The Bible opens with a Paradise and closes with one. The Bible opens with the Adamic or Edenic Paradise, which was ruined by sin and utterly destroyed. The Bible closes with a Paradise of God where no sin will ever enter—that city foursquare, that beautiful, wonderful Paradise. Seven times in those two chapters in Revelation God describes that wonderful place called Heaven. In that City of God, the Lord's people will enjoy their rewards. In the midst of those two chapters, the Lord says, "And, behold, I come quickly; and my reward is with me, to give every man according as his work shall be" (Rev. 22:12).

When a Sunday school bus driver gets on that cold bus and drives down a snowy street—the Lord will reward him for that. When a fellow goes out calling, with the snow blowing and the wind cold—God will reward him for that. How do we know that?

Because Jesus said, 'Even a cup of cold water given in My name shall not go without reward.'

Isn't that wonderful! There is to be a place, God said, where His people can enjoy rewards forever.

VI. THE BIBLE GIVES A PROPHETIC DESCRIPTION OF HEAVEN

I know there is a place called Heaven because the Bible gives a prophetic description of Heaven. John, on the Isle of Patmos, received a prophetic vision from Heaven: "And I John saw the holy city, new Jerusalem, coming down from God out of heaven, prepared as a bride adorned for her husband" (Rev. 21:2).

Prophetically, the Bible looks forward and describes Heaven as a city foursquare. It has twelve gates. Each has a foundation bedecked with most precious stones. The city has streets of pure gold, gold so pure that it is almost transparent. When you go walking down the street in Heaven, you walk on gold. People kill for gold down here, but in Heaven we will walk on it!

Right through the middle of Heaven will be the River of Life flowing out from the throne of God. On each side will be fruit trees bearing twelve manner of fruits—all kinds. You can just throw a hook in the River of Life and catch a fish. You won't even need bait! (Don't look for that in the Bible.) But I believe it will be about like that.

Are you happy that you are on your way to Heaven?

I have often wondered what will make Heaven so wonderful. The main thing is that Jesus will be there. I have studied about Jesus for thirty-seven years, but have never seen Him. Someday I will! "Whom having not seen, ye love; in whom, though now ye see him not, yet believing, ye rejoice with joy unspeakable and full of glory" (I Pet. 1:8).

I had often wondered what will make Heaven so wonderful. Then it dawned on me that one of the things will be some of the things that will *not* be there. John said, "God shall wipe away all tears from their eyes; and there shall be no more death, neither sorrow, nor crying, neither shall there be any more pain: for the former things are passed away" (Rev. 21:4).

I have imagined myself in Heaven. After being there for awhile, I think one day I may say to anyone who will listen, "Everyone here seems to always be happy. I have never seen a cheek stained with a tear, never heard a sob from quivering lips. Why?" I will get this answer: "No tears in Heaven."

After I have been there awhile, I may say, "I have never seen a funeral procession. No tombstones mark the hillsides. Why?" And I will hear, "No death in Heaven."

After I have been there awhile, I may say, "Everyone here is so happy. Everyone has a radiant countenance and a happy look. Why?" The answer will come: "No sorrow in Heaven." Who has not had sorrow? But no one is going to sorrow in Heaven.

After I have been there awhile, maybe I will say to another, "You know, I have never heard a groan, nor anyone suffering pain. No one seems to hurt here." The person will answer, "No pain in Heaven."

"...for the former things are passed away" (Rev. 21:4).

Thank God for Heaven! I believe there is a Heaven because the Bible gives a prophetical description of Heaven.

VII. THE BIBLE AND REASON DEMAND
A PLACE OF PERFECTION

You have never seen anything perfect—that is, of this world. You will never know perfection until you have it. You have never seen a perfect environment, not even Eden, because the Devil has always come. The church is not a perfect environment, though it is the best place I know on earth.

No one on earth has ever had a perfect body, but in Heaven every Christian will have a perfect body.

The world has never known peace. One of the brothers of the first family on this earth committed fratricide and killed his own brother. From that hour until this, this world has never known peace—and it never will. You can have your United Nations, your peace treaties, but as long as there are people on this earth, there will be no peace. There will never be peace, will never be perfection until we are in God's City.

One day He is going to let it down out of the sky, and King Jesus is going in, and we are going in with Him. Then forever and forever and forever, world without end, while ages roll, we are going to be in Heaven!

I am glad that I am on my way from the bloody garden of this earth to the Upper Room of God's eternal City, all through the grace of our wonderful Saviour.

"And if I go and prepare a place for you, I will come again, and receive you unto myself; that where I am, there ye may be also."—John 14:3.

Chapter XI

Why I Know a True Believer Can Never Be Lost

Romans 8:32-39

Notice in this chapter of Romans a question and an answer. The question is in verse 35:

"Who shall separate us from the love of Christ?"

The answer is in verses 38 and 39:

"For I am persuaded, that neither death, nor life, nor angels, nor principalities, nor powers, nor things present, nor things to come, Nor height, nor depth, nor any other creature, shall be able to separate us from the love of God, which is in Christ Jesus our Lord."

The question is, "Who shall separate us from the love of Christ?" Paul answers that no created thing on earth or in the heavens or under the sea can ever separate a true believer from the love of Christ.

This subject is vital, and I would not be speaking on it if I did not believe it.

It is a misunderstood subject. People say there are two views: the Calvinistic view—that once you are saved, you are always saved; the Arminian view—that you can be saved and lost again.

I do not believe the Arminian view is true. Theologians, Bible students and others have been saying for centuries that there are two views. I don't believe there are. I believe there is the plain, clear teaching of the Word of God.

This is one of the most misunderstood subjects in the Bible.

When I say a true believer, I do not mean a church member, a person who has religion, someone who has had only an emotional experience, but a person who is born again. Can a true believer ever lose his or her soul?

I know of no subject that has been as abused as this one. People say, "Those folks who believe in eternal security believe you can be saved, then do anything you want to do; it doesn't make any difference."

The expression "eternal security" is not found in the Bible, although "eternal life" is found many times. I have never met a truly born-again Christian who believes one can be saved, then do anything he wants to do. I don't believe that, and the Word of God doesn't teach such a thing.

This subject is feared by many. They do not want to touch it. Some preachers and Bible students won't go to the Bible and find what it says on this subject, though it is a needed subject. Many who are saved wonder whether they are saved or not. Things happen in their lives which make them think they are lost when really they are not.

Then some who believe they are saved, are not saved—Proverbs 14:12: "There is a way which seemeth right unto a man, but the end thereof are the ways of death." The work of the Devil is to get lost people who have some religion thinking they are saved, and to get saved people thinking they are lost. The Bible clearly defines this matter of eternal life in Christ Jesus the Lord.

There are four ways to look at the Scriptures. You can look at them and see that there are some things God wants you to understand right now. Says II Timothy 2:15, "Study to shew thyself approved unto God, a workman that needeth not to be ashamed, rightly dividing the word of truth." If you rightly divide the Word of truth, you will find that right now God can help you know that you are saved.

There is not a more unworthy recipient of salvation than this preacher. I don't deserve to be saved. Sometimes we hear people say, "I want my rights!" I don't, for if I received "my rights," I would be on my way to Hell. I will say, though, that I am just as sure of Heaven right now as if I were already there, for Ephesians 2:6 says, "And hath raised us up together, and made us sit together in heavenly places in Christ Jesus." God wants you to know that right now. The Bible says in I John 5:11, "And this is the record, that God hath given to us eternal life, and this life is in his Son." Then verse 13 says, "These things have I written unto you that believe on the name of the Son of God; that ye may know that ye have eternal life, and that ye may believe on the name of the Son of God."

God wants us to know that we have eternal life. No one is going to learn all depths of the Bible. There are things that we do not understand right now, for we are finite creatures with finite minds. But this is an infinite Book, written by the infinite Spirit of Almighty God.

A Christian should read his Bible every year, from Genesis to Revelation. A preacher ought to read it more than that. If you get saved by the time you are twenty and God lets you live threescore years and ten, you could read your Bible through fifty times. A person who reads and studies it with all his heart can understand what God wants him to know.

There was a period in my life when I read a minimum of ten chapters a day out of the Word of God. Then when I began studying it a little more closely, I didn't read quite that much; but I would read it, study it and meditate on it until God spoke to my heart. But a Christian will never know all there is to know about the Bible. It is written with the infinite mind of God for finite minds; so we will never understand it all, "For now we see through a glass, darkly; but then face to face: now I know in part; but then shall I know even as also I am known."

The day will come when we will know the truth of God just as much as God knows us right now. Some things we will never know while here on this earth. "The secret things belong unto the Lord our God: but those things which are revealed belong unto us and to our children for ever, that we may do all the words of this law," says Deuteronomy 29:29.

Then, some things are hard to know. Simon Peter, a better Christian than most of us, believed that; for he said in II Peter 3:15,16:

"...even as our beloved brother Paul also according to the wisdom given unto him hath written unto you; As also in all his epistles, speaking in them of these things; in which are some things hard to be understood, which they that are unlearned and unstable wrest, as they do also the other scriptures, unto their own destruction."

The Bible says that "some things are hard to be understood."

Salvation is not hard to understand. If you are saved, you will never be lost. John 10:28 says, "And I give unto them eternal life; and they shall never perish, neither shall any man pluck them out of my hand." God can help you to know that you will never lose your soul. That knowledge will make you a better Christian.

What is a true believer? A true believer is one in whom several things have happened. He believes the Gospel in his heart.

"That if thou shalt confess with thy mouth the Lord Jesus, and shalt believe in thine heart that God hath raised him from the dead,

thou shalt be saved. For with the heart man believeth unto righteousness; and with the mouth confession is made unto salvation. "—Rom. 10:9,10.

A Christian is one who believes the Gospel in his heart. There has never been a day when I did not believe the Gospel. I believed it as a twenty-year-old Alabama boy, yet lost without God and without hope, and I believe it now. Had someone come to me before I was saved and asked, "Do you believe Jesus came and died upon a cross, was buried in a tomb and arose from the grave?" I would have answered, "Yes, I believe that." But I believed it in my head. Then just before I became twenty, in August, 1935, I believed it in my heart—believed that God raised Christ from the dead and brought Him off a bloody cross to save me from sin. From that moment until this, I have believed that I am a child of God.

One has to believe in his heart. Many church members believe in their heads. You say, "A head belief—what do you mean by that?" Let me illustrate.

If a fellow were to say to his wife, "I love you with all my head," she would say, "I married a nut!"

If you were to say to your best friend, "With all of my head, I believe that you are a good neighbor," he would answer, "I don't want to talk to that fellow. He'll get me confused!"

The heart is the seat of man's emotions. If you do not believe in your heart, you are never going to believe. When I say a *"true believer,"* I mean one who has believed in his heart, I mean one who has been born again.

We live in a day when people are saying that certain terms are archaic and are no longer to be used. You do not now hear many preachers using the term *"born again."* They talk about *committal.* (To me that means that you bury someone.) They say that committal is what happens when you get saved, when you commit yourself. *"Commit yourself"* to me has always meant that you were committed to an institution! Some preachers are afraid to talk about being saved, being washed in the blood, being born again. But that term has never changed.

Jesus said to Nicodemus, "Verily, verily, I say unto thee, Except a man be born again, he cannot see the kingdom of God" (John 3:3). "I don't understand that," you say. Neither did Nicodemus understand it, for in verse 4 he asked, "How can a man be born when he is old? can he enter the second time into his mother's womb, and be born?" Jesus answered him in verse 5, "Verily, verily, I say unto thee, Except a man be born of water and of the Spirit, he cannot enter into the kingdom of God."

When I say a true believer, I mean one who can never lose his soul. A true believer is one who has had the new-birth experience by the Holy Spirit of God. A true believer is one who has had a divine nature imparted unto him. In II Peter 1:4, we read, "Whereby are given unto us exceeding great and precious promises: that by these ye might be partakers of the divine nature, having escaped the corruption that is in the world through lust."

God has imparted unto us a divine nature. When we got saved, God gave us a new nature; but He didn't take away our old one. Those educated beyond their intelligence will say, when a fellow gets a little off in some ways, "Well, he has a dual personality." I hear people say, "When I got saved, I lost my old nature." No, you didn't. You still have dandruff. You still have to wear bifocals. You have bunions and bulges and bifocals and bridges! When you got saved, you did not get rid of the old nature, but you got a new one, which lives in triumph over the old one. You became a schizophrenic, as far as this world is concerned. That divine nature imparted unto you is as eternal as the God who gave it.

When we talk this way, some fellow is thinking of one who had a prominent part in religion, then ran off with someone else's wife or embezzled money or got put in jail for murder. That behavior has nothing to do with the divine nature.

A true believer is one to whom God has given a divine nature, says II Corinthians 5:17: "Therefore if any man be in Christ, he is a new creature: old things are passed away; behold, all things are become new." That new creature can never be lost. He is a "true believer."

You ask, "Preacher, if it is so plain and clear, why do some people not believe that a true believer can never lose his soul?"

First, everyone has human weaknesses and failures. The Apostle Paul said in Romans 7:24, "O wretched man that I am! who shall deliver me from the body of this death?"

You say, "I thought Paul was a good Christian." Yes, that is why he said this. He didn't go around singing and shouting all the time; he had the peace of God in his heart and knew the joy of the Lord. When Paul said, "O wretched man that I am! who shall deliver me from the body of this death?" Paul was saying, "Who shall deliver me from this dead body? I want deliverance from this dead body."

From the time Paul was saved, he knew he carried around with him that dead body. You, too, have that dead body, but you, too, have a new nature. Because of human weaknesses and failures, some people think they are not eternally saved. Many times people do not understand what happens when a Christian sins. God does not "kick you out." There is no license to sin—Romans 6:1,2: "What shall we say then? Shall we continue in sin, that grace may abound? God forbid."

When a Christian sins, he grieves God, and if that person is a true Christian, he will come to the throne of grace and seek God's forgiveness; but that does not mean that the Christian loses his soul.

Some people believe that one is saved but not forever, because of human weaknesses and failures. Some do not believe people are saved forever because they knew some who had been saved and then had fallen away. Jesus talked about these in Matthew 7:21: "Not every one that saith unto me, Lord, Lord, shall enter into the kingdom of heaven; but he that doeth the will of my Father which is in heaven." He said, 'Many will say to Me in that day, "Lord, Lord, have we not prophesied in Thy name? Have we not preached in Thy name, cast out devils in Thy name, wrought miracles in Thy name?" ' But, sadly, Jesus answers in Matthew 7:23, "And then will I profess unto them, I never knew you: depart from me, ye that work iniquity."

Not everyone who says, "Lord, Lord," is truly saved; and some who appear to be saved and fall away, have never been saved. "What about Judas Iscariot?" you ask. I will deal with him at a later point in this message.

Often I have had people quote Matthew 24:13 to me: "But he that shall endure unto the end, the same shall be saved." You may say, "Preacher, I've got you here! You will have to admit that it says, '. . . he that endureth to the end shall be saved.' If a person doesn't endure, what about it?"

Matthew 24 is dealing with the Great Tribulation. "But he that shall endure unto the end, the same shall be saved" is talking of the period of time after the Lord comes and takes His church out and all hell breaks loose on earth. It is talking about the time of verse 22: "And except those days should be shortened, there should no flesh be saved. . . ." It is talking about flesh being saved; it is talking about enduring to the end of the Tribulation. The Jews who believe, endure to the end; unless they do, they will not even be saved physically. This verse is not talking about whether your soul is saved or not, but about the dispensation of grace.

Many Christians have lost the blessings of all their Christian experience because they say, "The Bible says you have to endure to the end to be saved," or "Brother, you have to hold on." But

I have something better than holding on: I have Someone who has hold of me!

Paul said, "But I keep under my body, and bring it into subjection: lest that by any means, when I have preached to others, I myself should be a castaway" (I Cor. 9:27). *Castaway* comes from a Greek word meaning "put on the shelf" or "disapproved." Paul said, "I don't want the day to ever come that, when I preach to others, I will be put on the shelf myself and not be able to preach anymore." This verse has nothing to do with a man's soul.

Hebrews 6:4-6 appears to some to teach that a person can be saved, then be lost. It speaks of Israel that tasted the good Word of God, tasted of the Holy Ghost and went along with the things of God; then they went back. They had that experience at Kadesh-Barnea, and God let them wander in the wilderness forty years until they died physically (all those twenty years old and older). This has nothing to do with whether one is saved or not. If Hebrews 6 were dealing with what we are talking about—whether or not one is saved for time and eternity—it would plainly teach that, if we ever got saved and fell away one time, we could never be saved again.

"For it is impossible for those who were once enlightened, and have tasted of the heavenly gift, and were made partakers of the Holy Ghost, And have tasted the good word of God, and the powers of the world to come, If they shall fall away, to renew them again unto repentance; seeing they crucify to themselves the Son of God afresh, and put him to open shame."—Heb. 6:4-6.

Matthew 24:13 is not talking about the matter of eternal life. Hebrews 6:4,5 is not speaking of a person in this church age being saved, then being lost again. It is written for us and written to the Hebrews who hesitated between the Old Testament ritual and the pure grace and liberty of the Gospel of Christ. That is why God's Word says, "Study to shew thyself approved unto God, a workman that needeth not to be ashamed, rightly dividing the word of truth'' (II Tim. 2:15).

You ask, ''What about Galatians 5:4 which says that you fall from grace?'' That verse says, ''Christ is become of no effect unto you, whosoever of you are justified by the law; ye are fallen from grace.'' Galatians has to do with the true Gospel against the false gospel and people who taught that you had to be saved by keeping the Law. Paul said, ''When you preach that you are saved by keeping the law'' (there are those who do that today), ''you are fallen or departed from grace.'' The verse does not teach nor say that a person was saved by grace and then fell out of it and lost his soul. God never said it. The Word of God teaches that a true believer can never lose his or her soul.

You may ask about Acts 1:25: ''That he may take part of this ministry and apostleship, from which Judas by transgression fell, that he might go to his own place.''

They held an election and elected Matthias to take a place as an apostle because ''Judas by transgression fell, that he might go to his own place.'' What did he fall from? He fell from the ministry and from being an apostle.

You can be a minister and not be saved. If you don't believe that, go to some of them and ask them if they believe in being washed in Jesus' blood and in being born again by the Spirit of God. Then you will know. Because a man wears a black suit and a black tie and puts his shirt on backwards does not necessarily mean that he is saved.

One day Jesus said, ''Ye are clean, but not all.'' Jesus ''knew who should betray him; therefore said he, Ye are not all clean'' (John 13:11). Notice John 6:70, ''Jesus answered them, Have not I chosen you twelve, and one of you is a devil?'' These words were spoken of Judas Iscariot, who was never saved. Many preachers are never saved. There will be many preachers in Hell.

Many preachers have been turned out in some "preacher factory" who are not saved and cannot preach the Gospel of saving grace and keeping power.

You ask, "Why don't people believe that a true believer can't be lost?" Because they think some Scriptures seem to teach otherwise. Some think it a strange doctrine and that, if you preach it, people will just live like hell and do as they please. But this needs to be preached because the unsaved need it.

I have had many say to me, "Preacher, I would like to be a Christian, I really would; I would like to be saved and to know that my sins are forgiven—but I can't hold out. I don't believe I could live up to it."

Even a lost person needs to see the sweet truth that God not only saves but that He keeps and He satisfies. A Christian needs to accept this truth in order to be a good soul winner. How on earth can a Christian win someone to the Lord and urge someone to be saved unless he himself believes that God can save and keep him?

There are seven reasons why I believe a true believer can never be lost.

I. BECAUSE OF THE ETERNAL PURPOSE OF GOD FOR BELIEVERS

I believe a true Christian can never be lost because of the clear teaching of the Bible on the eternal and sovereign purpose of God for believers. I do not know of anything more misunderstood than this often-asked question, "What did God save me for?" If you ask a hundred Christians, probably ninety-nine would say, "God saved me to get me to Heaven."

That answer is not what the Bible teaches. God has a purpose for you, that you be like Christ. That is what predestination and election are all about. God saved you to be like Jesus—Jesus, who, in the form of God, came in the form of man, that you might be made like Him. He became like you that you might be made like Him.

Romans 8:29 teaches this purpose of God: "For whom he did foreknow, he also did predestinate to be conformed to the image of his Son...."

Ephesians 1:4 says: "According as he hath chosen us in him before the foundation of the world, that we should be holy and without blame before him in love."

God saved us so that someday we will be perfect. I am a long way from it now, but I am going to be perfect someday. I am going to be like Christ. "Beloved, now are we the sons of God, and it doth not yet appear what we shall be: but we know that, when he shall appear, we shall be like him; for we shall see him as he is" (I John 3:2).

We read in II Timothy 1:9, "Who hath saved us, and called us with an holy calling, not according to our works, but according to his own purpose and grace, which was given us in Christ Jesus before the world began."

Your calling was not according to works. It is a good thing that this is taught in the Bible. If it were because of good works, I know that some of our people would not make it! Many of our members are like James and John who sent their mother to Jesus to request that He let one sit on the right hand and the other on the left hand of Jesus in Heaven. Baptists have been praying their prayer ever since: "Let me sit. Lord, we pray that we may sit!" They hold down a seat. But someday when they meet the Lord, wouldn't it be wonderful to have done something for Him other than just hold down a seat! Wouldn't it be wonderful if they could say, "Lord, I won someone else. I served You. I helped spread Your Word to the ends of the world. I helped to honor You. I tried to lift You up!"

Salvation is not according to works. So if it is not according to works that you are saved, it is not according to works that you are lost.

I read "that the purpose of God according to election might stand" (Rom. 9:11). God's Word is going to stand. Whatever God saved you for, that is what is going to happen. You are not going to lose out. God saved you to be like Christ, and that is what is going to happen to you. That whole verse says: "For the children being not yet born, neither having done any good or evil, that the purpose of God according to election might stand, not of works, but of him that calleth."

Ephesians 1:11 tells us: "In whom also we have obtained an inheritance, being predestinated according to the purpose of him who worketh all things after the counsel of his own will."

One time two men were discussing whether we can be lost after we have been saved. One fellow believed exactly the way I do. He believed what I have been talking about in this message; the other believed differently. He believed that you couldn't know that you were saved for sure until you stood in His presence in Heaven. He believed that you could be saved and lost, saved and lost.

One said, "Jesus said, 'And I give unto them eternal life; and they shall never perish, neither shall any man pluck them out of my hand. My Father, which gave them me, is greater than all; and no man is able to pluck them out of my Father's hand' " (John 10:28,29). This same man continued: "Suppose I were out in a boat with my little two-year-old boy. He doesn't know that, if he falls over the boat into the water, he will drown. So I am not going to permit him to run up and down in the boat and do whatever he wants to do. I will get him on my lap and hold him."

The other man said, "But suppose you do hold him because you don't want him to fall out of the boat and drown; but suppose he wiggles loose and falls over into the water. Suppose he wiggles out of his coat and gets away from you.''

The first man said, ''Sir, you don't understand. I wouldn't be holding onto his coat; I would be holding onto *him*.''

Friends, the Lord has a hold of you, and He is never going to turn you loose. You might as well forget the world because you have been spoiled for the world. The Lord is never going to let go of a Christian. Hallelujah! Thank God forever!

In August of 1935, the Lord reached down His nail-scarred hand, and I reached my hand to Him. He took hold of mine. It is not my holding on and holding out; it is that He got a grip with that hand that was nailed to the cross and that hand that flung worlds into space and made everything that was made. He laid hold on me. When mountains crumble to dust, and stars from the heavens fall, and time shall be no more, Jesus will still be holding on. Hallelujah! What a Saviour! He saves, He keeps, He satisfies.

"Who shall separate us from the love of Christ?"

II. BECAUSE SALVATION IS ALTOGETHER
OF GRACE

I believe a true believer can never be lost because salvation is altogether of grace. All of us know that the word *grace* means ''unmerited favor'' or ''undeserved favor''—no one deserves to be saved; but notice that the Bible teaches salvation by grace— Ephesians 2:8,9: ''For by grace are ye saved through faith; and that not of yourselves: it is the gift of God: Not of works, lest any man should boast.''

Remember that being saved by grace means you were not saved because of any works of your own. God says that we are saved by grace, not by our works. That means that faith is not even of yourselves. God gives you that faith whereby you are saved.

No one in Heaven can boast of being there because of works. If you are not saved by works in the first place, neither are you kept by works in the second place. To be saved by grace means to be completely saved by grace—from the moment of your conversion until you see the Lord: "Not by works of righteousness which we have done, but according to his mercy he saved us, by the washing of regeneration, and renewing of the Holy Ghost" (Titus 3:5).

Many people think of grace as merely a New Testament subject. That is not true. We have a wonderful illustration of grace in the Old Testament. The first time the word *grace* is found is in chapter 6 of the book of Genesis: "But Noah found grace in the eyes of the Lord" (vs. 8). Noah, who had seen the wickedness of the world, said, "All flesh is going to be destroyed." But for some unexplainable reason, we read that Noah found grace in the eyes of the Lord. What good was there in Noah? Nothing. What good work had he already done? Not one. Noah found grace in the eyes of the Lord—in the unmerited favor of God!

God said, "Noah, build an ark, and when the judgment waters and the floods come, you will be saved by grace." No one in the Old Testament or the New Testament has ever been saved any way other than by grace.

You say, "But Jesus had not died on the cross in the Old Testament." But Old Testament saints were saved by looking *forward* to Calvary. You and I are saved by looking *backward* to Calvary.

All who have ever been saved were saved by the unmerited kindness of God Almighty. No one deserved it. Works had nothing to do with it. So if works had nothing to do with your being saved, the same Bible also teaches that your works had nothing to do with keeping you saved.

When you are saved and love the Lord Jesus, you will work for Him, but not in order to keep saved. You work because you are saved.

Notice this: "Noah found grace in the eyes of the Lord." When the ark was finished from the inside, God gave this invitation to Noah to come into the ark with all his family:

"Come thou and all thy house into the ark."—Gen. 7:1.

"But with thee will I establish my covenant; and thou shalt come into the ark, thou, and thy sons, and thy wife, and thy sons' wives with thee."—Gen. 6:18.

Noah went into the ark. Now tell me—who closed the door of that ark? ". . .the Lord shut him in" (Gen. 7:16); ". . .he that openeth, and no man shutteth; and shutteth, and no man openeth" (Rev. 3:7).

Noah is on the inside with a door closed that God has shut, and no one can open that door.

You say, "Couldn't Noah have gotten out if he had wanted to?" Here is the water destroying the whole world, and here is a man in a boat that can save him: does he want to jump out? That is about the way some people reason on the things of God. Can you imagine Noah beating at the door and yelling, "I want out of here!"

That is like a fellow saying, "I know the Bible says God will give unto us eternal life and that no man shall pluck us out of His hand, but a Christian could walk out."

Here is Noah in the hands of God, with judgment all around him, a worldwide Flood; then someone says, "He could walk out." Can you even imagine Noah trying to get out of the ark? I don't even think he was holding on. Can you imagine Noah saying, "Now, everyone, get hold of a peg in the wall and hold on"? I think he sat back and said, "God gave the instructions about how to make the ark, a type of our blessed Lord Jesus, and God shut that door; I found grace in His eyes, so I am going to relax."

There is no rest in the world like soul-rest.

That is what Paul experienced when he was shipwrecked. There were 276 people on that boat, and God told Paul that not one of them would drown. And when God said it, He meant it. There were not enough devils in Hell, nor enough wind, nor storm to drown even one. God said, "Not one shall be lost."

Paul said, "You had better stay in this ship if you don't want to drown." There is the sovereign purpose of God; then there is human responsibility to live for Christ. God has said that the believer who is hidden with Christ is saved for eternity. "For ye are dead, and your life is hid with Christ in God. When Christ, who is our life, shall appear, then shall ye also appear with him in glory" (Col. 3:3,4).

We are saved by grace apart from works. Anytime you read of grace in the Bible, you are reading of something that is the very opposite of death, of works, of the Law, of human merit, of the energy of the flesh and of the religion of man. Salvation does not go from man to God; it comes from God to man. When God saves a soul, He does an eternal work.

"Who shall separate us from the love of Christ?"

III. BECAUSE THE REDEMPTIVE WORK OF CHRIST IS PERFECT AND COMPLETE

I believe a true believer can never be lost because the redemptive work of Christ is perfect and complete. Paul wrote to the church at Colosse, "For in him dwelleth all the fulness of the Godhead bodily. And ye are complete in him, which is the head of all principality and power" (Col. 2:9,10).

If you can be saved for awhile, then be lost, you are not complete in Jesus; but the above verses say you are. The redemptive work of Christ is perfect and complete.

In Romans 4:25 we read, "Who was delivered for our offences, and was raised again for our justification." Justification does not take place inside me. God's Word teaches that we are justified. He was raised for our justification. Justification, which means to be declared perfectly righteous in the eyes of God, takes place in Heaven. As God looks upon us hid in Christ, He is looking at us through the spotless, perfect righteousness of the Son of God. He sees us complete and perfect in Him.

When Jesus died, among the last words that He said were, "It is finished" (John 19:30). In this verse we find three words, but in the Greek New Testament there is but one word, *telestai.*

Recently I read an article in which someone had asked a Greek scholar, "Is there any other word that *telestai* could be translated into that would mean the same as *finished?*" The Greek scholar answered, "Yes, actually there is a word more descriptive of what Jesus said, even more descriptive than the word *finished.* It is the word *paid.*"

When Jesus died and the Scriptures had been fulfilled relative to His death, He cried, "Paid for! Paid for!" Thank God, they are all paid for!

Someone says, "Preacher, I can understand that about the sins I committed up to now and up to the time I was saved, but what about future sins?" When Jesus died, all your sins were future. You had never committed a sin, because you weren't even born; but He "was delivered for our offences, and was raised again for our justification" (Rom. 4:25). And, "Who being the brightness of his glory, and the express image of his person, and upholding all things by the word of his power, when he had by himself purged our sins, sat down on the right hand of the Majesty on high" (Heb. 1:3).

He died to save you; He lives to keep you.

"Wherefore he is able also to save them to the uttermost that come unto God by him, seeing he ever liveth to make intercession for them."—Heb. 7:25.

"My little children, these things write I unto you, that ye sin not. And if any man sin, we have an advocate with the Father,

Jesus Christ the righteous: And he is the propitiation for our sins: and not for our's only, but also for the sins of the whole world." —I John 2:1,2.

So when Jesus died, His redemptive work was complete, and we are saved because of the complete work He did on the cross.

"Who shall separate us from the love of Christ?"

IV. BECAUSE SALVATION IS AN ETERNAL WORK

I know that a true believer can never be lost because the Bible teaches that salvation is an eternal work.

A verse quoted by every Sunday school scholar is John 3:16: "For God so loved the world, that he gave his only begotten Son, that whosoever believeth in him should not perish, but have everlasting life." If I did not have anything else but "everlasting life," I would have to believe that what I got when I came to Calvary and what I got when I believed on Christ is going to last me forever and forever. Hallelujah! It does not say "intermittent life." It does not say "life while you hold out." It does not say "life if you do good." It says that, if you are saved, you have "everlasting life."

If I did not have anything else, I would have to believe that a true believer is saved for time and eternity.

In Hebrews 5:9 we read, "And being made perfect, he became the author of eternal salvation unto all them that obey him."

Then Hebrews 9:12 says, "Neither by the blood of goats and calves, but by his own blood he entered in once into the holy place, having obtained eternal redemption for us."

Then in the same chapter of Hebrews, notice verse 14: "How much more shall the blood of Christ, who through the eternal Spirit offered himself without spot to God, purge your conscience from dead works to serve the living God?"

Here I have read four verses that say "everlasting life," "eternal salvation," "eternal life" and "eternal redemption." Then I read to you one verse that speaks about the eternal Holy Spirit.

Have you ever heard someone say, "I don't believe the Holy Spirit will hold onto me forever"? The same words that say 'eternal Spirit of God' describe the eternality of our salvation and the life we have in Christ Jesus.

Now, will one argue that the Holy Spirit is not eternal? God used the same identical words to describe everlasting life, everlasting redemption, etc. So according to the Bible, salvation is an eternal work.

Paul wrote: "And the Lord shall deliver me from every evil work, and will preserve me unto his heavenly kingdom: to whom be glory for ever and ever. Amen" (II Tim. 4:18). The Lord's work of preservation is just as clear on the pages of the Word of God as the work of salvation.

"Who shall separate us from the love of Christ?"

V. BECAUSE OF HIS MANY PROMISES GUARANTEEING SECURITY

I know a true believer can never be lost because of His many promises guaranteeing our security. Again and again the Lord gives us this wonderful promise: "All that the Father giveth me shall come to me; and him that cometh to me I will in no wise cast out" (John 6:37). When you were saved, God gave you as a love gift to Jesus. This verse means that, if you come, the Lord will take you.

A young lady recently handed me her Bible and asked me to sign it. I wrote my name and Romans 8:32 after it. Since she had some other things written on that page, I happened to notice one of her statements. She had the date of her salvation, then this statement following it: "That day the Lord received me."

We ordinarily think about our receiving the Lord, but the Lord receives us, too. This verse doesn't mean that, just the moment you come, God is going to say, "No, I don't want you. No, I am not going to take you." It means that never is He going to cast you out. "All that the Father giveth me shall come to me; and him that cometh to me I will in no wise cast out."

God promises us in His Word that He never casts away one of His own. In John 10, the Great Shepherd chapter, Jesus says, "My sheep hear my voice, and I know them, and they follow me: And I give unto them eternal life; and they shall never perish, neither shall any man pluck them out of my hand" (vss. 27,28). They will never perish—the Lord said that. Then He said in verse 29, "My Father, which gave them me, is greater than all; and no man is able to pluck them out of my Father's hand."

In John 17, Jesus is praying, and He says in verse 12: "While I was with them in the world, I kept them in thy name: those that thou gavest me I have kept, and none of them is lost, but the son of perdition [talking about Judas Iscariot]; that the scripture might be fulfilled." God saves you for time and eternity.

Paul wrote to the Philippian church, "Being confident of this very thing, that he which hath begun a good work in you will perform [accomplish] it until the day of Jesus Christ" (Phil. 1:6)—that is, He will accomplish it until the day of redemption of the body. From the time the Lord saves your soul, He preserves you until He saves your body—that is, when He comes and you are translated and God gives you a new body.

So again and again, there is a promise in the Word of God that we have security in Christ.

In II Timothy 1:12 Paul said, "For the which cause I also suffer these things: nevertheless I am not ashamed: for I know whom I have believed, and am persuaded that he is able to keep that which I have committed unto him against that day"—the day of His coming and the day of the redemption of the body.

"Who shall separate us from the love of Christ?"

VI. BECAUSE OF OUR VITAL UNION
WITH CHRIST

I know that a true believer can never be lost because of our vital union with Christ. Notice how the Lord talks about it in His Word: "I am the vine, ye are the branches: He that abideth in me, and I in him, the same bringeth forth much fruit: for without me ye can do nothing" (John 15:5).

God speaks of a union that defies description between a believer and the Lord. He also describes Himself as the Head of the church or the groom, and us as the bride. "What therefore God hath joined together [that is, the groom and the bride], let not man put asunder" (Mark 10:9). God has formed an eternal union between His Son and you, which is unbreakable and indissoluble. Our union with Christ teaches us that we are saved for time and eternity.

"Who shall separate us from the love of Christ?"

VII. BECAUSE OF THE ETERNAL WORK
OF THE HOLY SPIRIT

In the last place, I believe that a true believer can never be lost because of the eternal work of the Holy Spirit.

The Lord has placed in our bodies His blessed Holy Spirit. Let us notice three Scriptures that deal with the work of the Holy Spirit of God in our lives.

John 14:16 says, "And I will pray the Father, and he shall give you another Comforter, that he may abide with you for ever."

You say, "I had a preacher teach me out of the Word of God that one can be saved and then be lost, be saved and then be lost." That thought is impossible. One passage preachers use is Hebrews 6:4-6:

"For it is impossible for those who were once enlightened, and

*have tasted of the heavenly gift, and were made partakers of the
Holy Ghost, And have tasted the good word of God, and the powers
of the world to come, If they shall fall away, to renew them again
unto repentance; seeing they crucify to themselves the Son of God
afresh, and put him to an open shame."*

That chapter alone teaches that, if you could lose your salvation, you could never get it again. There is no such thing in the
Bible as being saved more than one time, any more than you can
be born in the flesh more than one time. Every time God's Word
talks of salvation, it is forever. "And I will pray the Father, and
he shall give you another Comforter, that he may abide with you
for ever" (John 14:16). Verse 17 says, "Even the Spirit of truth;
whom the world cannot receive, because it seeth him not, neither
knoweth him: but ye know him; for he dwelleth with you, and
shall be in you." That is what Romans 8 says. The Holy Spirit
Himself beareth witness with our spirit, that we are the children
of God.

Do you have that witness? When people ask me how I know
I am saved, I tell them I know because the Bible tells me that I
am. It is my title and deed to what I have.

But I have something more—the witness in my heart. "The Spirit
itself [himself] beareth witness with our spirit, that we are the
children of God" (Rom. 8:16).

When the Spirit of God speaks to me, He says, "Tom Malone,
you are saved." Even if I am not close to Him and even if I do
not feel good, even if I do not have His joy for that moment, the
Spirit of God says to me, "Tom Malone, you belong to Me."
Even if I grieve Him, He says, "Because I am in you, you belong
to Me."

The witness of the Spirit—do you have that? Oh, the blessed
Comforter who comes in and abides forever!

Ephesians 1:13 tells us, "In whom ye also trusted, after that ye heard the word of truth, the gospel of your salvation: in whom also after that ye believed, ye were sealed with that holy Spirit of promise.'' Then Ephesians 4:30 warns, ''And grieve not the holy Spirit of God, whereby ye are sealed unto the day of redemption.''

I heard a story about a man's wayward, prodigal, sinful son. Another man said to the father of this son, ''If he were my son, I would throw him out.''

This loving, tender father said, ''If he were your son, I would throw him out, too. But he is mine.''

Friends, this blessed Book tells me that we are His. Hallelujah!

Someone may say, ''Preacher, if you are His forever, then you can do anything you want to do.'' The wonderful thing about being saved is that it changes your whole life, including your desires.

We are saved forever, according to the Word of God. Do you have the witness in your heart that you have eternal life in Him?

''Who shall separate us from the love of Christ?''—Rom. 8:35.

Chapter XII

Why I Know a Believer Shall Be Delivered From the Wrath of God

(Preached in the Emmanuel Baptist Church, Sunday, January 10, 1971)

READ: Matthew 24:1-22

"For then shall be great tribulation, such as was not since the beginning of the world to this time, no, nor ever shall be."—
Matt. 24:21.

The expression "great tribulation," as it refers to this time, is found only twice in the New Testament. First, it is found in Matthew 24:21, "For then shall be great tribulation, such as was not since the beginning of the world...." God is talking about a Tribulation period, the like of which has never been on this earth. The Flood that destroyed the world, the fire and brimstone that destroyed Sodom and Gomorrah, cannot compare to this Tribulation period.

Then Revelation 7:14 mentions the Great Tribulation again: "These are they which came out of great tribulation, and have washed their robes, and made them white in the blood of the Lamb." This speaks of a time of great trouble that is coming to the world. If the coming of the Lord be imminent—that is, if the Lord could come today—then that time of great trouble could start today.

I wish I could draw you an elementary chart that shows you the chronological unfolding of the ages and God's dealing with the world in certain ages.

Calvary ended the dispensation of law and began the dispensation of grace. The second coming of our Lord, the personal, visible, literal second coming of our Lord, will end the dispensation of grace and begin the Tribulation period, a period which is spoken of very often in the Bible.

The book of Jeremiah talks about this Tribulation period. God says, "Alas! [talking about something cataclysmic, some awful judgment, some period of judgment time the like of which the world will never know before or since]—Alas! for that day is great, so that none is like it: it is even the time of Jacob's trouble, but he shall be saved out of it" (Jer. 30:7).

Daniel 12:1 says it is a time of trouble: "...and there shall be a time of trouble, such as never was since there was a nation even to that same time...."

That period of time called the Tribulation is marked out by the coming of the Lord for His church and with His church. You understand that the second coming of Christ is like one tremendous drama that will take place in two acts. The first act is when Jesus comes and takes away His church. This is called the rapture of the church, although the word *rapture* is not one time found in the Word of God. All through the ages, saints of God who looked for the coming of Christ have called it "the rapture of the church." It is expressed in I Thessalonians 4:17: "Then we which are alive and remain shall be caught up together with them in the clouds, to meet the Lord in the air: and so shall we ever be with the Lord."

Then sets in the time of Jacob's trouble, the worst judgment that this world has ever known, seven awful years of judgment.

Those seven years are marked out, beginning when the Lord

comes for His church and ending when the Lord comes with His church. Jude 14 speaks of the Lord coming "with ten thousands of his saints." That will be the end of this Tribulation period.

There are two sides to look upon. There will be a Heaven's side, when we will be with the Lord at the marriage supper of the Lamb. Then the judgment seat of Christ will take place up there, while all hell breaks loose on earth for seven years.

Many things characterize this great time of judgment. No thinking person, no reasonable person would want to take any chance whatsoever of being left behind when Jesus comes, to go into that awful Tribulation. It will be a time of awful judgment. In the greatest prophetical book in the Bible, from chapter 4:1 to 19:11 of the last book of the Bible, God uses fifteen chapters to describe the awful judgment. Water is turned to blood; stars fall from their sockets in the sky; the moon and sun refuse to shine; fire and hail fall from heaven. God will bring on this earth every plague ever mentioned in the Bible. The heavens will roll up like a scroll, and He will bring judgment on a world that crucified His Son. There will be an awful judgment, where there will be no Holy Spirit abiding, because the Holy Spirit and the church will have been taken out. I don't want to live on this earth when the Holy Spirit has gone. But when the church is taken up, His abode will be taken up; for He lives in the bodies of redeemed, blood-washed people. According to II Thessalonians 2:8, "...then shall that Wicked [man of sin] be revealed, whom the Lord shall consume with the spirit of his mouth, and shall destroy with the brightness of his coming."

The Antichrist, that smooth-talking man of sin, shall rule the world. Satan will be unrestrained. Now he is restrained. Here is the Emmanuel Baptist Church that, for thirty years, has sounded out the Word of God. Here hundreds and thousands of people have been born again, washed in the blood, lived in the Word and have stood and resisted the power of the Devil all these years. But when this awful day of judgment comes, there will be no restraints. Satan will be unrestrained.

The Bible says that God, in His infinite holiness, and God, in judging this world, will literally cause men to believe a lie that they might be damned. If you don't believe, then you argue with God; for II Thessalonians 2:11,12 says, "And for this cause God shall send them strong delusion, that they should believe a lie: That they all might be damned who believe not the truth, but had pleasure in unrighteousness."

It is a fearful thing to take God's Word, hold it in unrighteousness and say you do not believe it; to take God's Son, hold Him at naught and say you will not accept Him. God says that He will judge people for that.

During this period, there shall be a time of delusion, and people shall believe a lie. It will be a judgment not only upon human beings, but upon this physical earth, such an awful judgment that the Bible says no flesh will be saved. It will look as though no human being will survive, so God said He will cut that day short for fear that not one bit of flesh should be saved. "And except those days should be shortened, there should no flesh be saved: but for the elect's sake those days shall be shortened" (Matt. 24:22).

Let no one say that the Bible teaching concerning the Tribulation period is not important. God has given much emphasis to it in His Word. Several passages in the Old Testament deal with this period of seven years, and several passages in the New Testament, such as Matthew 24, Luke 21 and Mark 13. In fact, a thorough understanding of the teaching concerning the time of Tribulation helps to unlock many other passages in the Word of God.

When I was a country boy, saved in a little country church down in North Alabama, I had never heard a lot of this phraseology and these theological terms.

Some folks say, "I am a pre," while some say, "I am a post." When they say, "I am a pre," they mean they believe the Lord is coming previous to this Tribulation period. When they say, "I am a post," they believe that the Lord is coming at the close of this Tribulation period.

Then there are a few fuzzy-minded ones who believe in the "mid-tribulation rapture"—that is, they believe the Lord is coming right in the middle of the whole thing. You might as well try to prove that Simon Peter was an Irishman as to try to prove that there is any such thing as the mid-tribulation rapture.

I feel as Dr. R. G. Lee felt when he went to the doctor with a sore throat. When the doctor said, "Say ah," Dr. Lee said, "I'd die first!" The " 'ah'-millennialists" believe in no Tribulation, no millennium; so they are called amillennial.

I am a *pre* all the way. I am predestinated, so how could I be anything else? I am preserved, so how could I be anything else? I am prepaid for Heaven. Not only am I prepaid, but I am prepared, premillennial and pretribulation. So I couldn't be anything else but a "pre."

The Lord is coming before this awful time ever comes upon the world.

Notice five things that tell why I know a believer shall be delivered from the wrath to come. These five things prove to me that the church will not go through the Tribulation.

I. THE JUDGMENT FOR BELIEVERS HAS ALREADY TAKEN PLACE

Romans 8:1 says, "There is therefore now no condemnation to them which are in Christ Jesus, who walk not after the flesh, but after the Spirit."

This chapter begins with no condemnation. Verse 35 of the same chapter says that tribulation shall never separate us from the love of the Lord Jesus Christ: "Who shall separate us from the love of Christ? shall tribulation, or distress, or persecution, or famine, or nakedness, or peril, or sword?" Then the answer comes in verse 37: "Nay, in all these things we are more than conquerors through him that loved us." So Romans 8 begins with no condemnation and ends with no separation.

I know I am not condemned because I am in Christ. I cannot be separated from Him because I am in Christ. When He is above, I will be above. There is not one bit of reason to believe that the Lord will ever let His people go through more judgment. The judgment for believers has already passed. Says I Thessalonians 5:9, "For God hath not appointed us to wrath [the believers], but to obtain salvation by our Lord Jesus Christ." Judgment for Christians has already passed. When Jesus cried on the cross, "It is finished," He meant that the payment for sin had been paid, and the one who comes to Christ and trusts Him has his judgment taken care of once and for all times.

When civilization was pressing out across the East toward the West in this great land of ours, there were two explorers and an Indian guide pressing toward the western plains. One day they heard a fearful roar. "What is this?" they wondered. They had never heard anything like it. There were no clouds in the sky.

But then the Indian pointed miles away across the plains to a prairie fire. That huge volcano of fire that literally swept the earth clean as it went, was coming toward them. "Where shall we go? There are no mountains in which to hide, just acres and acres of prairie grass burning."

It is said that the white men became frustrated and afraid, but their Indian guide had no fear; he knew exactly what to do. As the fire came closer and closer, he dropped down on his knees, struck two flints together and set another fire right at their feet.

The explorers stood in amazement as they saw a fire kindling, and coming toward them another fire from which there was no escape.

They watched that fire burn in a little black circle and saw the Indian step in it and motion for them to do the same. They stepped in that black circle and watched that mountain of fire grow and become more intense and burn a wider circle around them. By that time the mountain of fire had reached them; but when it came to where it had already been burned, it broke and went around, and they stood sheltered from it all because you cannot burn what has already been burned.

Thank God, two thousand years ago, robed in blood and crowned with thorns, Jesus hung upon the old rugged cross and God laid upon Him your sin and mine. He paid that debt to the full satisfaction of God. And a holy, righteous God would never demand that anyone pay for something again that has already been paid for once. Praise His name! It is all finished!

I know the church shall not go through further judgment because a believer's judgment has already taken place.

II. TYPOLOGY SHOWS DELIVERANCE
BEFORE JUDGMENT

Then, all typology related to the Bible shows deliverance before judgment. All the great types of the Bible that give us a tremendous story of salvation, all give us the same picture—that is, deliverance before judgment.

Take, for example, Noah and the Flood. God said to Noah after the ark had been made, "Come thou and all thy house into the ark; for thee have I seen righteous before me in this generation" (Gen. 7:1). Noah and his family went into that ark. The same thing that happened then is going to happen to you and me. Noah and his family went into that ark, and the fountains of the deep were broken up, the windows of Heaven were opened, and God sent a Flood to destroy the world. But now, where are the Lord's people? Safe in the ark. And the only door in it was closed by God Himself. Noah did not close the door. If he had, he might have opened it! God closed the door, and that ark rode above the judgment waters.

Hallelujah! That is where we are going to be—above! We will be astronauts someday, and not have to go through all that rigid training to be one! We are going up, going to make contact; then we won't have a re-entry. We will be coming back with Him when He returns in His revelation.

Everything in the Bible indicates that Christians will be above. That is always the picture in all the typology of the Bible. Always God shows the believer *above* it all and the sinner *in* it all.

That happened when God destroyed Sodom and Gomorrah. Listen to what God said to Lot: "Escape for thy life; look not behind thee, neither stay thou in all the plain; escape to the mountain..." (Gen. 19:17). God said, "Flee to the mountains; don't stay in the plains. Don't stay down, go up!"

Lot started out, but his wife turned back and turned into a pillar of salt. Then Lot and his two daughters, the only believers in Sodom, were delivered out of the city. Lot, that rebellious, backslidden, carnal, worldly Christian said, "Don't make me leave this plain; I've loved it here." He had, but it brought about the destruction of his family and did nothing for the deliverance of the Sodomites.

God said, "Here is a little city called Zoar; stay in it for awhile." I read that, and I say, "Now Lord, it looks like the type is broken," but keep reading. When Sodom and Gomorrah are just about destroyed, God comes to Lot in Zoar again and says, "Lot, to the mountains with you." Remember: always in the Bible, the Christian is up and judgment is down. "And Lot went up out of Zoar, and dwelt in the mountain, and his two daughters with him" (Gen. 19:30).

The Lord has put a difference between a saved person and a lost person, just like God put a difference between Israel and Egypt, as Exodus 11:7 tells us: ". . .that ye may know how that the Lord doth put a difference between the Egyptians and Israel."

Thank God, we are going up! I can hardly wait for that trumpet to blow! I wish it were today! What does this world hold for a Christian? We are like the prodigal trying to feed in a hogpen. I long to go Home.

Mrs. Malone and I have stood for over thirty years and watched our loved ones one by one cross over, until today when we look across the river, we must say that we have more riches on the other side. I want the Lord to come. We are going up. What a day that will be! I can't wait!

"For this we say unto you by the word of the Lord, that we which are alive and remain unto the coming of the Lord shall not prevent [precede] them which are asleep. For the Lord himself shall descend from heaven with a shout, with the voice of the archangel, and with the trump of God: and the dead in Christ shall rise first: Then we which are alive and remain shall be caught up together with them in the clouds, to meet the Lord in the air: and so shall we ever be with the Lord. Wherefore comfort one another with these words."—I Thess. 4:15-18.

The graves will be open. The Bible says we are going up together. God is going to burn this old world up. If you would rather have it than have Jesus, go ahead, but God is going to burn it up. This earth shall melt with fervent heat, says II Peter 3:10: "But the day of the Lord will come as a thief in the night; in the which the heavens shall pass away with a great noise, and the elements shall melt with fervent heat, the earth also and the works that are therein shall be burned up."

Years ago a missionary by the name of Long told the story of a fireman who one day looked at the school where his little daughter attended. It was an old-fashioned, wooden-framed building—a veritable fire trap.

He one day called the little girl to his knees and said, "Now, since your daddy is a fireman, it is my business to help prevent fires and put out fires and save people's lives. Someday that old school building may catch on fire. If it does while you are at school, don't run for the stairway. If you do, you will be trampled to death. Just wait for me."

Sure enough; one day the alarm sounded, and the old fire truck went down the street with bells sounding and sirens blowing. "Where is the fire?" someone asked. "I think it's the school house."

When they came to the school, smoke belched from every window and door. Consternation reigned. The stairway was gutted with little bodies who had suffocated. The fireman began his duties. He put his ladder against that window, and up the ladder he went. There amidst the smoke was a little face with folded hands. He reached in, took her in his arms, and down the ladder to safety he carried her. Why was she saved? Because when the fire bell rang, she said, "I'm gonna' wait for my daddy!"

Listen, I am waiting for my Father. I am waiting for the trumpet to blow, and the archangel to sound, and the shout, "Come up hither!"

If the Lord came today, saved people would be taken and lost people would be left. You may call me overdramatic if you wish, but if the Lord were to come at this moment, there would be trains hurtling down the railroad track whose Christian engineers were taken; there would be planes crashing all across the country because the Christian pilots were taken. Big block headlines of the papers would read, HUNDREDS AND THOUSANDS OF CHILDREN MISSING! Mother goes into a room with a little crib; the sheets are unruffled, but the little one is gone.

The headlines will read: MYSTERY OF MYSTERIES. HUN-
DREDS OF THOUSANDS OF PEOPLE MISSING! No mystery;
the Lord came! As John on the little island of Patmos said, "Even
so, come, Lord Jesus."

III. OUR POSITION IN CHRIST PROHIBITS THIS

A further reason why God will not let one single believer nor
allow the church to go through this Tribulation period is that our
position in Christ prohibits this.

Here is one sweet and wonderful truth that I fear many of the
Lord's people have never really gotten hold of: who we are, what
we have and where we are at this time in Christ Jesus. More than
twenty times, the first chapter of Ephesians mentions that the Christian is in Christ.

What does it mean for a Christian to be in Christ? Ephesians
2:6 tells us, "And hath raised us up together, and made us sit
together in heavenly places in Christ Jesus." In the mind, counsel
and sovereign purpose of Almighty God, every believer is now
seated in the heavenlies with the Lord.

You say, "I thought I was here on earth." That shows how
mixed up some folks can get. The Christian is seated in the
heavenlies in Christ Jesus. In the mind, counsel, purpose and
sovereign plan of the eternal God, it is as good as done. It is like
chapter 8 of the book of Romans teaches: He has not only justified
us; but clothed in the righteousness of Jesus and washed in His
blood, we are already glorified in the eyes of Almighty God.

If we are seated in the heavenlies, then earth judgment holds
no part for those of us who are saved. When a Christian dies, the
Bible tells us he has a change of address. He moves out of the
old body. "...absent from the body, and...present with the
Lord."

Jesus said, "I will never leave thee, nor forsake thee." There are not enough demons in Hell or under the sea or in the earth or in the air to take a Christian out of the hands of God. So from the time I was saved in 1935, throughout the endless ages of eternity, while the millions of years roll on and on, I am going to be with Jesus Christ.

So I need only to ask myself one question: "When all this judgment takes place on earth, where will Jesus be?" In the heavens, where I am going to be. It is unthinkable that a Christian could ever be separated from Christ. Where Jesus is, is where I am going to be.

Paul was talking about that in Philippians 3:20: "For our conversation [citizenship] is in heaven...."

Our very position is in Christ, and it demands that we go to no period of judgment. It is unthinkable that a Christian will ever go through the judgment which God will pour out on this world.

I think of Colossians 3:3: "For ye are dead, and your life is hid with Christ in God." We are hid from all judgment. We are protected from it. We are sealed from it. We are with Him, and wherever He is, there is no judgment for the child of God. All this victory is of the Lord.

When I was first saved, it seemed as if the Devil were knocking on my door all the time. I would answer the door and say, "Who is it? What do you want?" He would tell me what he wanted. I didn't want that, but he would work it around some way until he would get the best of me.

Then one day I heard an old saint say something that caused me to change my whole routine. When the Devil knocks on my door now, I just say, "Jesus, would You mind going to the door for me? It is the Devil, and You know how to handle him."

Listen! Jesus has never let him in one time. We are saved, and our position in Christ is that we are seated in the heavenlies with Him. That is why the whole book of Ephesians tells us what we have in Christ and is called the book of the heavenlies. We are seated with Him.

You say, "Preacher, I can see you." No, you can't. You are having an illusion! You are having a nightmare. You see 175 pounds of fat and blubber, but I am not here. I am seated in the heavenlies with Him, never to be separated from Him.

IV. NO MENTION OF EARTH RELATIONSHIP OF THE CHURCH IN THE TRIBULATION SCRIPTURES

I believe we shall not go through this period of judgment because there is no mention of earth relationship of the church in the Tribulation Scriptures.

There is far more said about this little period of time—seven years in duration—than any other period in the book of Revelation. From Revelation 4:1 to Revelation 19:11, more than fifteen chapters are devoted to what the Bible calls by several names, a period of seven years. It is called the time of Jacob's trouble; it is called Daniel's seventieth week, and twice in the New Testament (once in the book of Matthew, the first book, and in Revelation, the last book), this period of time is called the Great Tribulation.

It is divided into two periods of three and one-half years. You read in the book of Revelation of 1,260 days, and you read of 42 months. Thus, God divides this Tribulation period into two equal parts of three and one-half years.

Revelation 7:4 tells of 144,000 who will be saved during the Tribulation. The next few verses of the same chapter tell us that there will be 12,000 from each of the twelve tribes of Israel— Jews, not Jehovah's Witnesses! The Jehovah's Witnesses started out to claim they were the 144,000; then when they outgrew that number, they were in one awful mess to explain it, and their explanation was even worse yet. They devised a company that they call the Jonadabs (these folks are mentioned in the Old Testament in II Samuel 13). They say, "Now we have the 144,000—and the Jonadabs." That makes as much sense to you as it does to me. There is no question at all about who the 144,000 are. They are Jews, 12,000 from each of the twelve tribes of Israel. Revelation, chapter 7, plainly teaches this.

There is a lot of misunderstanding about this period of time, and I do not mean that after this message it will be clear in your mind. But I have had many people ask me, "Will there be anyone saved in the Tribulation? Now this is after the Lord has come. Will there be anyone saved, anyone come to know the Lord, in this period of time?"

Yes, there will be folks saved after Jesus comes. But if there is anyone now who has heard the Word of God and has never come to a saving knowledge of the Lord Jesus Christ, there is not one verse of Scripture that gives you one ray of hope that you will be saved. If you reject Him until the day the trumpet blows and Jesus comes to receive His bride, you have no hope that you will ever be saved.

The Bible does teach that there will be people saved during the Tribulation period. We read of two groups in chapter 7 of the book of Revelation. There will be the 144,000. God said that He would seal them unto Himself, reserve them unto Himself. They will be saved. These are Jews saved during the Tribulation period. After they are saved, God will use them to fulfill the prophecy of Matthew 24:14: "And this gospel of the kingdom shall be preached in all the world for a witness unto all nations; and then shall the end come."

During this Tribulation period, these 144,000 Jews will become great evangelists and go around the world. These Jews, saved by the Lord, shall preach the message of the kingdom. As a result,

the Bible says there is a multitude which no man can number—
not Jews but Gentiles—who will be taken out of all nations and
all kindreds and all people and all tongues, and they shall be saved.

When one asks the question, "Who are these?" the answer
comes in Revelation 7:14, "These are they which came out of
great tribulation, and have washed their robes, and made them
white in the blood of the Lamb." So during the Tribulation period,
there will be people saved.

But the question is often asked, "Will the people who make up
the body of Christ, the born-again people of this dispensation of
grace, enter into that Tribulation? Will they know, will they feel
any of His judgment?"

Not one bit in the world. As I said before, I am what is known
as a "pre." I have been predestinated, prepaid, preserved,
prepared, and I am one who believes in the pre-tribulation rapture
—that the Lord will come before He ever pours out all this hot
judgment upon this wicked world.

I have read the book of Revelation many times. I used to say
to the Lord what I have heard many people say, "Lord, I just
don't get it!" I will admit to you that Revelation is not an easy
book to understand, but one day the Lord gave me one little bit
of truth that seemed to unlock the book for me. When we read
this last book of the Bible, this great prophetical book, and come
to Revelation 4:1, we read these words: "After this I looked, and,
behold, a door was opened in heaven: and the first voice which
I heard was as it were of a trumpet talking with me; which said,
Come up hither, and I will shew thee things which must be
hereafter." That is the rapture of the church.

So in chapter 4, verse 1, of the book of Revelation, the church
is taken up; then all the rest of the book of Revelation, to chapter
19, is not on this earth but up in Heaven. We do not see the church
anymore in the book of Revelation until we get to chapter 19. We

see a sealed group of Jews, a multitude which no man can number; but we do not see the blood-bought body of our Lord Jesus Christ. Not here do you see them, but we see them appear in chapter 19.

Notice that chapter. Verse 7 tells about the marriage of the Lamb. Then verse 11 says, "And I saw heaven opened, and behold a white horse; and he that sat upon him was called Faithful and True, and in righteousness he doth judge and make war."

Revelation 4:1 is the rapture—that is, His coming for the church. Revelation 19:11 is the revelation—that is, the Lord coming with His church. Notice He comes riding a white horse.

"And I saw heaven opened, and behold a white horse; and he that sat upon him was called Faithful and True, and in righteousness he doth judge and make war. His eyes were as a flame of fire, and on his head were many crowns; and he had a name written, that no man knew, but he himself. And he was clothed with a vesture dipped in blood: and his name is called The Word of God."—Rev. 19:11-13.

Where do we come in? Look at Revelation 19:14: "And the armies which were in heaven followed him upon white horses, clothed in fine linen, white and clean." The armies of Heaven are coming on white horses someday to rule this world. The Battle of Armageddon will take place, and there is not one shadow of doubt about who will win. It will be God's people. Heaven will triumph over earth, and Jesus will reign wherever the sun doth his successive journeys run.

So there is no mention of the church in the passages of the Bible that deal with the Tribulation time. We are going to be delivered from it.

In 1914, there began a war that people said would end all wars. I remember as a young man how my grandparents sent two boys into the service. I remember them talking about how World War I was supposed to end all wars.

Since World War I, there was World War II in which more people were killed than all other wars put together. Following World War II by a few years was the Korean War in which many American boys lost their lives. Now there was a war in Viet Nam in which fifty thousand young American boys gave their lives.

There will be no real peace on this earth. Not one thing in the Bible ever indicates it. There is not a man or a group of men, nation or nations, that can bring peace until the Lord ends all wars. When Jesus comes riding upon a white horse and the armies of Heaven behind Him, when He comes in His revelation, wars will all be over.

V. PAUL AND ALL NEW TESTAMENT WRITERS SPEAK OF THE IMMINENT RETURN OF CHRIST

No seven-year period, no great period of judgment is to take place before the Lord can come. The Bible teaches that He can come at any moment.

In I Corinthians 15:51,52, Paul says:

"Behold, I shew you a mystery; We shall not all sleep, but we shall all be changed, In a moment, in the twinkling of an eye, at the last trump: for the trumpet shall sound, and the dead shall be raised incorruptible, and we shall be changed."

Everyone is not going to die. They use the old expression, "As sure as death and taxes," but death is not sure for a Christian. I hear many songs today about the coming of the King and the coming of the Lord, but these songs are more than a doctrine, more than a song: they are a reality. The Lord could come at any moment.

This verse says "in the twinkling of an eye" we shall be changed. A twinkling of the eye is very quick. Just that quick it is all going to take place.

That is all the time it will take for the Lord to come, an angel to shout, the trumpet to blow, and for us to be caught up to be with the Lord in the air. So shall we ever be with the Lord!

Over three-fourths of this Bible is prophetic, and three-fourths of that prophecy has already been fulfilled. If I were a betting man and someone were to say to me, "Here is a fellow who has predicted a lot of things, three-fourths of which have already come to pass just exactly like He said it would," I would count on the other coming to pass, too, just as He predicted.

Not one thing in the Bible has ever failed. All of the Word of God has come to pass just exactly like God said it would.

A barometer tells you when it is going to rain and when it is going to be dry, when it is going to be wet and when it's going to be windy. The hand on the barometer points to the kind of weather that it is going to be. A fellow on Long Island in 1938 bought a barometer. When the hand on that barometer turned to hurricane, he shook that thing until he nearly ruined it. Then he said, "On Long Island, there is not going to be any hurricane!"

He sat down and wrote a red-hot letter to the company that built the barometer. But the hand on the barometer kept pointing to hurricane.

He had to go into the city of New York the next day to work, and he mailed the letter he had written to the company while he was in the city. When he got home from work that night, he didn't have a barometer because a hurricane had come in 1938, on Long Island, and blown his house, his barometer and the whole works away.

Listen! This Bible points to a coming King. Bless God, He is coming whether it looks like it to this old world or not! Thank God, He is coming. A Deliverer is coming.

There was an old man of God who used to preach in New York. One time one of his members came to him and said, "What do you think the hope of this sinful world is, this world with its awful mess?"

The old preacher looked as if he had that answer prepared forever. He said, "Dictator."

"Dictator?"

"Yes, that's what we need—a dictator."

The man said, "In order to have a dictator who could straighten things out and rule over everyone, he would have to be a superman."

The old preacher said, "Exactly right. That's the kind we need."

The man said, "Do you really mean a dictator?"

The preacher said, "Yes."

"In order to have a dictator, he would have to know all the problems of all of the people and have the power to do something about it."

"Exactly right. That's the kind we need."

"You mean a real dictator?"

"Yes," the old preacher said.

"But do you realize all the opposition we would have to overcome, if a dictator were to take over in this country?"

"Yes, that's the kind we need, and that's the kind I'm looking for—King Jesus."

He is the One I too have pinned my hopes on. I am looking for Him. John closed the Holy Writ with these words, "Even so, come, Lord Jesus" (Rev. 22:20).

That is my prayer, that the Lord will come. He is coming. Are you ready for His coming?

"For then shall be great tribulation such as was not since the beginning of the world to this time, no, nor ever shall be."— Matt. 24:21.

For a complete list of books available from the Sword of the Lord, write to Sword of the Lord Publishers, P. O. Box 1099, Murfreesboro, Tennessee 37133.